ARGO BROTHERS

New York City

Specialized High Schools Admissions Test

Test Prep for Advanced Students

• Anayet Chowdhury • Jesse Gelburd-Meyers • Corey Harrilal
• Vladislav Suleyman

Authors	**Anayet Chowdhury**
	Jesse Gelburd-Meyers
	Corey Harrilal

| Interior Design | **Vladislav Suleyman** |

| Cover Design | **Vladislav Suleyman** |

Contributing Editors   **Mirza Mohsin, Abid Syed, Shafat Choudhury, Jacqueline Lukonina**

ARGO BROTHERS

TABLE OF CONTENTS

INTRODUCTION

The Specialized High Schools Admissions Test (SHSAT) is an exam that students take in order to gain admission into one of the New York Specialized High Schools. Out of the nine Specialized High Schools, eight of the schools admit students solely on the SHSAT score. Fiorello H. LaGuardia High School of Music & Art and Performing Arts (LaGuardia), is the only specialized high school which admits based on an audition and academic review.

Here is a list if the Specialized High Schools along with their contact information.

The Bronx High School of Science
75 West 205th Street, Bronx, New York 10468
Contact Number: (718) 817-7700
www.bxscience.edu

Brooklyn Technical High School
29 Fort Greene Place, Brooklyn, New York 11217
Contact Number: (718) 804-6400
www.bths.edu

The Brooklyn Latin School
223 Graham Avenue, Brooklyn, New York 11206
Contact Number: (718) 366-0154
www.brooklynlatin.org

High School for Mathematics, Science & Engineering at the City College of New York
240 Convent Avenue, New York, New York 10031
Contact Number: (212) 281-6490
www.hsmse.org

High School for American Studies at Lehman College
2925 Goulden Avenue, Bronx, New York 10468
Contact Number: (718) 329-2144
www.hsas-lehman.org

Queens High School for the Sciences at York College
94-50 159th Street, Jamaica, New York 11433
Contact Number: (718) 657-3181
www.qhss.org

Staten Island Technical High School

485 Clawson Street, Staten Island, New York 10306

Contact Number: (718) 667-3222

www.siths.org

Stuyvesant High School

345 Chambers Street, New York, New York 10282-1099

Contact Number: (212) 312-4800

stuy.enschool.org

Fiorello H. LaGuardia High School of Music & Art and Performing Arts

100 Amsterdam Avenue, New York, New York 10023

Contact Number: (212) 496-0700

www.laguardiahs.org

The SHSAT is a 2 hour and 30 minute timed multiple choice test with two sections, verbal and math.

Number of Questions	Content	Total Point Value
5	Section 1: Scrambled Paragraphs	10
10	Section 1: Logical Reasoning	10
30	Section 1: Reading	30
50	Section 2: Math	50
	Total Points	**100**

The Importance of Ranking Schools

When you take the SHSAT test, you will be required to rank the Specialized High Schools you want to attend. It is extremely important that you know ahead of time which schools you would like to attend. You will only be admitted into one school if your score meets the level. Acceptance is based on the score you get on the SHSAT exam followed by your choices of schools.

When making the decision to rank the schools, some important things to think about are:

- How far away is the school from you?
- Does the school have a program you are interested in?
- Is there a certain sport or activity you would like to do in high school?
- Is the school a good fit for you? Each school differs in class size and specialty.

What do I need on test day?

You will need to bring your signed Admission Ticket which will have your school choices. There are **no calculators** permitted on the exam. Have more than one number 2 pencil, an eraser and a watch to keep track of time. Water and snacks are allowed, however you must wait until your proctor gives you permission to eat the snacks. Most importantly, bring your confidence! If the exam seems difficult, do not stress. Give it your best shot and have fun!

How can I study for this exam?

The first thing you need to understand is to do well on this exam, you must put in the time and effort to study. This is a challenging exam, so here is a list of a few important tips.

- **Practice and PRACTICE!**
  Take as many practice exams as you can find. Taking simulated exams will give you a very good idea on the type of questions that will be asked during the exam and will make you more confident.

- **Read Books**
  The best way to raise your score in the Verbal Section of the exam is to read books, articles and newspapers. You will develop a better vocabulary list and find it easier to read the passages provided in the exam.

- **Learn from your mistakes**
  When you go over your practice exams, make sure you understand **why** you got the question wrong. Did you read the corrections correctly? Was it a simple calculation error? Try to understand why you got the answer wrong.

Test Day Strategies

There is no penalty for wrong answers, so **do not** leave anything blank. If you do not know the answer to a question, then circle the question and move on. When you are done with all solvable questions, return to the circled questions. If you still do not know the answer, make an educated guess.

If you still have time after finishing all questions, then check your answers. First, check all the arithmetic questions in the math section. Next, go to the reading comprehension section and find the line numbers associated with each answer. Is your answer directly from a line in the passage? Finally, check simple logic games and spend the rest of your time ensuring that you have explanations for each sentence in your scrambled paragraphs.

While you practice, find roughly fifteen questions from throughout your practice that you believe to exemplify the test. You should know how to answer these questions perfectly. On test day, use these fifteen questions as a warmup. Make sure that you go through all steps when going through the question. You should be able to explain why each wrong answer is wrong.

You do not need to take the exam in the order that it is presented. Take the test in the order that you believe will maximize your time on those questions which you are most likely to get correct. If you feel you are slow in the scrambled paragraph section, then do these questions after all other sections. If you are terrific at logical reasoning and math, but perform worse on reading comprehension and scrambled paragraphs, then do logical reasoning, then math, then reading comprehension, and then scrambled paragraphs. It is better to spend time on questions you know you can get right than spending an excessive amount of time on questions that you find more difficult.

SHSAT ENGLISH SECTION

The SHSAT English Language Arts section consists of three sections, totaling 45 questions. Out of these three sections, two are largely unique to the SHSAT: scrambled paragraphs and logical reasoning. Reading comprehension—the third and final section—is similar in format and difficulty to a seventh grade state ELA exam.

SCRAMBLED PARAGRAPHS:

The first section to appear on the exam is "scrambled paragraphs." Every test has five scrambled paragraph problems. Each paragraph is worth two points if perfectly reconstructed. No points are given for partially correct answers.

Scrambled paragraphs are a unique test component that you may not have seen before. Traditionally, this section is considered the most difficult section of the exam; however, by remembering a few important details and approaching the paragraphs a certain way, you can master this section.

Things to remember:

1. There must always be a correct order.
2. The test relies on these paragraphs having a lot of information in them, making it difficult to keep all information in one's head.

Authors of the exam ensure that there is a correct answer by utilizing pronouns, referential nouns and transition words.

Pronouns include words such as he, she, they, this, that, those, and them. A pronoun takes the place of a noun. Most importantly, a pronoun must always take the place of an "antecedent noun." An antecedent noun is the most recent noun discussed, often in the previous sentence. If you see a pronoun near the beginning of a sentence, think about what word the pronoun is replacing. That word must be in the previous sentence!

Referential Nouns "point" to another noun. Sometimes, referential nouns are accompanied by words such as this, those, and they. For example, a sentence may begin: "This painting was..." In this example, the painting noted is a particular painting that must have been discussed in the directly previous sentence. "The potato," "This discovery," and "These techniques" all utilize referential nouns.

Transition words consist of words such as "for example," "moreover," "regardless," and "additionally." These words cue the reader into the type of sentence they are about to read and the sentences relationship to the previous sentence. If we see the phrase "for example," then we know that the example presented must relate to the principle or concept discussed in the previous sentence. By far the most common transition word is "however." Sentences prior and after the word "however" will always have distinct claims, opinions or positions. As such, when we see however, we should not only look to place it after the phrases it most clearly seems to counter, but also make sure that it is breaking up two positions. A quick tip: If all sentences run counter to the introductory sentence, then "however" must be in the first sentence.

Using these three sentence mechanics, we can fully recognize the ordering of the sentence. Unfortunately, simply seeing the words that must link to past sentences can often not be enough. Paragraphs consist of six full sentences with a multitude of words in each sentence, and it is easy to experience input overload. To avoid overloading ourselves with information, we will treat scrambled paragraphs as logical sequencing games.

Scrambled Paragraphs as Logical Sequencing

Step 1: Read initial sentence. Restate in own words.
Step 2: Set up sequential ordering game, i.e.: _ _ _ _ _
Step 3: Circle the pronouns, referential nouns, and transition words in each sentence.
Step 4: Read each sentence, one at a time. If a sentence cannot follow the introductory sentence, then place it under the line and cross it out. Remember that a pronoun, referential noun, and transition word must directly follow that to which it is referring.
Step 5: Place sentences that could be first above the line. Maybes are OK!
Step 6: Using circled clues from step 3, determine which sentence is first. Repeat steps for following lines.

By the time you are done, your page may look like:

Additional: If one sentence must be before another due to rules of referential cues, make it into a logical sequencing game rule. Use this to your advantage to help determine order!

LOGICAL REASONING:

The second section to appear on the exam will always be logical reasoning. The logical reasoning section consists of ten questions, all intended to test a student's ability to use rules and information so as to prove certain statements. Most students taking the SHSAT have never seen a logical reasoning question prior to preparing for the exam. However, with a little practice, they can quickly become the easiest problems on the exam.

The logical reasoning section largely utilizes four different question types. Mastering the format of these games and questions will prepare you for any hybrid questions that may appear on the exam. The question types are as follows:

If/Then Statements

An if/then statement relies on the logical laws of causality. When one states "if ...., then...." two things will always be true. First, as long as the first statement is true, the second will always follow. Second, as long as the second is not true, then the first will always be not true. In order to master these phrases, think of one that makes sense to you!

An important note to keep in mind is that this exam only tests "validity." In order for a phrase to be valid, it must only follow the causal laws. Phrases need not be "sound." To be sound, a premise within the if/then phrase would have to be true in reality. Do not worry whether or not a statement made in the exam is true in the real world. Finally, if/then statements can chain together.

It is important that you learn to write out all phrases using formal logic. Formal logic sounds complicated, but for the sake of this exam, it simply requires putting an arrow pointing from the "if" statement to the "then" statement. Keep in mind that if the "if" is in the second half of the sentence, then that information is on the "if" side of the logical equation.

Some valid statements:

If I study for the exam, then I will not do poorly. If I did poorly, then I did not study for the exam.

Study→ ~~poorly~~; poorly→ ~~study~~

If I have milk in the house, then someone must have gone grocery shopping. If no one has been grocery shopping, then I will not have milk in the house.

Milk → went shopping; ~~shopping~~ → ~~milk~~

We will go to the beach if it does not rain. If we do not go to the beach, then it must have rained.

~~Rain~~ → go to beach; ~~beach~~ → rain

If I miss the bus, then I will be late for school. If I am late for school, then Mrs. Grant will be angry.

Mrs. Grant will send me to detention if she is angry. If I go to detention my parents will be furious.

Miss bus → late for school → Grant angry → sent to detention → parents furious

~~Parents furious → detention → Mrs. Grant angry → late for school → miss bus.~~

7

Pairing games

Pairing games require the student to place sets of "players" into groups. A normal pairing game will consist of two to three groups, each holding two to four players. Games rely heavily on knowing exactly how the board is set up, and knowing exactly how the rules interact with the players.

Sequencing games

Sequencing games are similar to pairing games in that they will have a "board" to set up, players that fill the board, and rules that dictate the location of the board. Sequencing games differ in that rather than the board focusing on which players go into a certain group, the board instead is oriented towards the order of all players. Many times, games will have elements of both pairing and sequencing games. In these instances, it is important to pay special attention to how the board is set up.

For both games types, follow these simple steps:

Step 1: Determine what kind of game you are playing.

Step 2: Set up game board. Complicated games throughout this book will have the game set up in the explanations section.

Step 3: Write out all rules for the games using shorthand.

Step 4: Solve game to completion. In order to solve the game, you may need to set up multiple boards. Don't be afraid to make boards just so that you can try out rules!

Step 5: After filling out whole game to completion, look at corresponding questions.

Coding Games

Coding games consist of three to four pairs of lines. In nearly all instances, one line will consist of a letter or symbol, and the corresponding line will consist of words. These questions can, at first glance, seem daunting, but these games are the simplest to master.

Before diving into these games, make sure to note the stated rules. They are not always the same! Generally, there are two different rule types. Depending on the rules — and in particular the third rule — your approach should be slightly different.

The first rule type will state that each letter/symbol corresponds to a word in the line below and that the symbol may or may not be directly above the corresponding word. For these versions of the game, follow these rules:

Step 1: Scan the lines for letters/symbols that occur in all line pairs. Write down these symbols.

Step 2: Scan the lines for words that occur in all line pairs. Write these down as potential equivalents.

Step 3: If multiple words/symbols exist in all lines within this ruleset, then there will be no way to determine which symbol is paired with each word. Move on to symbols that appear in the next most line pairs. If there are four total line pairs, then we will now be looking for symbols that appear in three. As in step 1 and step 2, write down all the symbols and then put down the potential word pairings next to the symbol.

Step 4: We can now begin to determine which words that appear in these many line pairs correspond to which word. Take one symbol at a time and look at all lines with that symbol. If a symbol does not have words currently listed as potentials paired with it, then cross off that word. Do this to all symbols appearing in this many lines. If at the end there are multiple words and letters appearing in identical line pairs, then those must be left unfinished. If a symbol/word pair is determined, then cross them off from the game.

Step 5: Continue this process. Find symbols that appear in a decreasing amount of line pairs. As line pairs are left with individual symbols/words, pair them.

Finish the entire game before looking at the questions. As you get better at these games, they will be completed very rapidly, allowing you to know with certainty that you are getting the answers correct and saving time for future problems. When the game is completed, your code board may look something like:

A = Tom
B = Joe / Sam
C = Joe / Sam
D = Carl, Derick, Francine
E = Carl, Derick, Francine
F = Carl, Derick, Francine

The second rule type will be similar to the first, except that it will disallow symbols from being directly over the word that it is supposed to be paired with. These games will often have fewer line pairs than the first rule type. To solve these games, follow the same steps as the previous rule set, but when you find symbols that occur in the same amount of line pairs as a word, look at whether or not the symbol is directly above the word in any pairs. If a symbol is directly over a potential word, then cross it out.

READING COMPREHENSION

Reading comprehension makes up the majority of ELA questions on the SHSAT. The reading comprehension section will contain five passages, with six questions for each passage. In any given passage, you will always have one "main idea" question, three to five "hunt the passage" questions, and zero to two "inference" questions.

Main Idea Questions will always appear as the first question in a passage. These questions can always be answered by finding the answer choice that appears explicitly in the most paragraphs. Do not get tricked into picking a general topic that the whole passage relates to, but which is not explicitly discussed within the passage.

Hunt the Passage Questions require you to find the answer directly in the passage. Unlike most exams, the SHSAT will rarely give you a line number. In order to find the proper line, look in the question for the noun or phrase that is most likely to be unique within the passage and find the lines that relate to this noun. The answer will be in these lines.

Inference Questions tend to be the most challenging question type for students within the reading comprehension section of the exam. These questions will ask you to choose a statement or opinion based on which would most likely be true based on the information provided in the passage. Similar to "hunt the passage" questions, inference questions will normally relate to a particular line or paragraph of the passage. When answering these questions, determine if there is a single paragraph that most deals with the topic of the question, and select an answer that most relates to that paragraph.

Extreme Language: Whenever taking an exam with reading comprehension questions, be on the look-out for extreme language in the answer choices. Extreme language quantifies something in an immutable way. Examples of extreme language are "all," "none," "never," and "always." An answer can only be true while using extreme language if explicitly noted in the passage. If a passage states "nearly all participants were successful," then the answer cannot be "no participants were unsuccessful."

Your exam will contain 50 math questions, which cover a variety of topics including arithmetic, algebra, geometry, probability and statistics.

BASIC MATH TERMS YOU MUST KNOW

There is no reference sheet provided during the exam, so you must know all the formulas and be familiar with the words and methods.

Please look at the following terms that we have provided you with. This is not a comprehensive list, however these are a few terms that you must understand.

INTEGERS	Whole numbers that are positive or negative, and include zero. Example: -1 , 0 , 1 , 4.0, $\frac{-20}{2}$ are all integers.
CONSECUTIVE INTEGERS	1, 2, 3, 4 are consecutive integers. 4, 6, 8, 10 are consecutive even integers. 1, 3, 5, 7 are consecutive odd integers.
WHOLE NUMBERS	These are counting numbers, including 0. There are no negative numbers in whole numbers. Example: 0, 1, 2, 3, 4...
RATIONAL NUMBERS	All integers, fractions, decimals, repeating decimals and terminating decimals. Example: 1, 0.121212, $\frac{1}{8}$, 191.01
IRRATIONAL NUMBERS	These numbers cannot be written as fractions. These are non-repeating decimals. Example: 0.162728..., $\sqrt{2}$, π
SCIENTIFIC NOTATION	When you have a large number, it is easier to express it in scientific notation. You must know how to correctly convert numbers into scientific notation for the exam. Example: 281,000,000 = 2.81 x 10^8
PEMDAS	Parenthesis, Exponents, Multiplication, Addition, Subtraction This is the order of operations that must be followed to get the correct answer.
PRIME NUMBERS	A positive integer greater than 1, whose factors are 1 and the number itself. Example: 2, 3, 5, 7, 11 Note: 1 is not a prime number. Make sure you know that!

COMPOSITE NUMBERS

A number that has more than two factors.
Example: 4, 10, 20, 55

GREATEST COMMON FACTOR

It is the largest number that is a factor of two or more numbers. In order to find the GCF, list all the prime factors of each number and multiply the factors that both numbers have in common. Example: If we wanted to find the GCF of 12 and 15, you need to list the prime factors of both numbers.

Prime Factors of 12: 2 • 2 • 3
Prime Factors of 16: 2 • 2 • 2 • 2

The only numbers that are common in both sets is 2 and 2, so when you multiple 2 • 2 , you get 4. Therefore, 4 is the greatest common factor of 12 and 16.

LEAST COMMON MULTIPLE

It is the lowest common multiple between two or more numbers. In order to find the LCM, list all the prime factors of each number and multiply the factors by the greatest number of times it appears. For example, if you are finding the LCM of 8, 10 and 25; first list their respective prime numbers.

Prime Factors of 8: 2 • 2 • 2
Prime Factors of 10: 2 • 5
Prime Factors of 25: 5 • 5

2 is a factor of both 8 and 10, however, the greatest number of times 2 appears in a set is three times. Therefore, we want to multiply 2 • 2 • 2 when finding the LCM. 5 is a factor of both 10 and 25, however, the greatest number of times 5 appears in a set is two times. Therefore, we want to multiply 5 • 5 when finding the LCM. Combining this, we get:

2 • 2 • 2 • 5 • 5 = 200
Therefore, 200 is the LCM of 8, 10 and 25.

RULE FOR EVEN AND ODD INTEGERS

Even + Even = Even
Even + Odd = Odd
Odd + Odd = Even

Even • Even = Even
Even • Odd = Even
Odd • Odd = Odd

PERCENTAGES

Percent means "out of 100". There are a few key things you need to know for percent problems.
If you are given the question: 15 is what percent of 60?
You need to always remember that **"is"** means an equal sign and **"of"** means multiply. Now simply set up the equation.
15 = ? % • 60. The variable here is the percentage, so if you solve for that you get .25 or 25%

PERPENDICULAR LINES

Lines that intersect to form a 90° angle.
Example: Lines AB and CD are perpendicular.

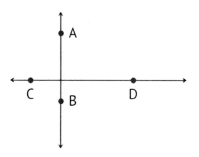

PARALLEL LINES

These lines never intersect.
Example: Line segments AB and CD are parallel.

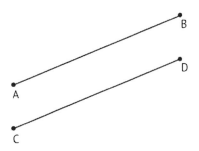

ALTERNATE INTERIOR ANGLES

If you have two parallel lines which are intersected by transversal line, you create alternate interior angles.

Example: Angles B and C are alternate interior angles. If Angle B has a measure of 40°, then Angle C also has a measure of 40°. Please note that angles A and D are also alternate interior angles.

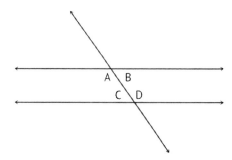

ALTERNATE EXTERIOR ANGLES

Once again, the diagram must have two parallel lines that are intersected by a transversal line. In this case, the angles are outside of the parallel lines.

Example: Angles A and D are alternate exterior angles. If Angle A has a measure of 50°, then Angle D also has a measure of 50°. B and C are also alternate exterior angles.

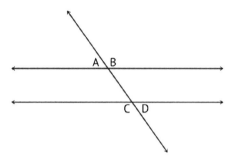

TRIANGLES

An **equilateral** triangle has three equal sides and angles. Each of the angles for an equilateral triangle measure 60°.

An **isosceles** triangle has two sides that is always equal, and therefore two angles that are also equal.

A **scalene** triangle has no equal sides or angles.

Acute angles are less than 90°.

Obtuse angles are greater than 90°.

Right angle measures 90°.

CONGRUENT VS SIMILAR

Congruent figures have the same length and angles.
Similar figures have different length but same angles.

PYTHAGOREAN THEOREM

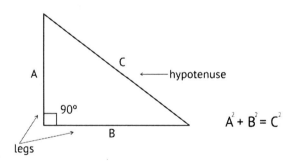

$$A^2 + B^2 = C^2$$

FORMULAS FOR AREA

Rectangle: $A = l \cdot w$

Triangle: $A = \frac{1}{2}b \cdot h$

Parallelogram: $A = b \cdot h$

Square: $A = l \cdot w$

Trapezoid: $A = \frac{1}{2}(b_1 + b_2) \cdot h$

Circle: $A = \pi r^2$

14

30-60-90 TRIANGLE

If you have a 30-60-90 triangle, the ratio of the sides will be
$$x : x\sqrt{3} : 2x$$

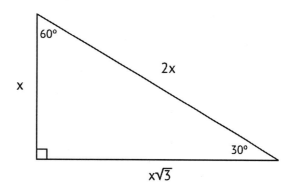

45-45-90 TRIANGLE

If you have a 45-45-90 triangle, the ratio of the sides will be
$$x : x : x\sqrt{2}$$

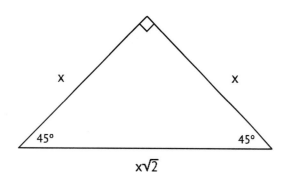

STATISTICS

If you want to find the average of a set of numbers, you must add them up and divide by the number of terms. Use the following formula: **Average = Sum of terms / Number of terms**

The average formula is very important to master, because the SHSAT math exam will contain questions that require you to manipulate this formula. For example, you should know that the **Sum = (Average) x (Number of terms)**.

Here is a very important rule to remember:
In a **consecutive** series of numbers, the **mean is also equal to the median.** This rule will help you answers quicker to save time on the exam.

For example: If the sum of 5 consecutive even integers is 280, then what is the largest value of the 5 consecutive even integers?

The first thing you need to realize is that, 280 is the sum, and there are 5 number of terms. You can easily find the average, by simply dividing 280 by 5, which is 56. Now, using the rule we just learned, we know that 56 is the median value in this consecutive integer series. That means 56 is the third consecutive even integer, and we want to find the fifth even integer. Using simple math, the 5th even integer is 60. Therefore, 60 is the largest value of the 5 consecutive even integers. If you practice using this rule, you will be able to solve these problems in under 45 seconds.

Average Rate is a little different from the usual average formula. If you want to find the average rate or speed, the formula you need to use is: **Average Speed = $\dfrac{\text{Total Distance}}{\text{Total Time}}$**

For example: If you are trying to find the average speed for 100 miles at 50 mph and 100 miles at 25 mph, you cannot just average the two speeds given. You must figure out the total distance and then divide it by the total time. The total distance is simply 100 miles + 100 miles = 200 miles. Don't get confused when finding out the total time. If you are going 50 mph and traveled 100 miles, that is 2 hours. If you are going 25 mph and traveled 100 miles, that is 4 hours. Therefore, a total of 6 hours. The average speed, then, is $\dfrac{200}{6} = 33.33$ mph.

The **Median** is a number that is in the middle of the set, and the set must be in sequential order.

For example: If we are given the numbers 5, 3, 1, 7, and 9 then what is the median value? First order them in sequential order and then find the middle value.
1, 3, 5, 7, 9 so the median is 5.

The **Mode** is a number that appears the most often in a set of numbers. You can have more then one Mode, if one or more number shows up the same number of times.

For example: 1, 1, 2, 5, 6, 7, 6
The Mode for this set of numbers is 1 and 6.

PROBABILITY

Probability = $\dfrac{\text{Favorable Outcomes}}{\text{Total Possible Outcomes}}$

EXPONENT RULES

If you are multiplying, and have the same base, you need to add the exponents and keep the same base.

Example: $y^2 \cdot y^3 = y^{2+3} = y^5$

If you are dividing, and have the same base, you need to subtract the exponents and keep the same base.

Example: $\dfrac{y^{10}}{y^5} = y^5$

If you are raising a power to a power, then you must multiply the exponents.

Example: $(y^2)^3 = y^{2 \cdot 3} = y^6$

ABSOLUTE VALUE

Absolute Value of a number is defined as the distance from zero on the number line. Since the value is a distance, distance can never be negative. Therefore, absolute value is **always positive**. Example: Absolute Value of -7 is 7.

DIFFERENCE OF SQUARES

This is an important concept to master. Realize that $a^2 - b^2 = (a - b)(a + b)$, and therefore if you are given the expression, $x^2 - 16$, you can factor that to $(x + 4)(x - 4)$.

FOIL

Anytime you are multiplying a binomial, use the FOIL method. **F**irst, **O**uter, **I**nner, **L**ast.

DISTANCE FORMULA

Distance Formula:

$$d = \sqrt{(x_1 - x_2)^2 + (y_1 - y_2)^2}$$

SLOPE	If you are given two points, you can find the slope by using the formula **Slope = Change in Y** / **Change in X**
	If you want to write an equation in slope-intercept form, the formula you need to use is $y = mx + b$
MIDPOINT OF LINE	If you are trying to find the midpoint of a given line segment, use the following formula:

$$\frac{x_1 + x_2}{2} \ , \ \frac{y_1 + y_2}{2}$$

CIRCUMFERENCE OF A CIRCLE	Circumference = $2\pi r$
LENGTH OF AN ARC	Length of an arc = $\dfrac{n}{360} \cdot 2\pi r$
VOLUME OF A CUBE	Volume of a cube = s^3
VOLUME OF A CYLINDER	Volume of a cylinder = $\pi r^2 h$
VOLUME OF A SPHERE	Volume of a sphere = $\dfrac{4}{3}\pi r^3$
SURFACE AREA OF A SPHERE	Surface area of a sphere = $4\pi r^2$
SURFACE AREA OF A SYLINDER	Surface area of a cylinder = $2\pi rh + 2\pi r^2$

SHSAT
PRACTICE TESTS

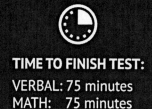

TIME TO FINISH TEST:
VERBAL: 75 minutes
MATH: 75 minutes

— This exam is 2 hours and 30 minutes long. Try to take this full exam in one sitting to simulate real test conditions.

— While taking this exam, refrain from hearing music or watching T.V.

— Please note, calculators are not permitted! You are permitted to answer questions in any order you see fit.

— Not all answers need take the same amount of time. Allocate your test time accordingly.

— Concentrate and GOOD LUCK!

To calculate your score visit our web site and download excel calculator:
www. einstein-academy.com/calc

SHSAT PRACTICE TEST 1
ANSWER SHEET

PART 1 (VERBAL)

SCRAMBLED PARAGRAPHS

Paragraph 1

The first sentence is   Ⓠ Ⓡ Ⓢ Ⓣ Ⓤ
The second sentence is   Ⓠ Ⓡ Ⓢ Ⓣ Ⓤ
The third sentence is   Ⓠ Ⓡ Ⓢ Ⓣ Ⓤ
The fourth sentence is   Ⓠ Ⓡ Ⓢ Ⓣ Ⓤ
The fifth sentence is   Ⓠ Ⓡ Ⓢ Ⓣ Ⓤ

Paragraph 2

The first sentence is   Ⓠ Ⓡ Ⓢ Ⓣ Ⓤ
The second sentence is   Ⓠ Ⓡ Ⓢ Ⓣ Ⓤ
The third sentence is   Ⓠ Ⓡ Ⓢ Ⓣ Ⓤ
The fourth sentence is   Ⓠ Ⓡ Ⓢ Ⓣ Ⓤ
The fifth sentence is   Ⓠ Ⓡ Ⓢ Ⓣ Ⓤ

Paragraph 3

The first sentence is   Ⓠ Ⓡ Ⓢ Ⓣ Ⓤ
The second sentence is   Ⓠ Ⓡ Ⓢ Ⓣ Ⓤ
The third sentence is   Ⓠ Ⓡ Ⓢ Ⓣ Ⓤ
The fourth sentence is   Ⓠ Ⓡ Ⓢ Ⓣ Ⓤ
The fifth sentence is   Ⓠ Ⓡ Ⓢ Ⓣ Ⓤ

Paragraph 4

The first sentence is   Ⓠ Ⓡ Ⓢ Ⓣ Ⓤ
The second sentence is   Ⓠ Ⓡ Ⓢ Ⓣ Ⓤ
The third sentence is   Ⓠ Ⓡ Ⓢ Ⓣ Ⓤ
The fourth sentence is   Ⓠ Ⓡ Ⓢ Ⓣ Ⓤ
The fifth sentence is   Ⓠ Ⓡ Ⓢ Ⓣ Ⓤ

Paragraph 5

The first sentence is   Ⓠ Ⓡ Ⓢ Ⓣ Ⓤ
The second sentence is   Ⓠ Ⓡ Ⓢ Ⓣ Ⓤ
The third sentence is   Ⓠ Ⓡ Ⓢ Ⓣ Ⓤ
The fourth sentence is   Ⓠ Ⓡ Ⓢ Ⓣ Ⓤ
The fifth sentence is   Ⓠ Ⓡ Ⓢ Ⓣ Ⓤ

LOGICAL REASONING

11 Ⓐ Ⓑ Ⓒ Ⓓ Ⓔ
12 Ⓕ Ⓖ Ⓗ Ⓙ Ⓚ
13 Ⓐ Ⓑ Ⓒ Ⓓ Ⓔ
14 Ⓕ Ⓖ Ⓗ Ⓙ Ⓚ
15 Ⓐ Ⓑ Ⓒ Ⓓ Ⓔ
16 Ⓕ Ⓖ Ⓗ Ⓙ Ⓚ
17 Ⓐ Ⓑ Ⓒ Ⓓ Ⓔ
18 Ⓕ Ⓖ Ⓗ Ⓙ Ⓚ
19 Ⓐ Ⓑ Ⓒ Ⓓ Ⓔ
20 Ⓕ Ⓖ Ⓗ Ⓙ Ⓚ

READING

21 Ⓐ Ⓑ Ⓒ Ⓓ Ⓔ
22 Ⓕ Ⓖ Ⓗ Ⓙ Ⓚ
23 Ⓐ Ⓑ Ⓒ Ⓓ Ⓔ
24 Ⓕ Ⓖ Ⓗ Ⓙ Ⓚ
25 Ⓐ Ⓑ Ⓒ Ⓓ Ⓔ
26 Ⓕ Ⓖ Ⓗ Ⓙ Ⓚ

27 Ⓐ Ⓑ Ⓒ Ⓓ Ⓔ
28 Ⓕ Ⓖ Ⓗ Ⓙ Ⓚ
29 Ⓐ Ⓑ Ⓒ Ⓓ Ⓔ
30 Ⓕ Ⓖ Ⓗ Ⓙ Ⓚ
31 Ⓐ Ⓑ Ⓒ Ⓓ Ⓔ
32 Ⓕ Ⓖ Ⓗ Ⓙ Ⓚ

33 Ⓐ Ⓑ Ⓒ Ⓓ Ⓔ
34 Ⓕ Ⓖ Ⓗ Ⓙ Ⓚ
35 Ⓐ Ⓑ Ⓒ Ⓓ Ⓔ
36 Ⓕ Ⓖ Ⓗ Ⓙ Ⓚ
37 Ⓐ Ⓑ Ⓒ Ⓓ Ⓔ
38 Ⓕ Ⓖ Ⓗ Ⓙ Ⓚ

39 Ⓐ Ⓑ Ⓒ Ⓓ Ⓔ
40 Ⓕ Ⓖ Ⓗ Ⓙ Ⓚ
41 Ⓐ Ⓑ Ⓒ Ⓓ Ⓔ
42 Ⓕ Ⓖ Ⓗ Ⓙ Ⓚ
43 Ⓐ Ⓑ Ⓒ Ⓓ Ⓔ
44 Ⓕ Ⓖ Ⓗ Ⓙ Ⓚ

45 Ⓐ Ⓑ Ⓒ Ⓓ Ⓔ
46 Ⓕ Ⓖ Ⓗ Ⓙ Ⓚ
47 Ⓐ Ⓑ Ⓒ Ⓓ Ⓔ
48 Ⓕ Ⓖ Ⓗ Ⓙ Ⓚ
49 Ⓐ Ⓑ Ⓒ Ⓓ Ⓔ
50 Ⓕ Ⓖ Ⓗ Ⓙ Ⓚ

PART 2 (MATHEMATICS)

MATHEMATICS PROBLEMS

51 Ⓐ Ⓑ Ⓒ Ⓓ Ⓔ
52 Ⓕ Ⓖ Ⓗ Ⓙ Ⓚ
53 Ⓐ Ⓑ Ⓒ Ⓓ Ⓔ
54 Ⓕ Ⓖ Ⓗ Ⓙ Ⓚ
55 Ⓐ Ⓑ Ⓒ Ⓓ Ⓔ

56 Ⓕ Ⓖ Ⓗ Ⓙ Ⓚ
57 Ⓐ Ⓑ Ⓒ Ⓓ Ⓔ
58 Ⓕ Ⓖ Ⓗ Ⓙ Ⓚ
59 Ⓐ Ⓑ Ⓒ Ⓓ Ⓔ
60 Ⓕ Ⓖ Ⓗ Ⓙ Ⓚ

61 Ⓐ Ⓑ Ⓒ Ⓓ Ⓔ
62 Ⓕ Ⓖ Ⓗ Ⓙ Ⓚ
63 Ⓐ Ⓑ Ⓒ Ⓓ Ⓔ
64 Ⓕ Ⓖ Ⓗ Ⓙ Ⓚ
65 Ⓐ Ⓑ Ⓒ Ⓓ Ⓔ

66 Ⓕ Ⓖ Ⓗ Ⓙ Ⓚ
67 Ⓐ Ⓑ Ⓒ Ⓓ Ⓔ
68 Ⓕ Ⓖ Ⓗ Ⓙ Ⓚ
69 Ⓐ Ⓑ Ⓒ Ⓓ Ⓔ
70 Ⓕ Ⓖ Ⓗ Ⓙ Ⓚ

71 Ⓐ Ⓑ Ⓒ Ⓓ Ⓔ
72 Ⓕ Ⓖ Ⓗ Ⓙ Ⓚ
73 Ⓐ Ⓑ Ⓒ Ⓓ Ⓔ
74 Ⓕ Ⓖ Ⓗ Ⓙ Ⓚ
75 Ⓐ Ⓑ Ⓒ Ⓓ Ⓔ

76 Ⓕ Ⓖ Ⓗ Ⓙ Ⓚ
77 Ⓐ Ⓑ Ⓒ Ⓓ Ⓔ
78 Ⓕ Ⓖ Ⓗ Ⓙ Ⓚ
79 Ⓐ Ⓑ Ⓒ Ⓓ Ⓔ
80 Ⓕ Ⓖ Ⓗ Ⓙ Ⓚ

81 Ⓐ Ⓑ Ⓒ Ⓓ Ⓔ
82 Ⓕ Ⓖ Ⓗ Ⓙ Ⓚ
83 Ⓐ Ⓑ Ⓒ Ⓓ Ⓔ
84 Ⓕ Ⓖ Ⓗ Ⓙ Ⓚ
85 Ⓐ Ⓑ Ⓒ Ⓓ Ⓔ

86 Ⓕ Ⓖ Ⓗ Ⓙ Ⓚ
87 Ⓐ Ⓑ Ⓒ Ⓓ Ⓔ
88 Ⓕ Ⓖ Ⓗ Ⓙ Ⓚ
89 Ⓐ Ⓑ Ⓒ Ⓓ Ⓔ
90 Ⓕ Ⓖ Ⓗ Ⓙ Ⓚ

91 Ⓐ Ⓑ Ⓒ Ⓓ Ⓔ
92 Ⓕ Ⓖ Ⓗ Ⓙ Ⓚ
93 Ⓐ Ⓑ Ⓒ Ⓓ Ⓔ
94 Ⓕ Ⓖ Ⓗ Ⓙ Ⓚ
95 Ⓐ Ⓑ Ⓒ Ⓓ Ⓔ

96 Ⓕ Ⓖ Ⓗ Ⓙ Ⓚ
97 Ⓐ Ⓑ Ⓒ Ⓓ Ⓔ
98 Ⓕ Ⓖ Ⓗ Ⓙ Ⓚ
99 Ⓐ Ⓑ Ⓒ Ⓓ Ⓔ
100 Ⓕ Ⓖ Ⓗ Ⓙ Ⓚ

ARGO BROTHERS

VERBAL
SCRAMBLED PARAGRAPHS

DIRECTIONS: This section requires you to rearrange five given sentences, such that they form a proper paragraph. The introductory sentence for each paragraph will be given.
An appropriate answer will order sentences so that they are logical and grammatically sound.
Credit is exclusively given for answers perfectly correct. There are no partially correct answers.

Scrambled Paragraphs
Practice Test 1 (Paragraphs 1-5)

Paragraph 1

Traditionally, world governing bodies have used Gross Domestic Product (GDP) in order to compare the wealth and success of nations.

 _____ **Q.** This metric successfully shows researchers how much money is circulating through a certain body of people, but fails to account for many related items.

 _____ **R.** A plethora of alternative metrics have been developed in response to these pitfalls, but most continue to bias analysis in ways detrimental to sound governing practice.

 _____ **S.** Nations with incredible bifurcation in wealth distribution can have high GDP, while maintaining low standards of living for the vast majority of the population.

 _____ **T.** Furthermore, GDP does not consider the cost of living when studying the wealth of a nation.

 _____ **U.** Firstly, it fails to show distribution of wealth.

CONTINUE ON TO THE NEXT PAGE ➡

Paragraph 2

It is hard to be a successful visual artist.

_____5_____ **Q.** These degrees are necessary for a multitude of reasons.

_____3_____ **R.** Besides needing immense talent, successful artists have often also spent thousands of dollars on professional degrees in fine arts.

_____4_____ **S.** However, even if they have received a degree from one of these elite MFA programs, they will often still find it difficult to recuperate the expense.

_____6_____ **T.** Furthermore, the social bonds created during the program can heavily influence an artist's prospective representation.

_____2_____ **U.** Critiques, giving throughout the student's tenure, strengthen their artistic statements.

Paragraph 3

Although there are many different songs created every day within the rock genre, almost all follow the same standard form.

_____6_____ **Q.** This quick transition is today perhaps the most recognizable turnaround in all of music.

_____4_____ **R.** In this progression, musicians play within the confines of three chord structures, alternating depending on the bar.

_____5_____ **S.** Good musicians can focus on different elements of these three chords, but they will often maintain the core integrity of them at the required moments in the song.

_____2_____ **T.** This form originates from blues music, and is thus labeled the blues chord progression.

_____3_____ **U.** The only progression that is potentially more noticeable in the rock genre is an innovation that developed simultaneously in blues and jazz in which musicians move from the second chord in a key, to the forth, and finally land back on the first chord of the primary key; however, rather than this progression occurring throughout the song, it may occur only for one or two bars in between verses.

CONTINUE ON TO THE NEXT PAGE ➡

Paragraph 4

Roads are a dangerous place for pedestrians.

_____ 2 **Q.** At first, it was difficult to navigate with a car due to the prevalence of humans on streets.

_____ 6 **R.** This all changed with the introduction of the automobile.

_____ 4 **S.** However, it was not always the case that you could not walk in the middle of the road.

_____ 5 **T.** Until the turn of the century, roads were explicitly places for walking traffic, and carriages would be required to give way to the slower pedestrian travelers.

_____ 3 **U.** With the effort of the American Automobile Association(AAA), laws were introduced to change these practices, leading to the present distinction between roads and sidewalks.

Paragraph 5

Chinese history is flooded with one of the largest varieties of flutes across historical civilizations.

_____ 4 **Q.** The practice of associating higher pitch instrumentation with happier sentiments can be seen across cultures, as even European musical analysis tended to interpret high pitch music as "flighty" and "light."

_____ 3 **R.** This distinction by size and pitch is not a coincidence.

_____ 6 **S.** These emperors believed that a higher pitch would be interpreted by the people as happier, and thus indicate the prevalence of a happier time in history.

_____ 5 **T.** As new emperors began their rule, they would periodically order their royal musicians to cut down the flute's size, so that it would tend to play at a high pitch.

_____ 2 **U.** These flutes are all largely built of the same bamboo material, but are often of varying sizes and operating pitches.

CONTINUE ON TO THE NEXT PAGE ➡

Logical Reasoning
Practice Test 1 (Paragraphs 11-20)

DIRECTIONS: This section requires you to closely analyze the problems and choose the correct answer choice. Exclusively use premises provided within the text. Pay close attention to the rules, setups, and wording.

11. If Kawai plays soccer, then he will play the forward position. If he plays the forward position, then he will score at least one goal.

    What must be true?

    A. If Kawai is not playing forward, then he will not score any goals.

    B. If Kawai plays any other sport he will also play forward.

    C. If Kawai is not playing forward then he will not play soccer.

    D. Kawai was not always able to score every game.

    E. Kawai is the best scorer on his team.

Questions 12, 13 and 14 all relate to the following scenario:

The United Nations is holding a round table discussion concerning international taxation policy. There are eight countries: Armenia, Hungary, China, Estonia, Denmark, Georgia, Bosnia, and France. The table is shaped as an octagon, and all eight countries are represented by a diplomat who is facing inwards. Armenia is sitting across from Hungary. China is sitting directly to the left of Armenia. Estonia is sitting directly across from Denmark. Estonia and China are not sitting next to each other. Lastly, Hungary is sitting directly to the left of Germany.

12. Who is sitting to the right of Denmark?

    F. Germany

    G. Armenia

    H. France

    J. China

    K. Hungary

CONTINUE ON TO THE NEXT PAGE ➡

13. Who is sitting to the left of China?

    A. Denmark

    B. Germany

    C. Hungary

    D. Armenia

    E. Cannot be uniquely determined

14. Who is sitting to the left of Estonia?

    F. Armenia

    G. China

    H. Bosnia

    J. France

    K. Cannot be uniquely determined

Questions 15 and 16 refer to the following information:

Uncover the code below. Each letter corresponds to a word in the line directly below it. A letter **may not** be directly above its corresponding word.

C	E	D	B	means...
Lion	Cow	Cat	Dog	
D	E	F	C	means...
Cat	Goldfish	Lion	Dog	
C	A	B		means...
Rabbit	Dog	Cow		
F	G	D	E	means...
Lion	Goldfish	Cat	Hamster	

15. What word corresponds to A?

    A. Cow

    B. Goldfish

    C. Hamster

    D. Dog

    E. Rabbit

16. What word corresponds to G?

    F. Cow

    G. Cat

    H. Hamster

    J. Cow

    K. Hamster or Cow

CONTINUE ON TO THE NEXT PAGE ➡

17. There are five houses in a row

red, yellow, green, blue, orange

1. The red house is first.
2. The yellow house and blue house have one house in between them.
3. The green house is not next to the red house.
4. The orange house is not next to the red house.

Based on the information above, what must be true?

A. The yellow house is third

B. The blue house is fifth

C. The blue house is fourth

D. The green house could be in the third or fifth position

E. The yellow house is fifth

18. Some of Grant's friends are in the computer science club. If you are in the computer science club, then you receive a free tablet. If you do not have a tablet, then you are not able to play the new game, "Tablet Game." Grant wants to play Tablet Game with his friend Jake, but Jake says he is not able to play.

What **must** be true?

F. Jake does not have a tablet.

G. Jake is not in the computer science club.

H. Grant is in the computer science club.

J. If Jake was in the computer science club, then he would be able to play Tablet Game.

K. None of the above.

19. Six high-school seniors—Anne, Brian, Cardinal, Derrick, Enok, and Frenchie—have been accepted to six different universities—Georgetown, Harvard, Idaho University, Jamestown College, Kent College, and Lehigh.

1. Brian got into Jamestown.
2. Cardinal got into Kent College.
3. Anne got into either Lehigh or Idaho University.
4. Derrick got into either Lehigh or Harvard.
5. Enok did not get into Georgetown, Lehigh, or Idaho University.

Based on the above information, what must be true?

A. Derrick got into Lehigh

B. Frenchie got into Harvard

C. Anne got into Lehigh

D. Derrick got into Harvard

E. Frenchie got into Lehigh

20. Tom is either going to camp or going on vacation this summer. If he goes to camp he will be gone for exactly two weeks. If he goes on vacation he will be gone exactly one week. Without being gone for exactly two weeks, he will be forced to go to a family reunion. What must be true?

F. If Tom goes on vacation, then he will be forced to go to the reunion.

G. Tom secretly wants to go to the reunion.

H. If Tom does not go to the family reunion, then he will not go to camp.

J. If Tom does not go on vacation, then he will not go to the family reunion.

K. Not enough information provided.

CONTINUE ON TO THE NEXT PAGE ➡

Reading
Practice Test 1 (Questions 21-50)

DIRECTIONS: Analyze the passages below, and answer the commensurate questions. Only use information provided within the passage for your answers. There is only one answer for each question.

The opinion that absolute power is essential to the state is very prevalent among statesmen and publicists. They disagree, however, as to who should be invested with this absolute
5 power, the executive or the people; but they agree in the opinion that it should be lodged somewhere.

Without absolute power, they say, there is no peace, no unity in the state, no authority which
10 is either final or supreme. Absolute power and sovereignty are sometimes called synonymous. There are whole families of nations, with which a high respect for absolute power seems to be a natural
15 tendency, which submit to it willingly and without reserve. It is not simply those today with less power that have submitted to an absolute ruler, but rather members of nations of all time. The democratic Greeks believed
20 that the authority of the people were absolute, just as the Romans understood the Caesars to ultimately have absolute power.

Individuals of great energy and superior intellect, when at the head of the
25 government, are most apt to be provoked to resistance by any limit imposed to their universal authority, and seek to justify their action whenever they overstep the limit imposed, by an appeal to the necessity of

30 absolute power. Instances of a leaning toward absolute power are, therefore, frequently met with in the history of modern European states, and were the provocations of a great many political events. And it is not
35 always bad men who incline toward absolutism.

What is the meaning of absolute power? Absolute, in the full sense of the word, means freedom from all limitation. Really, there is
40 nothing absolute but what is without beginning and end; a beginning and an end are limitations. The truly absolute, therefore, can be predicated only of a being unlimited and infinite, that is, only of God. Hence,
45 absolute power, in the real sense of the word, can be conceived only as divine omnipotence.

21. What is the main idea of this passage?

(A.) The nature of absolute power in states.

B. To illustrate that even those who mean well will abuse power

C. To show that there can never be a fair state.

D. To justify the actions of kings

E. To prove that only democratic nations, in which absolute power is lodged in the people, are legitimate.

22. The author compares the absolute power desired by historical political leaders to what?

   F. The Greek power
   G. The power of European leaders
   H. An omnipotent deity
   J. The power of a parent over his/her child.
   K. The power of medicine against disease.

23. What does the author imply about those who try to seize absolute power?

   A. They are evil.
   B. The always lead to war.
   C. They believe themselves as great as the gods.
   D. They do not always have bad intentions.
   E. They never have bad intentions.

24. What is the example, provided by the author, of absolute power lodged in an executive?

   F. The Greeks.
   G. Democratic Italy.
   H. Caesar
   J. The president of a contemporary nation.
   K. The executive chair of Coca-Cola.

25. Based on the passage, what may a leader attempting to gain absolute power argue so as to gain power?

   A. The ruler may argue that without absolute power he/she cannot obtain wealth.
   B. The ruler may argue that without absolute power he/she cannot invade neighboring territories.
   C. The ruler may argue that without absolute power he/she cannot collect wages
   D. The ruler may argue that without absolute power he/she cannot prevent a civil war.
   E. The ruler may argue that without absolute power he/she cannot rule effectively.

26. What word does the author claim to be similar to absolute power?

   A. Constitutional power
   B. Sovereignty
   C. Executive power
   D. People power
   E. All of the power

CONTINUE ON TO THE NEXT PAGE ➡

The bar is a term applied collectively to all who give professional assistance to others in legal controversies, and are licensed by some competent authority to do so. The term in this sense is variously ascribed to the fact that the space occupied by advocates in a court of justice is separated by a rail or bar from that which is appropriated to spectators.

As soon as a people emerge from barbarism, a body of people who make it their business to expound the law, and assist those who may need assistance in legal matters, is always observed to make its appearance. As one of the requisites of civilization and legal order, the state confers upon its members special and peculiar privileges by law, and at the same time places them under regulations more or less strict, for the protection of the public and of those who may place their interests in their care. In the earliest accounts we have of judicial investigations, the litigants are brought into court in person, and are permitted to give their own account of the controversy, and the judges, after inquiring further, proceed to give judgment. This places the ignorant and simple at the mercy of the cunning, crafty and designing, and it is easily made the means of perverting justice, and clothing wrong with the forms of law.

In the famous description of the shield wrought by Hephæstus for Achilles, the picture of a judicial trial is given, and we perceive, immediately, that the most persuasive voice is expected to succeed, whatever may be the merits, unless perhaps the clamor of partisans, who are active and noisy about the court, shall sway the action of the judges in the other direction. That this would be so is by no means unlikely in any case in which popular sympathy is aroused or popular prejudice strongly excited, or even where money or family influence was able to produce the appearance of strong popular feeling. In Athens there seems to have been no distinct class of men who made advocacy their business, and causes were expected to be managed by someone interested therein. However, friends sometimes appeared to support the cause of those who lacked the ability or the eloquence to speak on their own behalf, and sometimes a public prosecutor was appointed for a particular case, as Pericles was called upon by the people to prosecute Cimon, when the latter was accused of having been bribed to abandon the invasion of Macedon.

27. What is the main idea of this passage?

A. To discuss the historical origin and necessity of legal representation.

B. To discuss the origin of the beer bar.

C. To discuss the Greek origins of legal representation.

D. To argue for a buffering of the legal apparatus.

E. To dissuade those who dislike lawyers.

CONTINUE ON TO THE NEXT PAGE ➡

28. What is the origin of the term "bar?"

   F. The place people would go following
      a case.

   G. The gavel used to signal an end to a case.

   H. The tool used to adjudicate punishment
      to defendents.

   J. The railing separating those involved in
      the case from the public.

   K. The name of the Greek god of law, "Bar."

29. A member of the bar is both assigned
     special legal rights and ___?

   A. Responsibilities

   B. Payments

   C. Dividends

   D. Must be older than sixteen years of age.

   E. All of the above

30. What is Hephæstus shielding Achilles from?

   F. Popular opinion

   G. Arrows

   H. Trojans

   J. The plaintiff

   K. Himself

31. What does the author imply about
     Pericles?

   A. He was a bully.

   B. He was ahead of his time.

   C. He was a god.

   D. He was very good at arguing his legal
      case.

   E. People would believe him regardless
      of his argumentation.

32. Under what conditions would an Athenian
     call upon a friend for legal support?

   F. When their friend was a lawyer.

   G. When their friend was more
      persuasive than they were.

   H. When their friend was Pericles.

   J. When their friend could bribe the
      judges.

   K. When they were unable to speak.

The congress of the revolution and the confederacy was peripatetic, and at various *I many different places* times in its history held meetings at Philadelphia, Baltimore, Lancaster, York, Princeton, Annapolis, Trenton and New York. On June 21, 1783, a handful of insubordinate and unpaid militia marched into Philadelphia, where congress was sitting, and, unchecked by any efforts of the state or city authorities to keep the peace, broke up the session of congress by jeering the members and pointing muskets at the windows. This, among other incidents, gave an impulse to the desire to obtain a permanent home for the national legislature.

On October 7, 1783, congress resolved that a building for its use should be erected at some place near the falls of the Delaware. This was soon after modified, in deference to sectional jealousy, by requiring the erection of a suitable building near the falls of the Potomac, so that the meetings of congress might alternate between the two places. After long and warm debate, congress returned to its first resolution, and decided that there should be but one capital, and commissioners were appointed to lay out a federal town near the falls of the Delaware.

December 23, 1784, it was resolved to meet regularly in New York city until the new town was completed. But, while money was wanting for more pressing demands, congress was unable to go any further than the plan. The commissioners made their report, but no action was taken upon it.

The successful establishment of the constitution, with the prospect of a federal government whose wealth and resources would surpass any previous experience in America, revived the notion of a federal town. Objection was made to New York city as a permanent capital by many of the delegates from agricultural districts, who considered a commercial metropolis very ineligible, because of the direct influence which the moneyed interest might exert on congress; and objections were also made to Philadelphia by many of the southern members, who were affronted by the assiduity of the Quakers in preparing and presenting to congress propositions for the abolition of slavery.

When the new congress also came to the conclusion to fix the location of the federal town in the north, placing it this time on the banks of the Susquehanna, the decision roused intense anger among the southern delegates, and Madison declared that if this action had been foreseen, his state might never have entered the Union. As a compromise, it seemed probable that congress would drift back again to the plan of two capitals, and of alternate meetings north and south, an arrangement excellently adapted for preserving the two sections in their separate integrity, and for facilitating their ultimate separation.

33. What is this passage mostly about?

A. Why the Capital was in New York City.

B. Why there were arguments over the location of the nation's capital.

C. How special interests threatening the federal government was a concern at the nation's founding.

D. The history of the U.S. Capital prior to its locationing in Washington, D.C.

E. To illustrate discontent between the north and south during the country's origin.

CONTINUE ON TO THE NEXT PAGE ➡

34. Which of the locations was not listed as a potential location for the Capital?

   F. Falls of the Delaware

   G. New York City

   H. Boston

   J. Philadelphia

   K. Off the banks of the Susquehanna

35. New York City was rejected most fiercely as the location of the Capital by what group?

   A. Confederates

   B. Yankees

   C. Agriculturists

   D. Bankers

   E. Britain

36. By the end of the passage, how many Capitals does the author suggest was most likely to be built?

   F. One

   G. Two

   H. Three

   J. Four

   K. Five

37. What was the main reason noted by the author for why southerners rejected Philadelphia as the location of the Capital?

   A. It was in the north.

   B. It was a center of commerce.

   C. It was not owned by the United States of America.

   D. The abolitionist beliefs held by Quakers.

   E. Southerners preferred having no Capital.

38. What does the author imply about the relationship between the north and south at the time directly following the American Revolution?

   F. The north and south were strong allies.

   G. Southern leaders did not trust Northern leaders.

   H. People did not consider a difference between the north and south.

   J. There were no ideological differences between the leading figures in the north and south.

   K. They were deeply unified.

CONTINUE ON TO THE NEXT PAGE ➡

The division of employments is a natural consequence of the life of man in society. It is, moreover, an element of productive power and of intellectual development. In the infancy of society each individual, each family, manufactures with difficulty and in an imperfect manner the objects it needs; the wisest, the old man of the tribe, preserves in his head the treasure, as yet very meagre, of acquired knowledge, which he endeavors to transmit by word of mouth to those who are to survive him. But as tribes grow larger, and improve, they come to sanction and maintain the right of the individual property of each man in the fruit of his labor; they come to understand the utility of exchanges freely consented to; and henceforth each man can devote himself to the special occupation for which he feels himself peculiarly fitted.

He achieves greater results in the branch of labor to which he thus devotes himself, and produces more than is personally necessary to him; he lacks, on the other hand, everything that his individual labor is unable to supply, and exchange provides him with the means of establishing an equilibrium between what he produces himself and what he wants but cannot produce; he gives his surplus in return for what he requires, and thus barters the services which he renders for those which he himself has occasion for.

When nations become greater and more developed, the division of labor becomes more marked. Certain individuals now devote themselves to hunting, to fishing, to the cultivation of the soil, others to manufactures: others there are again who devote themselves exclusively to the culture of the mind: these latter discover the laws of nature which God has placed at the service of man, whom he has charged to discover them

and turn them to useful account. Thus they effectively help in the production of the wealth, upon the aggregate of which society subsists.

39. What is the main idea of this passage?

A. To detail the many professions available to humans.

B. To give a historical background of todays industrialized society

C. To introduce the idea of a division of labor, and discuss its historical origins

D. To justify the profession of those who do not work with their hands.

E. To give an explanation as to the origin of academia.

40. Why does the author imply it is more productive to focus on an individual trade?

F. People will naturally trend towards professions they are most apt to perform.

G. As people perform an individual skill more, they will continue to perfect that skill.

H. When producing more of a single item, you can create techniques permitting one to scale the operation successfully.

J. Less time is wasted changing actions when a worker continues to perform one task.

K. It is easier to develop technology in a field where there are individuals focused on that field.

41. What is an example of the division of labor becoming "more marked" in modern society?

    A. A teacher who teaches the whole village from youth until adulthood.

    B. A political leader who knows all the laws and tales of the tribe by memory

    C. A neuroscientist studying the brains response to pain.

    D. A parent who must know what a good diet is for his/her child, how to teach the child language, and how to ensure a good future for that child.

    E. A hunter who turns the hide into clothing.

42. What would be an example of how a surplus of goods can be used to exchange for other goods?

    F. A hunter turning their hides into clothing.

    G. A chef cooking for someone else.

    H. A lottery ticket winner exchanging his/her ticket for cash.

    J. A blacksmith trading a horseshoe for a loaf of bread.

    K. A starving farmer trading in a portion of his crops for the protection of the army.

43. What is the "treasure" that the old man holds?

    A. Gold

    B. Silver

    C. Food

    D. Knowledge

    E. All the surplus created by his tribe.

44. What would the author consider a worker creating "culture of the mind?"

    F. Hunter

    G. Theologist

    H. Wall builder

    J. Farmer

    K. Bridge builder

CONTINUE ON TO THE NEXT PAGE ➡

The large standing army was concentrated on the frontier and defended the interior of the empire against foreign invasions.

As far as was possible, the Roman imperial administration attempted to make the Roman armies as productive as possible. Some units operated brick factories, tile manufactories, lead and iron smelters, and many other enterprises. They were often allowed to remain headquartered in the same garrison town almost permanently and often drew their recruits from the local population. Someone who had joined the Roman army had decided upon his life's work since the standard enlistment was for twenty-five years.

Since many recruits came from poor and isolated regions far from the centers of Roman life, the army literally taught them from the bottom up. They learned to dress properly, to speak Latin, to practice personal hygiene, as well as learning at least one and perhaps more than one trade. Along with this, however, it was even more important that they learn of the greatness of Rome and of the majesty of its institutions. Their year was marked off by great rituals in which they honored Roma, a goddess who was the exemplification of Rome, as well as for the peace of the imperial family, its security, the loyalty that bound the army to the service of the emperor, and so on.

Indeed, in times when Rome itself fell in disorder or when the imperial administration had fallen into the depths of corruption or ineffectiveness, the army's reverence for the ideal of Rome remained undiminished even though they might acclaim their general as emperor and march upon Rome to clear up the mess there. Consequently, they invested their spare time and effort in turning the towns that sprang up along

their fortresses into little Romes, or at least close to what the soldiers believed the essence of Rome to be. Stationed on the frontier, they were set to the task of creating the transportation and communication networks - roads, bridges, beacons, canals, ports, aqueducts, - as well as numerous other public works throughout the empire.

45. What is the main idea of this passage?

   A. To inform readers of the many trades known by members of the Roman Army

   B. To illustrate why the Roman army was so powerful

   C. To demonstrate the ways by which Rome generated loyalty amongst its population

   D. To illustrate the myriad ways that the Roman army supported both the infrastructure and idea of Rome.

   E. To demonstrate to readers how massive the Roman army was.

46. What was not a task noted in the passage as one performed by members of the Roman army?

   F. Creating bricks

   G. Creating canals

   H. Creating bridges

   J. Forging iron

   K. Adjudicating municipal legal affairs

CONTINUE ON TO THE NEXT PAGE ➡

47. What is implied about the standard recruit to the Roman army?

A. They did not grow up knowing Latin.

B. They were trained in combat from an early age.

C. They always knew that they wanted to be members of the Roman army.

D. They were skilled in a trade before joining the army.

E. They were of noble backgrounds.

48. In what way was the Roman army's reverence for the idea of Rome beneficial to the continuation of the Empire?

F. It allowed for the center of power—the army—to maintain integrity in the face of nefarious political happenings.

G. It permitted the members of the army to fight ferociously.

H. It spread the romance languages.

J. The Roman emperor was often at one time a member of the army.

K. Rome would not have an industry if it was not for the Roman Army's hard work.

49. What was the name of the god to whom many Roman soldiers prayed?

A. Athena, the goddess of wisdom

B. Mars, the god of war

C. Roma, the god of Rome

D. Belona, goddess of war and conquest

E. Jupiter, god of gods

50. Roman soldiers were located on the frontier to protect the home land and____.

F. Spread the technology and ideas of Rome.

G. To more readily invade neighboring territories.

H. To keep the military, mostly comprising of non-Romans, out of the capital.

J. To keep them near their homeland.

K. They were only kept on the frontier during times of peace.

CONTINUE ON TO THE NEXT PAGE ➡

MATHEMATICS
INSTRUCTIONS

75 MINUTES • 50 QUESTIONS

Select the best answer from the choices given by carefully solving each problem. Bubble the letter of your answer on the answer sheet. Please refrain from making any stray marks on the answer sheet. If you need to erase an answer, please erase thoroughly.

Important Notes:

1. There are no formulas or definitions in the math section that will be provided.
2. Diagrams may or may not be drawn to scale. Do not make assumptions based on the diagram unless it is specifically stated in the diagram or question.
3. Diagrams are not in more than one plane, unless stated otherwise.
4. Graphs are drawn to scale, therefore, you can assume relationships according to the graph. If lines appear parallel, then you can assume the lines to be parallel. This is also true for right angles and so forth.
5. Simplify fractions completely.

Practice Test 1 (Questions 51-100)

51. Convert $\dfrac{7}{20}$ to decimal form.

A. 0.0035
B. 0.035
C. 0.35
D. 3.50
E. 35.0

52. The value of 500,000 + 400 + 5 is

F. 500,450
G. 540,005
H. 540,500
J. 500,405
K. 540,450

CONTINUE ON TO THE NEXT PAGE ➡

53. If $x = 4$ and $y = 3$, what is $(x + y)^2$?

$(4 + 3)^2$

- A. 25
- B. 32
- C. 7
- **D.** 49
- E. 50

54. $(\sqrt{144})(\sqrt{16}) =$

- F. 16
- **G.** 48
- H. 12
- J. 32
- K. 20

55.

$$1 \text{ Knot} = 3 \text{ Vines}$$
$$2 \text{ Shings} = 4 \text{ Knots}$$

How many Shings are in 9 Vines?

- A. $\dfrac{4}{5}$
- B. $\dfrac{2}{3}$
- C. $\dfrac{5}{4}$
- **D.** $\dfrac{3}{2}$
- E. $\dfrac{1}{2}$

56. What number is halfway between $2 \cdot (\dfrac{3}{6})$ and 4 ?

- F. 2
- **G.** 2.5
- H. 3.5
- J. 3
- K. 1.5

57.

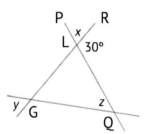

In the figure shown above LGQ is a triangle. What is z in terms of y?

- **A.** $30 - y$
- B. $y + 150$
- C. $2y + 30$
- D. $2y - 30$
- E. $180 + y$

58. $-2 + 5(-18 \div 3 + 9) - 13 =$

- F. 3
- G. -4
- H. 13
- **J.** 0
- K. -15

CONTINUE ON TO THE NEXT PAGE ➡

59. The area of a square is equal to the area of a circle, whose diameter is 10. What is the length of a side of the square?

    A. $\pi r \sqrt{5}$

    B. $25\pi r$

    C. πr^2

    D. $5\sqrt{\pi}$

    E. $25\sqrt{\pi r}$

60. $4a(3b - 6)$

    F. $7ab - 6$

    G. $7ab - 2a$

    H. $12ab - 6$

    J. $12b - 24$

    K. $12ab - 24a$

61. $\dfrac{(-39)^2}{13^3} =$

    A. -3

    B. $\dfrac{-1}{13}$

    C. $\dfrac{9}{13}$

    D. $\dfrac{12}{13}$

    E. 3

62. In a scaled diagram, 1 inch represents 20 feet. How many square inches on the diagram represent 1 square foot?

    F. 0.0025

    G. 0.04

    H. .4

    J. 0.05

    K. 400

63. What is the greatest common factor of 2,240 and 3,360?

    A. 105

    B. 280

    C. 1,120

    D. 2,240

    E. 6,720

64. If 50% of $2y$ is 12, what is y^2 ?

    F. 36

    G. 6

    H. 16

    J. 144

    K. 256

CONTINUE ON TO THE NEXT PAGE ➡

65.

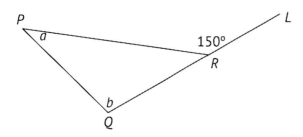

In the figure above ∡ PRL is 150°. What is

$$\frac{a^2 - b^2}{(a - b)} \ ?$$

A. 30
B. 120
C. 150
D. 160
E. 180

66. If $y = \frac{3}{4}$ and $xy^2 = \frac{9}{16}$, what is $(x - 4)$?

F. -3

G. $\frac{-13}{4}$

H. $\frac{-9}{16}$

J. -4

K. 0

67. If P is an odd integer, which of the following must be an even number?

A. $\dfrac{P^2 - \left(\frac{P}{4}\right)}{P^2 \cdot P^4}$

B. $\dfrac{P - 2P^2}{2P + 5}$

C. P^2

D. $\dfrac{2P^2 - 2P^3}{2P}$

E. $3P$

68 If the diameter of a circle is P, and $\dfrac{P^2}{4} = 2$, what is the area of the circle?

F. 4π
G. 8π
H. $2\pi\sqrt{2}$
J. 2π
K. 16π

69. If a regular polygon has (N - 10) sides, where, $N = \left(\dfrac{40}{10}\right)^2$, what is the measure of one of its angles?

A. 120°
B. 160°
C. 240°
D. 340°
E. 720°

70.

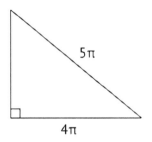

If the perimeter of the triangle shown above is the circumference of a circle, then what is the radius of the circle?

F. 12
G. 9π
H. 4
J. 6
K. 6π

71. If $x = \dfrac{7}{x}$, what is the value of $14 (14)$?

A. 0.25
B. 0.50
C. 7
D. 14
E. 196

72. What is the least common multiple of 4, 16, 25 and 30?

F. 30
G. 160
H. 240
J. 480
K. 1200

73. How many positive integers are between $\dfrac{-7}{3}$ and $\dfrac{5}{2}$?

A. 0
B. 1
C. 2
D. 3
E. 4

74. The perimeter of a rectangle is 80 inches. If the width is 18 inches, what is the area of the rectangle?

   F. 22 sq.in
   G. 80 sq.in
   H. 324 sq.in
   J. 396 sq.in
   K. 6,400 sq.in

75. $7|-x - 3| = b$, If $x = -3$, what is b ?

   A. 24
   B. 40
   C. 42
   D. 26
   E. 0

76. $1 + 2 + 3 + 4 + 5 + ... + 100 =$

   F. 1010
   G. 5050
   H. 101
   J. 5000
   K. 1000

77. After a 10% increase, a population was 55. What was the population before the increase?

   A. 44
   B. 50
   C. 40
   D. 45
   E. 51

78. The length of a rectangular solid is 10. The width, w and the height, h follow the relationship, $w^3 h^3 = 27$. What is the volume of the rectangular solid?

   F. 270
   G. 30
   H. 90
   J. 60
   K. 33

CONTINUE ON TO THE NEXT PAGE ➡

79.

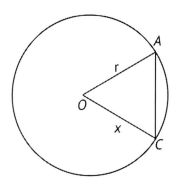

Figure not drawn to scale.

$\overline{AC}$ has a length of 10 and r, the radius, is 7.
What is x?

A. 5
B. 7
C. $7\sqrt{2}$
D. 10
E. 17

80.

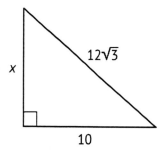

Figure not drawn to scale.

Find the length of x?

F. $2\sqrt{3}$
G. $\sqrt{83}$
H. $2\sqrt{83}$
J. $2\sqrt{332}$
K. 332

81. If $A = 3r^2h^2$, and (rh) increases by 100%, then the new A is how many times greater than the old A?

A. 2
B. 3
C. 4
D. 5
E. 12

82. If $x^a = \sqrt[q]{x^p}$, what is $\frac{p^2}{q^2}$?

   F. $\sqrt{a}$

   G. $a^{1/3}$

   (H.) a^2

   J. a

   K. a^3

83. Set $A = \{\,1, 2, 3, a\,\}$

Set $B = \{\,2, 4, 5, a^2, b\,\}$

What is $A \cap B$?

   A. $\{\,2, a\,\}$

   B. $\{\,2, a^2, b\,\}$

   C. $\{\,2, \frac{b}{a}\,\}$

   (D.) $\{\,2\,\}$

   E. $\{\,2, \frac{a}{b}\,\}$

84. $2\sqrt{75} - (\sqrt{25})(\sqrt{3})$

   (F.) $5\sqrt{3}$

   G. $10\sqrt{3}$

   H. $\sqrt{70}$

   J. $2\sqrt{3}$

   K. 5

85. Express $\frac{0.0345}{10}$ in scientific notation.

   A. 3.45×10^{-2}

   B. $.0345 \times 10^{-2}$

   (C.) 3.45×10^{-3}

   D. 0.345×10^{-3}

   E. $.00345 \times 10$

86. ☆ x ☆ = $3x$, if x is even and negative **OR**

☆ x ☆ = $4x$, if x is odd.

Following the rule above, what is the value of ☆ - 23 ☆ ?

   F. 92

   (G.) -92

   H. 529

   J. -529

   K. 1587

CONTINUE ON TO THE NEXT PAGE ➡

ARGO BROTHERS

87. $y = x^3$

The only possible values of x are those in the set $\left\{ \dfrac{-1}{3}, \dfrac{1}{2}, \dfrac{1}{3} \right\}$

What is the maximum value of y?

A. $\dfrac{1}{27}$

B. $\dfrac{-1}{27}$

C. $\dfrac{1}{4}$

D. $\dfrac{1}{8}$

E. $\dfrac{1}{6}$

88. What is $\dfrac{x^3 y^2 z^4}{z^3 y^3}$ equal to

F. $x^3 yz$

G. $\dfrac{x^3}{3}$

H. $x^3 yz^2$

J. $\dfrac{x^3 z}{y}$

K. $\dfrac{x^3 y}{z}$

89.

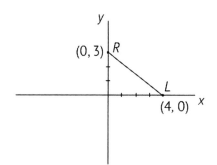

What is the length of $\overline{RL}$?

A. 3

B. 6

C. 5

D. 4

E. 7

90. In a triangle, the sum of two angles equals the third. Find the measure of the third angle.

F. 45°

G. 60°

H. 90°

J. 30°

K. 180°

CONTINUE ON TO THE NEXT PAGE ➡

91. If Anthony and Bridget take turns watching T.V. every 4 hours and Anthony's third watch was at 10: 00 P.M. and Bridget was the first to watch T.V., then when did Bridget begin her second watch?

    A. 6:00 P.M.

    B. 2:00 P.M.

    C. 10:00 A.M.

    D. 10:00 P.M.

    E. 6:00 A.M.

92. There are a total of 9 bicycles and unicycles in a path. There are 13 wheels in total. If x is the number of bicycles, what is x^2 ?

    F. 16

    G. 12

    H. 23

    J. 13

    K. 9

93. A boy moves 4 miles south. Then he turns 90° to the left. He moves forward 6 miles. He turns 90° to the left. He moves forward 4 miles. How far is he now than from his starting point?

    A. 4 miles

    B. 3 miles

    C. 6 miles

    D. 5 miles

    E. 8 miles

94.

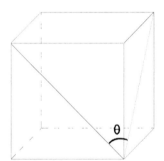

Note: The angle is between the two diagonal lines of the cube

In the figure above, what is the angle, θ?

    F. 45°

    G. 56°

    H. 60°

    J. 90°

    K. 30°

CONTINUE ON TO THE NEXT PAGE ➡

95.

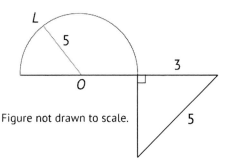

Figure not drawn to scale.

$\overline{OL}$ is the radius. What is the perimeter of the figure above?

A. $12 + 5\pi$
B. $12 + 25\pi$
C. $6 + 25\pi$
D. $22 + 5\pi$
E. $22 + 25\pi$

96. What is $0.\overline{53} - 0.\overline{36}$?

F. $\dfrac{7}{50}$

G. $\dfrac{17}{100}$

H. $\dfrac{7}{99}$

J. $\dfrac{17}{99}$

K. $\dfrac{7}{9}$

97. The sum of two positive numbers is 6 times their difference. What is the reciprocal of the ratio of the larger number to the smaller?

A. $\dfrac{5}{7}$

B. $\dfrac{7}{5}$

C. $\dfrac{5}{2}$

D. $\dfrac{2}{5}$

E. $\dfrac{9}{5}$

98. The mean weekly salary of 9 teachers in a school is $1,000. If there are 9 teachers and 11 assistant principals and the mean weekly salary for assistant principals and teachers is $1,275, what is the mean salary of the assistant principals?

F. $1,100
G. $1,500
H. $1,137.50
J. $1,300
K. $1,000

CONTINUE ON TO THE NEXT PAGE ➡

99. Given $x_n = x_{n-1} + x_{n-2}$, what is $\dfrac{x_6}{x_5}$, knowing that $x_4 = 3$ and $x_5 = 2$?

    A. $\dfrac{3}{2}$

    B. $\dfrac{5}{8}$

    C. $\dfrac{8}{5}$

    D. $\dfrac{2}{3}$

    E. $\dfrac{13}{5}$

---

100. $f(x) = \dfrac{1-x}{1-x}$, which of the following set is not a possible domain for the given function?

    F. $\{\,2, 3, 5\,\}$

    G. $\{\,1, 0, 6\,\}$

    H. $\{\,\pi, 2.17, 10\,\}$

    J. $\{\,2\pi, \pi^2, 0.65\,\}$

    K. $\{\,4, 6, 10\,\}$

THIS IS THE END OF THE TEST. IF THERE IS TIME REMAINING, YOU MAY CHECK YOUR ANSWERS TO PART 1 OR PART 2.

SHSAT PRACTICE TEST 1
ANSWER KEY

PART 1 (VERBAL)

Scrambled Paragraphs

1. Q, U, S, T, R
2. R, Q, U, T, S
3. T, R, S, U, Q
4. S, T, R, Q, U
5. U, R, T, S, Q

Logical Reasoning

11. C
12. J
13. A
14. K
15. E
16. H
17. D
18. K
19. A
20. F

Reading

21. A	44. G
22. H	45. D
23. D	46. J
24. H	47. A
25. E	48. F
26. B	49. C
27. A	50. F
28. J	
29. A	
30. F	
31. D	
32. G	
33. C	
34. H	
35. C	
36. G	
37. D	
38. G	
39. C	
40. F	
41. C	
42. J	
43. D	

PART 2 (MATHEMATICS)

Math

51. C	63. C	75. E	87. D	99. C
52. J	64. J	76. G	88. J	100. G
53. D	65. C	77. B	89. C	
54. G	66. F	78. G	90. H	
55. D	67. D	79. B	91. C	
56. G	68. J	80. H	92. F	
57. A	69. A	81. C	93. C	
58. J	70. J	82. H	94. H	
59. D	71. A	83. D	95. D	
60. K	72. K	84. F	96. J	
61. C	73. C	85. C	97. A	
62. F	74. J	86. G	98. G	

To calculate your score visit our web site
and download excel calculator:
www. einstein-academy.com/calc

Practice Test 1 (Answers and Explanations)

SCRAMBLED PARAGRAPHS

1. Q, U, S, T, R

Q: "This metric" refers to GDP as discussed in the introductory sentence.

U: "Firstly" is the first of the "related items" discussed in sentence Q.

S: S provides a further discussion of the topic introduced in sentence U.

T: "Furthermore" indicates a following issue, and must thus follow Q, U, and S.

R: "These pitfalls" refers to the two discussed and must thus follow Q, U, S, and T.

2. R, Q, U, T, S

R: This sentence introduces the idea of art schools, and must thus be prior to all other sentences.

Q: "These degrees" refers to degrees mentioned in sentence R.

U: U provides a first of the reasons noted in sentence Q.

T: "Furthermore" indicates that it is not the first reason, thus must be the second.

S: "However" indicates something different from the previous sentences. As no other sentences expand on the statement made in S, it must be the final sentence.

3. T, R, S, U, Q

T: "This form" refers to the form mentioned in the introductory sentence.

R: "This progression" refers to the blues progression of sentence T.

S: "These three chords" again refers to the blues progression. As it provides additional information it must follow R.

U: U discusses a new progression. This progression is done for only "one or two bars" and can thus be assumed to not deal with sentences R or S.

Q: "Quick transition" refers to the progression in sentence U.

4. S, T, R, Q, U

S: "However" in sentence S establishes the change in content from the introductory sentence that leads to the following sentences.

T: T provides an example to buffer sentence S.

R: R provides a transition from T to Q and U.

Q: "At first" indicates that it is the first of the two sentences discussing cars.

U: "These practices" is a reference to sentence Q.

5. **U, R, T, S, Q**

> **U:** "These flutes" is a reference to the flutes noted in the introductory sentence.
>
> **R:** "This distinction" is a reference to the varying sizes and operating pitches noted in sentence U.
>
> **T:** T provides the explanation as to why the distinction in size and pitch "is not a coincidence."
>
> **S:** "These emperors" refers to the emperors of sentence T.
>
> **Q:** Q builds on the discussion started in sentence S. It relies on the introduction of a discussion concerning the relationship between pitch and happiness.

LOGICAL REASONING

11. **C** The logical statements should read as following:

$$[S \to F; \cancel{F} \to \cancel{S}] \; [F \to G; \cancel{G} \to \cancel{F}]$$

These formulas should in turn be chained, such that they read:

$$[S \to F \to G; \cancel{G} \to \cancel{F} \to \cancel{S}]$$

Not forward only leads to not soccer. It does not lead to not goal.
A logical phrase must only be valid;

it does not need to be sound. Thus, B is incorrect.
Not F leads to not S. Thus, C is correct.
D is irrelevant.
E is irrelevant.

12. **J** 12, 13, and 14 all rely on the same game. This game is simultaneously a pairing and sequencing game. It relies heavily on establishing a proper board and recognizing that all players are facing "inwards." First set up the board as an octagon:

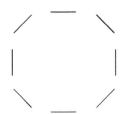

Player location is only important relative to other players in this game, so you can fill in the rules starting at any chair. First, place A and H directly across from each other. Next, place C to the left hand side of A. Make sure that you are not only thinking about "your" left, but A's left. After this, start writing out rules. The rules should like similar to:

E – D

H G

Place Hungary directly to the left of Georgia. At this point your board should look like:

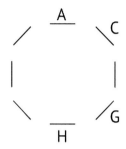

E needs to be across from D, but cannot be next to C; thus, D must be next to C and E must be across from D. The final two countries, Bosnia and France, have no additional information concerning them and can thus alternate in the two final seats. The board should look like:

A
B/F   C
E   D
B/F   G
H

China is sitting to the right of Denmark, thus the answer to 12 is J.

13. A Denmark sits to the left of China.

14. K Estonia is surrounded by either Bosnia or France, but it cannot be determined which. Thus, K is the correct answer.

15. E For 15 and 16, we must first solve the full game, finding what all letters stand for. First look for letters prevalent in all four pairs of rows. There are no letters that exist in all four letter rows, so start looking for letters that occur in three rows. E, D, and C all occur three times. Next, find the three words that occur three times. Lion, cat, and dog occur in all three. So far your game should look like:

E = Lion, Cat, Dog
D = Lion, Cat, Dog
C = Lion, Cat, Dog

Dog is not in the final row with E or D, thus neither E nor D can be dog. Accordingly, C must be dog. Cross out all C's and dogs from the board. There are no further rules to determine E and D, thus they can both be either lion or cat. Cross out E, D, lion, and cat off from the chart. B is alone, thus it must be Cow. F must be goldfish. A must be rabbit. G must be hamster. The final list should read:

E = Lion, Cat, ~~Dog~~
D = Lion, Cat, ~~Dog~~
C = ~~Lion, Cat,~~ Dog
B = Cow
F = Goldfish
A = Rabbit
G = Hamster

A is Rabbit; thus, the answer is E.

16. H   G is hamster; thus, the answer is H

17. D   Problem 8 is a sequencing game. Set up the game as such:

$$\overline{}\ \overline{}\ \overline{}\ \overline{}\ \overline{}$$
$$5\quad 4\quad 3\quad 2\quad 1$$

Plug R into slot 1. Rule 2, 3 and 4 should be written as such:

$$Y\overset{\wedge}{\_}B,\quad \boxed{\not{G}R},\quad \boxed{\not{O}R}$$

If in doubt, draw out the two possible board games:

$$\frac{Y/B}{5}\ \frac{}{4}\ \frac{Y/B}{3}\ \frac{}{2}\ \frac{R}{1}$$

$$\frac{}{5}\ \frac{Y/B}{4}\ \frac{}{3}\ \frac{Y/B}{2}\ \frac{R}{1}$$

As you can see, the first option is not viable, since neither G nor O can fit in position 2. Thus, the second board the correct board, and G or O can alternatively fit in 5 or 3. Thus, answer D is correct.

18. K   The logical statements should read as following:

$$[CS \rightarrow FT;\ \not{F}\not{T} \rightarrow \not{C}\not{S}]$$
$$[\not{T} \rightarrow \emptyset;\ G \rightarrow T]$$
$$[J \rightarrow \emptyset;\ G \rightarrow \not{J}]$$

The logical result of being Jake is that you cannot play the game. However, not G only exists as a consequence, and thus does not lead to further truths. F, G, and H are thus not true.
Being in the computer science club ensures you have a tablet, but does not ensure that you are able to play the game. Thus, K is correct.

19. A   This is a pairing question. After first inserting the rules, the board should look similar to:

A	B	C	D	E	F
L	J	K	L	~~E~~	
I			H	~~V~~	
				~~X~~	

E only has H left, so must be paired accordingly. If H is with E, then D must be with L. If D is with L, then A must be with I. This leaves F with G. Derrick did indeed get into Lehigh, thus A is correct.

20. F All statements are bi-conditional because Tom must either be at camp or go on vacation. If he goes on vacation he will be gone 1 week. If he is not gone for 2 weeks then he goes on a family reunion. 1 week is not 2 weeks, thus F is correct.

READING COMPREHENSION

21. A This passage discusses the nature of absolute power within the confines of states in all four paragraphs. All other answer choices occur in fewer paragraphs.

22. H The author notes that absolute power can only be understood as "divine omnipotence" in line 46. As these leaders wanted absolute power, we can assume that they wanted something similar to an omnipotent deity.

23. D This answer derives from lines 34-36.

24. H This answer derives from line 22.

25. E The author only provides the general argument that a ruler may argue that there is a "necessity of absolute power." As such, we can only choose the answer that similarly offers a general argument as to one's ability to rule without absolute power.

26. B This answer derives from lines 10-12, where he calls sovereignty and absolute power "synonymous."

27. A This is the topic of two paragraphs. C only appears in one paragraph.

28. J This answer derives from lines 4-8.

29. A This answer derives from lines 15-20.

30. F The trial discussed in the example is one in which popular opinion is set to overtake truth. The shield appears to protect Achilles from any issue stated within the trial.

31. D The passage notes that people would sometimes lobby for an individual to argue for a side in a case if they were particularly talented at legal argumentation. Pericles was asked to prosecute in a very important case.

32. G This answer derives from lines 49-51.

33. C All paragraphs discuss where the U.S. Capital should be placed. As at the end of the passage the Capital has not yet been placed in Washington, D.C., we can assume that this all takes place before its final placement.

34. H All other locations can be found explicitly noted within the passage.

35. C This answer derives from line 43.

36. G As noted in the final paragraph, plans had drifted back to the Capital being in two locations.

37. D This answer derives from line 50.

38. G Southern leaders did not want the capital in the north, because they did not trust northern leaders.

39. C The historical origins of the division of labor is discussed in the first paragraph, and the next two paragraphs discuss its importance. No other answer choice occurs in as many paragraphs.

40. F In lines 16-20, the author notes that individuals will devote themselves to occupations in which they find themselves peculiarly fitted.

41. C The passage notes that professions that use the mind and do not produce physical entities is a sign of a more marked division of labor. C best fits this description.

42. J J provides an example of an individual using a product he makes so as to buy an item he does not make. In F, the hunter is converting the objecting into something else himself. In G, there is no exchange of goods explicitly noted. In H, the individual did not themselves create a surplus of a good. In K, the farmer did not have a surplus of goods to trade.

43. D This answer derives from line 13.

44. G The author states that those devoted to the culture of the mind may try to uncover the nature of "God."

45. D This answer choice can be found in all paragraphs of the essay. No other answer is as prevalent.

46. J All other answers can be found within the passage explicitly stated.

47. A Line 21 notes that standard recruits needed to learn Latin. This implied that prior to joining, they did not know how to speak Latin.

48. F This answer derives from line 35.

49. C This answer derives from line 28.

50. F Lines 40-50 discuss the ways that Roman soldiers would spread technology and beliefs to the outposts where they were stationed.

Practice Test 1 (Answers and Explanations)

51. C $(\frac{7}{20}) \cdot (\frac{5}{5}) = (\frac{35}{100}) = 0.35$

52. J $500,000 + 400 + 5 = 500,405$

53. D Substitute and perform the respective operations.
$x = 4$
$y = 3$
$(4 + 3)^2 = (7)^2 = 49$

54. G $(\sqrt{144})(\sqrt{16}) = (12)(4) = 48$

55. D One approach to this type of problem is to look at the two equations and see what is common. Both equations have the word **Knot** in common.

Manipulate the equation so that both equations have the same number of Knots. You can do this by dividing the second equation by 4, to get
$\frac{1}{2}$ Shings = 1 Knot.

Therefore, 3 Vines = $\frac{1}{2}$ Shings.
Since you are trying to find out how many Shings are in 9 Vines, simply multiply the equation by 3 to get
9 Vines = $\frac{3}{2}$ Shings.

56. G Simplifying the first number gives us 1. So, the question is asking for what number is between 1 and 4. As a general rule for these types of problems, we must divide the difference of the numbers by 2 and add that value to the original number. This gives us:
$(\frac{4 - 1}{2}) + 1 = (\frac{1.5}{1}) + 1 = 2.5$

57. A $\angle GLQ = 150°$ since angles on a straight line add up to $180°$.
$\angle LGQ = y$ since vertical angles are always equal. Using this and the fact that the interior angles of a triangle add up to $180°$, find z in terms of y.

$y + 150° + z = 180°$ and by solving for z, you get
$z = 30 - y$, which is answer choice A.

58. J Use PEMDAS (Parenthesis, Exponents, Multiplication, Division, Addition, Subtraction).

59. D   You must remember the formula for the area of a circle and square. Given that the side of the square is, "s" and the radius and diameter of the circle are "r" and "D" respectively, we have:

A square = s^2
A circle = $(\pi)(r^2) = (\pi)(\frac{D^2}{4})$, since the radius is half the diameter (substitute the radius for $(\frac{D}{2})$).
We are given that the diameter is 10, and the areas are equal, so after setting both areas equal to each other, we have:

$s^2 = (\pi)(\frac{10^2}{4}) = 25\pi$, and solving for s, we get:
$s = 5\sqrt{\pi}$, which is answer choice D.

60. K   Use distributive property
$4a(3b - 6) = 12ab - 24a$

61. C   The trick here is to realize that 39 is the product of 13 and 3. Using that, we have:

$(\frac{(-3 \cdot 13)^2}{13^3}) = (\frac{(-3)^2 \cdot (13)^2}{13^3}) = $

$9 \cdot (\frac{13^2}{13^3}) = \frac{9}{13}$, which is answer choice C

62. F   If 1 inch represents 20 ft, you can square both sides to get 1 square inch represents 400 ft squared. We want to find how many square inches are in one square foot. Using this information, we can write a proportion:

$(\frac{1 in^2}{400 ft^2}) = (\frac{x in^2}{1 ft^2})$

and solving for x, we get:

$x = (\frac{1}{400}) = 0.0025$, which is answer choice F.

63. C   List the prime factors for each number
2240: $2^6 \cdot 5 \cdot 7$
3360: $2^5 \cdot 3 \cdot 5 \cdot 7$
Multiply the factors that are common in both sets.
$2^5 \cdot 5 \cdot 7 = 1,120$, which is answer choice C.

64. J   50% of $2y$ is half of $2y$, which is just y. So we have: $y = 12$, so then the square of y is 144. The answer choice is J.

65. C

We know that:
$(a + b) = 150°$ because of the rule that an exterior angle of a triangle is equal to the two opposite interior angles (a and b). And, simplifying:

$$\left(\frac{a^2 - b^2}{a + b}\right) = \left(\frac{(a - b)(a + b)}{a - b}\right) = (a + b)$$

$= 150°$, which is answer choice, C.

66. F

If $y = \left(\frac{3}{4}\right)$, then $y^2 = \left(\frac{9}{16}\right)$ which means x must equal 1 for $xy^2 = \left(\frac{9}{16}\right)$.
Now we just have to simplify $(x - 4)$ which is $(1 - 4)$, which is -3.
The answer choice is F.

67. D

We need to find which one is an even integer. An integer that is divisible by 2 is an even integer. If we can find an answer choice that is an integer multiplied by 2, then that answer choice is automatically an even integer. This is answer choice D, since each term is multiplied by 2 and if we were to divide by 2, we would be left with an integer.

68. J

If the diameter is P, then we know that the radius is $\left(\frac{P}{2}\right)$ and using the given information, we can substitute and find that the area is just:

$$A = \pi\left(\frac{P}{2}\right)^2 = \pi\left(\frac{P^2}{4}\right) = 2\pi,$$

which is answer choice J.

69. A

We must find what N is first. Simplifying, we find that $N = 16$ and so the polygon has (16-10) sides or 6 sides. Now we need to find the total number of degrees in this hexagon, and then divide by 6. We can use the formula:

Total number of Degrees = $(N - 2)180°$, and so when $N = 6$, this simplifies to 720°. Dividing this by 6, gives us:
120° for each interior angle. The answer is A.

70. J

It is important to note that this is a variation of a 3, 4, 5 right triangle. The fact that there is π multiplied with 4 and 5 does not change this relationship. Knowing this, the perimeter is 12π. This perimeter equals to the circumference of a circle, which gives way to this equation:

$12\pi = 2(\pi)r$, where r is the radius. Solving for the radius gives:
$r = 6$, so the answer choice is J.

71. A In this problem, we just need to plug into the formula. We get:

$(\frac{7}{14}) \cdot (\frac{7}{14})$,

which simplifies to a quarter, which is 0.25, or answer choice A.

72. K Since 25 can only go into 1200, K is the answer choice.

73. C We can simplify each fraction to a mixed number. Then, we are just looking for the positive integers that are bigger than $-2\frac{1}{3}$ and less than $2\frac{1}{2}$. If we wrote all the integers between those two numbers, we would get -2, -1, 0, 1, 2. Eliminating the negative ones gives us: 1 and 2, which is 2 integers giving us answer choice C.

74. J The formula of the perimeter of a rectangle is $2l + 2w$, where l and w are the length and width respectively. They give us the width as 18 inches and the perimeter at 80 inches. Which means when we solve for the length, we get 22 inches.
To get the area, we just need to multiply the length and width together, so we get 18in x 22in, which is 396 sq.inches or answer choice J.

75. E All we need to do is plug in $x = -3$ in the first expression. We then get $b = 7 \cdot |0|$, which is just 0.
The answer is E.

76. G Here, we need to find the sum:
$1 + 2 + 3 + 4 + ... + 100$.
Well, if we take the first and last number and add them, we get 101. If we take the 2nd and 99th number and add them, we get 101. If we continue this pattern, we will always get 101. So, we have 50 pairs of numbers that add up to 101 and we are adding them all up. So the answer is:
$50 \cdot 101 = 5050$, or answer choice G.

77. B Let's say that the original population was Y. Then we have that $1.1Y = 55$ because we increase Y by 10%.
Solving for Y gives us 50, or answer choice B.

78. G The volume of a rectangular solid is the product of the length, the width and the height.
$V = lwh$. We are given $l = 10$, so all we need is, wh. We can find this by taking the cube root of both sides of the equation below which is given to us:
$w^3h^3 = 27$ becomes $wh = 3$, so then:
$lwh = 30$, which is answer choice G.

79. B The key here is to realize that there are two radii of the circle drawn, *OA* and *OC*. All radii are equal, so $x = 7$. The answer is B.

80. H Using the Pythagorean Theorem, we get,
$x + 100 = 432$
$x = 332$
$x = \sqrt{332} = 2\sqrt{83}$, which is answer choice answer H.

81. C Another way of writing *A* is $A = 3(rh)^2$, and if we increase (rh) by 100%, we are actually doubling it, so we have for the new *A* called *A'*,
$A' = 3(2rh)^2 = 3 \cdot 4(rh)^2 = 12(rh)^2$
which is 4 times as large as the original *A*. The answer is C.

82. H We have,
$x^a = x^{\frac{p}{q}}$, which means $a = \dfrac{p}{q}$
so then,
$\dfrac{p^2}{q^2} = (\dfrac{p}{q})^2 = a^2$

The answer is H.

83. D The only common value(s) in both sets is 2. So the answer is {2} which is answer choice D.

84. F This can be simplified to
$2\sqrt{75} - \sqrt{25}\sqrt{3} = 10\sqrt{3} - 5\sqrt{3} = 5\sqrt{3}$
The answer is F.

85. C This can be reduced to 0.00345, which in scientific notation is
3.45×10^3.
The answer is C.

86. G Since -23 is odd, we must use the second rule. The answer is
$4(-23) = -92$.
The answer is G.

87. D The maximum value for *y* occurs when *x* is positive and large. This value of *x* is $(\frac{1}{2})$ giving us $y = (\frac{1}{8})$.
The answer is D.

88. J By simplifying, we get, $\dfrac{x^3 z}{y}$ or answer J.

89. C This is a special 3, 4, 5 right triangle. The length of *RL* must be 5. The answer is C.

90. H   If the sum of 2 angles equals the third, then the only value of the third angle that is possible is 90°.
One way of thinking of this is to realize that the sum of the third angle and the sum of the other two angles must be 180.°
The answer is H.

91. C   Bridget and Anthony take turns watching T.V. with 4 hour intervals. We progress in the order of Bridget (B), Anthony (A), Bridget (B), Anthony (A), etc. We can write a list where we know that Anthony's 3rd turn is at 10PM.

B-
A-
B-
A-
B-
A- 10PM

Now, we can work backwards to find Bridget's time for her second turn. That turns out to be at 10 AM.
The answer is C.

92. F   We can write a system of two linear equations. The first represents the number of bikes and unicycles as x and y respectively as a sum. The second represents the number of wheels for each bike and unicycle as a sum.

$x + y = 9$
$2x + y = 13$

Solving these equations by either substitution or addition, we get that $x = 4$. So, $x^2 = 16$
The answer is F.

93. C   The direction of his path is shown below.

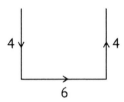

He is 6 miles from his starting point, which is answer choice C.

94. H   Since all the diagonals of a cube are equal, the angle is part of an equilateral triangle. So the angle measure is 60°.
The answer is H.

95. D   We must know the equation for the circumference of a semi-circle, which is simply half the circumference of a circle. We must also realize that the triangle is a special 3, 4, 5 right triangle. Adding the circumference of the semicircle, with the diameter of the semicircle and the perimeter of the triangle, we get the perimeter as $22 + 5\pi$.
The answer is D.

96. J   You must know that these repeating decimals can be simplified to,

$\frac{53}{99}, \frac{36}{99}$ respectively. Subtracting

these two repeating decimals, we get,

$\frac{17}{99}$, which is answer choice J.

97. A   We can set up an equation as follows, $(x + y) = 6(x - y)$ and solving for the ratio of y to x gives us:

$\frac{y}{x} = \frac{5}{7}$

The reason we want the ratio of y to x is because x is the larger number and we want the reciprocal of the larger number to the smaller number.
The answer is A.

98. G   We are given the mean weekly salary for the 9 teachers as $1,000. If x is the total for the salary of the teachers, then we have:

$\frac{x}{9} = 1000$

Now let's let y equal the total salary of the 11 assistant principals. Then we have:

$\frac{x + y}{9 + 11} = \frac{x + y}{20} = \frac{9000 + y}{20}$

= 1275 and solving for y, we get, $y = 16,500$. The mean weekly salary of the 11 assistant principals is just y divided by 11, giving $1,500 or answer G.

99. C   The recursion formula just requires us to take the two previous terms to get the next. So the 5th term is the sum of the 4th and 3rd terms, or 5. The 6th term is the sum of the 5th and 4th terms or 8.
The 6th term divided by the 5th

term is ($\frac{8}{5}$) or answer C.

100. G   We cannot divide by 0, so the set that is not a possible domain is any set with the value 1 in it, or answer G.

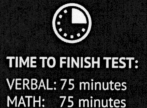

TIME TO FINISH TEST:
VERBAL: 75 minutes
MATH: 75 minutes

— This exam is 2 hours and 30 minutes long. Try to take this full exam in one sitting to simulate real test conditions.

— While taking this exam, refrain from hearing music or watching T.V.

— Please note, calculators are not permitted! You are permitted to answer questions in any order you see fit.

— Not all answers need take the same amount of time. Allocate your test time accordingly.

— Concentrate and GOOD LUCK!

To calculate your score visit our web site and download excel calculator:
www. einstein-academy.com/calc

SHSAT PRACTICE TEST 2
ANSWER SHEET

PART 1 (VERBAL)

SCRAMBLED PARAGRAPHS

Paragraph 1

The first sentence is ⓠ ⓡ ⓢ ⓣ ⓤ
The second sentence is ⓠ ⓡ ⓢ ⓣ ⓤ
The third sentence is ⓠ ⓡ ⓢ ⓣ ⓤ
The fourth sentence is ⓠ ⓡ ⓢ ⓣ ⓤ
The fifth sentence is ⓠ ⓡ ⓢ ⓣ ⓤ

Paragraph 2

The first sentence is ⓠ ⓡ ⓢ ⓣ ⓤ
The second sentence is ⓠ ⓡ ⓢ ⓣ ⓤ
The third sentence is ⓠ ⓡ ⓢ ⓣ ⓤ
The fourth sentence is ⓠ ⓡ ⓢ ⓣ ⓤ
The fifth sentence is ⓠ ⓡ ⓢ ⓣ ⓤ

Paragraph 3

The first sentence is ⓠ ⓡ ⓢ ⓣ ⓤ
The second sentence is ⓠ ⓡ ⓢ ⓣ ⓤ
The third sentence is ⓠ ⓡ ⓢ ⓣ ⓤ
The fourth sentence is ⓠ ⓡ ⓢ ⓣ ⓤ
The fifth sentence is ⓠ ⓡ ⓢ ⓣ ⓤ

Paragraph 4

The first sentence is ⓠ ⓡ ⓢ ⓣ ⓤ
The second sentence is ⓠ ⓡ ⓢ ⓣ ⓤ
The third sentence is ⓠ ⓡ ⓢ ⓣ ⓤ
The fourth sentence is ⓠ ⓡ ⓢ ⓣ ⓤ
The fifth sentence is ⓠ ⓡ ⓢ ⓣ ⓤ

Paragraph 5

The first sentence is ⓠ ⓡ ⓢ ⓣ ⓤ
The second sentence is ⓠ ⓡ ⓢ ⓣ ⓤ
The third sentence is ⓠ ⓡ ⓢ ⓣ ⓤ
The fourth sentence is ⓠ ⓡ ⓢ ⓣ ⓤ
The fifth sentence is ⓠ ⓡ ⓢ ⓣ ⓤ

LOGICAL REASONING

11 Ⓐ Ⓑ Ⓒ Ⓓ Ⓔ
12 Ⓕ Ⓖ Ⓗ Ⓙ Ⓚ
13 Ⓐ Ⓑ Ⓒ Ⓓ Ⓔ
14 Ⓕ Ⓖ Ⓗ Ⓙ Ⓚ
15 Ⓐ Ⓑ Ⓒ Ⓓ Ⓔ
16 Ⓕ Ⓖ Ⓗ Ⓙ Ⓚ
17 Ⓐ Ⓑ Ⓒ Ⓓ Ⓔ
18 Ⓕ Ⓖ Ⓗ Ⓙ Ⓚ
19 Ⓐ Ⓑ Ⓒ Ⓓ Ⓔ
20 Ⓕ Ⓖ Ⓗ Ⓙ Ⓚ

READING

21 Ⓐ Ⓑ Ⓒ Ⓓ Ⓔ
22 Ⓕ Ⓖ Ⓗ Ⓙ Ⓚ
23 Ⓐ Ⓑ Ⓒ Ⓓ Ⓔ
24 Ⓕ Ⓖ Ⓗ Ⓙ Ⓚ
25 Ⓐ Ⓑ Ⓒ Ⓓ Ⓔ
26 Ⓕ Ⓖ Ⓗ Ⓙ Ⓚ
27 Ⓐ Ⓑ Ⓒ Ⓓ Ⓔ
28 Ⓕ Ⓖ Ⓗ Ⓙ Ⓚ
29 Ⓐ Ⓑ Ⓒ Ⓓ Ⓔ
30 Ⓕ Ⓖ Ⓗ Ⓙ Ⓚ
31 Ⓐ Ⓑ Ⓒ Ⓓ Ⓔ
32 Ⓕ Ⓖ Ⓗ Ⓙ Ⓚ

33 Ⓐ Ⓑ Ⓒ Ⓓ Ⓔ
34 Ⓕ Ⓖ Ⓗ Ⓙ Ⓚ
35 Ⓐ Ⓑ Ⓒ Ⓓ Ⓔ
36 Ⓕ Ⓖ Ⓗ Ⓙ Ⓚ
37 Ⓐ Ⓑ Ⓒ Ⓓ Ⓔ
38 Ⓕ Ⓖ Ⓗ Ⓙ Ⓚ
39 Ⓐ Ⓑ Ⓒ Ⓓ Ⓔ
40 Ⓕ Ⓖ Ⓗ Ⓙ Ⓚ
41 Ⓐ Ⓑ Ⓒ Ⓓ Ⓔ
42 Ⓕ Ⓖ Ⓗ Ⓙ Ⓚ
43 Ⓐ Ⓑ Ⓒ Ⓓ Ⓔ
44 Ⓕ Ⓖ Ⓗ Ⓙ Ⓚ
45 Ⓐ Ⓑ Ⓒ Ⓓ Ⓔ
46 Ⓕ Ⓖ Ⓗ Ⓙ Ⓚ
47 Ⓐ Ⓑ Ⓒ Ⓓ Ⓔ
48 Ⓕ Ⓖ Ⓗ Ⓙ Ⓚ
49 Ⓐ Ⓑ Ⓒ Ⓓ Ⓔ
50 Ⓕ Ⓖ Ⓗ Ⓙ Ⓚ

PART 2 (MATHEMATICS)

MATHEMATICS PROBLEMS

51 Ⓐ Ⓑ Ⓒ Ⓓ Ⓔ
52 Ⓕ Ⓖ Ⓗ Ⓙ Ⓚ
53 Ⓐ Ⓑ Ⓒ Ⓓ Ⓔ
54 Ⓕ Ⓖ Ⓗ Ⓙ Ⓚ
55 Ⓐ Ⓑ Ⓒ Ⓓ Ⓔ

56 Ⓕ Ⓖ Ⓗ Ⓙ Ⓚ
57 Ⓐ Ⓑ Ⓒ Ⓓ Ⓔ
58 Ⓕ Ⓖ Ⓗ Ⓙ Ⓚ
59 Ⓐ Ⓑ Ⓒ Ⓓ Ⓔ
60 Ⓕ Ⓖ Ⓗ Ⓙ Ⓚ

61 Ⓐ Ⓑ Ⓒ Ⓓ Ⓔ
62 Ⓕ Ⓖ Ⓗ Ⓙ Ⓚ
63 Ⓐ Ⓑ Ⓒ Ⓓ Ⓔ
64 Ⓕ Ⓖ Ⓗ Ⓙ Ⓚ
65 Ⓐ Ⓑ Ⓒ Ⓓ Ⓔ

66 Ⓕ Ⓖ Ⓗ Ⓙ Ⓚ
67 Ⓐ Ⓑ Ⓒ Ⓓ Ⓔ
68 Ⓕ Ⓖ Ⓗ Ⓙ Ⓚ
69 Ⓐ Ⓑ Ⓒ Ⓓ Ⓔ
70 Ⓕ Ⓖ Ⓗ Ⓙ Ⓚ

71 Ⓐ Ⓑ Ⓒ Ⓓ Ⓔ
72 Ⓕ Ⓖ Ⓗ Ⓙ Ⓚ
73 Ⓐ Ⓑ Ⓒ Ⓓ Ⓔ
74 Ⓕ Ⓖ Ⓗ Ⓙ Ⓚ
75 Ⓐ Ⓑ Ⓒ Ⓓ Ⓔ

76 Ⓕ Ⓖ Ⓗ Ⓙ Ⓚ
77 Ⓐ Ⓑ Ⓒ Ⓓ Ⓔ
78 Ⓕ Ⓖ Ⓗ Ⓙ Ⓚ
79 Ⓐ Ⓑ Ⓒ Ⓓ Ⓔ
80 Ⓕ Ⓖ Ⓗ Ⓙ Ⓚ

81 Ⓐ Ⓑ Ⓒ Ⓓ Ⓔ
82 Ⓕ Ⓖ Ⓗ Ⓙ Ⓚ
83 Ⓐ Ⓑ Ⓒ Ⓓ Ⓔ
84 Ⓕ Ⓖ Ⓗ Ⓙ Ⓚ
85 Ⓐ Ⓑ Ⓒ Ⓓ Ⓔ

86 Ⓕ Ⓖ Ⓗ Ⓙ Ⓚ
87 Ⓐ Ⓑ Ⓒ Ⓓ Ⓔ
88 Ⓕ Ⓖ Ⓗ Ⓙ Ⓚ
89 Ⓐ Ⓑ Ⓒ Ⓓ Ⓔ
90 Ⓕ Ⓖ Ⓗ Ⓙ Ⓚ

91 Ⓐ Ⓑ Ⓒ Ⓓ Ⓔ
92 Ⓕ Ⓖ Ⓗ Ⓙ Ⓚ
93 Ⓐ Ⓑ Ⓒ Ⓓ Ⓔ
94 Ⓕ Ⓖ Ⓗ Ⓙ Ⓚ
95 Ⓐ Ⓑ Ⓒ Ⓓ Ⓔ

96 Ⓕ Ⓖ Ⓗ Ⓙ Ⓚ
97 Ⓐ Ⓑ Ⓒ Ⓓ Ⓔ
98 Ⓕ Ⓖ Ⓗ Ⓙ Ⓚ
99 Ⓐ Ⓑ Ⓒ Ⓓ Ⓔ
100 Ⓕ Ⓖ Ⓗ Ⓙ Ⓚ

ARGO BROTHERS

DIRECTIONS: This section requires you to rearrange five given sentences, such that they form a proper paragraph. The introductory sentence for each paragraph will be given.
An appropriate answer will order sentences so that they are logical and grammatically sound.
Credit is exclusively given for answers perfectly correct. There are no partially correct answers.

Scrambled Paragraphs
Practice Test 2 (Paragraphs 1-5)

Paragraph 1

Following World War Two, the allies that had previously presented a united front fractured and began what became known as the Cold War.

_____2____ **Q.** The Cold War eventually ended in a seemingly abrupt fashion, but its effects continue to influence geopolitics across the globe.

_____5____ **R.** Rather than engaging each other directly, the two formerly allied powers confronted each other using economic, political, and military influence on neighboring countries.

_____3____ **S.** This designation was made in contradiction to "hot" wars, in which political powers engage each other directly utilizing military might.

_____4____ **T.** Gaining influence often involved the use of military might, resulting in conflicts throughout the Middle East, the Caribbean, and Asia.

_____6____ **U.** By gaining power and influence over these previously neutral countries, both sides hoped to gain regional and international hegemony.

CONTINUE ON TO THE NEXT PAGE ➡

Paragraph 2

Most armchair economists believe that as more companies of a same kind enter the market, profits decrease.

_____ Q. In the previous case of the coffee shops, cultural shifts in use made them fill a niche in the market place for temporary work space, leading to a boom across the industry.

_____ R. As more consumers view an industry in a positive way, they become more apt to consume at a higher rate.

_____ S. Authors continue to debate over the specifics, but most largely agree that this economic paradox is culturally driven.

_____ T. However, sociologists and economists increasingly find that for many markets, the inverse is in fact the case.

_____ U. A study of the impact on local coffee chains by the influx of coffee chains, for example, found that as sit down coffee chains proliferated, previous competitors increased their sales and profits.

Paragraph 3

The Sophists are regularly demonized across the philosophic world.

_____ Q. Secondly, although they did charge for classes—unlike their primary competitor: Socrates—this was only unique in that traditionally educators taught exclusively for individual oligarchs and were paid with lavish lifestyles, housing, and influence.

_____ R. Noted as uninterested in truth, intellectual historians often label the Sophist tradition as one motivated by financial desires.

_____ S. Finally, rather than not being interested in truth, the Sophists taught both normative philosophies, and the ability to argue from multiple perspectives so that their students from the lower brackets of society could have a chance in public law cases when faced with more educated prosecutors.

_____ T. Firstly, the term "Sophists" hardly represents one group of instructors, but was rather the designation for all foreign educators working in Ancient Greece.

_____ U. This designation; however, is neither historically or philosophically accurate.

CONTINUE ON TO THE NEXT PAGE ➡

Paragraph 4

Most students across the world associate the name Berkley with a number of terrific schools across America, including University of California at Berkeley.

2 **Q.** Few of these students; however, would be able to discuss at any length the man for whom these schools are named.

6 **R.** To him, it was unimaginable that anything in the cosmos could be identifiable as anything besides a thought within the mind of a cognizant being, and thus everything must be composed of thoughts.

4 **S.** In these classes, they may learn that Bishop George Berkley famously argued against the revolution in science heralding the universe as being composed of identifiable matter.

3 **T.** In order to do so, they would likely need to take a class on theological principles, epistemology, or Scottish intellectual history.

5 **U.** To the contrary, Berkley argued that the very idea of matter was preposterous.

Paragraph 5

Technology does not always increase productivity as quickly as people believe.

4 **Q.** Instead, it took nearly twenty years for these industries to show clear gains due to the use of computing technology.

6 **R.** Despite spending these large sums on the new technological innovations, these companies seldom saw increases in worker productivity.

2 **S.** Without years of experience using computers and the software reinforcing the usefulness of the hardware, workers did little more on the computers than they previously would have using other means.

3 **T.** When the personalized computer hit the marketplace, for example, myriad industries spent huge amounts of capital on upgrading their hardware and training their employees.

5 **U.** As this example illustrates, technology can revolutionize the way things are done in the world, but only after a long period of development and learning.

CONTINUE ON TO THE NEXT PAGE ➡

Logical Reasoning
Practice Test 2 (Paragraphs 11-20)

DIRECTIONS: This section requires you to closely analyze the problems and choose the correct answer choice. Exclusively use premises provided within the text. Pay close attention to the rules, setups, and wording.

Questions 11 and 12 refer to the following scenario.

Six people are waiting to go down a water slide. Amy, Brady, Cacey, Derick, Enog and Felicity have all been waiting in a line and are now the next six to go down the slide. Enog and Felicity are standing on each side of Amy. Felicity is standing directly in front of Cacey. Brady is standing in front of Derick. Cacey is standing before Derick.

11. What position is Enog standing in?

   A. First

   B. Second

   C. Fourth

   D. Fifth

   E. Can be one of two positions

12. What position is Derick standing in?

   F. Fifth

   G. Second

   H. Third

   J. Sixth

   K. Can be one of two positions

CONTINUE ON TO THE NEXT PAGE ➡

13. Thomas is going to summer camp. Everyone who goes to summer camp has to play either soccer or basketball. No one at camp can play both sports. If you do not play basketball, then you will be eligible for the soccer tournament at the end of the summer. Thomas will not be eligible for the soccer tournament at the end of the summer.

A. Thomas is going to play basketball at summercamp.

B. Thomas does not like soccer.

C. Thomas does not want to be in the soccer tournament.

D. Thomas is going to play in the basketball tournament at the end of the summer.

E. If Thomas had not gone to camp he would not have been able to play soccer or basketball.

Questions 14, 15 and 16 refer to the following information.

Uncover the code below. Each letter corresponds to a word in the line directly below it. A letter **may** or **may not** be directly above its corresponding word.

B	F	A	E	G	means...
Tom	Farm	Store	Heat	Sam	

A	D	E	B	C	means...
Store	Bat	Farm	Tom	Carl	

H	B	C	D	G	means...
Sam	Store	Bat	Carl	Hope	

D	B	A	C	means...
Carl	Bat	Tom	Store	

14. Which word corresponds to D?

   F. Hope

   G. Farm

   H. Store

   J. Tom

   K. Bat or Carl

15. Which word corresponds to A?

   A. Tom

   B. Farm

   C. Hope

   D. Bat

   E. Store

16. Which word corresponds to G?

   F. Sam or Hope

   G. Bat or Carl

   H. Heat

   J. Store

   K. Sam

17. All of the people in Anna's school who are five feet and ten inches tall or taller have been invited to try-out for the basketball team. Three of Anna's friends at the school were invited to try out for the basketball team, but two were not. Anna is five feet and ten inches tall.

   A. Anna is going to play on the basketball team.

   B. Some of Anna's friends are just as tall, or taller than her.

   C. There are some students at Annas's school who are shorter than her.

   D. Some of Anna's friends will not be on a basketball team.

   E. If you are shorter than four feet tall then you will not be invited to the try-out.

18. Janette does not like dogs. All of Paul's friends like dogs. If you are not friends with Paul, then you will never be invited to the annual Tallahassee "Friends of Cats" party.

   F. If Janette liked dogs, then she would be friends with Paul.

   G. Janette wishes she were friends with Paul.

   H. Everyone invited to the Friends of Cats party likes dogs.

   J. If you are not friends with Paul then you do not like dogs.

   K. Janette can be friends with Paul despite not liking dogs.

CONTINUE ON TO THE NEXT PAGE ➡

19. Eight tennis players are competing in a mixed doubles competition. Four are females and four are males. Each team will consist of one male and one female. The four males are Carl, Greg, Devin, and Adam. The four females are Heather, Fiona, Elanor, and Biatrice. Heather and Carl are state champions and will continue to be on the same team. Devin will not play with Elanor or Fiona. Fiona refuses to play with Greg. Who will be on Elanor's team?

A. Carl

B. Greg

C. Devin

D. Adam

E. Cannot be determined

---

20. Every Friday, Jaryd goes to the carwash. Whenever he goes to the carwash he gets the superwash and a candybar. His favorite candy bar is Mounds. What statement is definitely true?

F. Jaryd eats a Mounds every Friday.

G. If Jaryd does not go to the carwash, then he cannot get a superwash.

H. 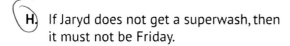 If Jaryd does not get a superwash, then it must not be Friday.

J. Jaryd only gets carwashes on Fridays.

K. If Jaryd did not get a carwash, then it can be any day but Friday.

CONTINUE ON TO THE NEXT PAGE ➡

Reading
Practice Test 2 (Questions 21-50)

DIRECTIONS: Analyze the passages below, and answer the commensurate questions. Only use information provided within the passage for your answers. There is only one answer for each question.

This text derives from an article authored in 1899.

The origin of the term caucus is obscure. It has been derived from the Algonquin word kaw-kaw-wus—to consult, to speak—but the more probable derivation makes it a
5 corruption of caulkers. In the early politics of Boston, and particularly during the early difficulties between the townsmen and the British troops, the seafaring men and those employed about the ship yards were
10 prominent among the towns-people, and there were numerous gatherings which may have very easily come to be called by way of reproach a meeting of caulkers after the least influential class who attended them, or from
15 the caulking house or caulk house in which they were held. What was at first a derisive description, came to be an appellation, and the gatherings of so-called caulkers became a caucus.

20 A caucus, in the political vocabulary of the United States, is primarily a private meeting of voters holding similar views, held prior to an election for the purpose of furthering such views at the election. With the
25 development of parties, and the rule of majorities, the caucus or some equivalent has become an indispensable adjunct of party government, and it may now be defined as a meeting of the majority of the electors

30 belonging to the same party in any political or legislative body held preliminary to a meeting thereof, for the purpose of selecting candidates to be voted for, or for the purpose of determining the course of the party at the
35 meeting of the whole body.

The candidates of each party are universally selected by caucus, either directly or indirectly through delegates to conventions chosen in caucuses. In legislative bodies the
40 course of each party is often predetermined with certainty in caucus, and open discussion between parties has been, in consequence, in some degree superseded. The caucus system is, in short, the basis of a complete electoral
45 system which has grown up within each party, side by side with that which is alone contemplated by the laws. This condition has in recent years attracted much attention, and has been bitterly denounced as an evil. It
50 was, however, early foreseen. John Adams, in 1814, wrote in the "Tenth Letter on Government": "They have invented a balance to all balance in their caucuses. We have congressional caucuses, state caucuses,
55 county caucuses, city caucuses, district caucuses, town caucuses, parish caucuses, and Sunday caucuses at church doors; and in these aristocratical caucuses elections have been decided."

ARGO BROTHERS

21. What is this passage predominantly about?

    A. The origin and political importance of caucuses in American politics.

    B. The origin of the American Revolution

    C. The etymological origin of the word caucus.

    D. The origin of congressional caucuses

    E. The importance of sailors in American Independence.

22. What is not provided as a possible etymological origin of the term, "caucus?"

    F. Algonquin roots.

    G. The name given to shipmen.

    H. The name given to the places where shipmen would meet.

    J. A Latin word meaning, "to discuss."

    K. A derivation of the word "caulker."

23. According to the passage, at what point in the election process does a caucus occur?

    A. A caucus is an election.

    B. A caucus occurs following an election, so that people may celebrate.

    C. A caucus occurs before an election.

    D. A caucus has no relevancy to an election.

    E. Caucuses are dangerous to elections.

24. What does John Adams imply to be an issue with caucuses?

    F. They do not include everybody.

    G. They involve only the most low class of citizens.

    H. They are time consuming.

    J. They allow aristocratic circles to decide elections.

    K. They are an outdated vestige of the revolution.

25. What would be an example of a caucus?

    A. A group of senators from one party meeting to discuss how they should vote on a bill.

    B. A group of people from different parties meeting so as to come to consensus.

    C. A group of people visiting a voting booth.

    D. A group of sailors on a ship.

    E. Any time a group of citizens from one party meets.

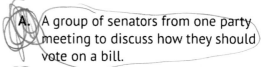

26. How frequently are presidential candidates of a party selected by caucus, according to the passage?

    F. Never

    G. Sometimes

    H. Only when the primary votes are inconclusive.

    J. Always

    K. Rarely

81

CONTINUE ON TO THE NEXT PAGE →

According to Denizart, a duel is a combat between two or more individuals, for reasons of a personal nature, at a place indicated in a challenge. According to Cauchy, a duel is a private war preceded by a challenge, by which each of the belligerent parties is warned to be on his guard and to resist force by force. John Reynaud describes a duel as a combat agreed upon in advance between two individuals, who, by this fact, place themselves without the pale of all social laws. Dupin is more severe, and his definition strongly resembles a judgment without appeal. According to him, "dueling is the savage state; it is not the right but the argument of the stronger and more adroit, and sometimes of the more insolent."

Little is known of the origin of dueling, and we shall not trace it back to Cain, who, according to some, was but a fortunate duelist. We find the first traces of it in Germany, whose inhabitants, says Montesquieu, "made war upon one another for murder, theft and injury. This custom was modified by subjecting these wars to rules. They were engaged in by order of the magistrate; this was preferable to a general license to fight." Gondebaud, king of the Burgundians, was the first to introduce into the code the judicial duel. A law called the Gombette law, promulgated in 501, regulated it. Charlemagne imitated this example, and this barbarous legislation can scarcely be said to have been seriously altered until during the reign of Philip the Fair in 1296. Duels properly so called, that is, duels to which any of the definitions given above may be applied, date from the period when tournaments and the judicial duel ceased.

The discourse of Brantome on duels furnishes us some curious information as to the rules which duelists recognized in the sixteenth century. The combatants, if they followed the advice of the malicious chronicler, should take good care not to fight without witnesses, first, in order not to deprive the public of a fine spectacle, and then, not to expose themselves to be prosecuted as murderers. "It is not necessary, in these matters, to speak of courtesy," says the author of Dames Galantes. "The man who enters the lists should propose to himself to conquer or die, and above all, never to surrender; for the vanquisher disposes of the vanquished as he pleases. He may drag him over the field, hang him, burn him, hold him as a prisoner, or dispose of him as a slave. A soldier may fight his captain, provided he has served two years and asked to leave the company. If a father accuses his son of any crime by which he might be dishonored, the son may justly challenge his father to a duel, since the father has done him a greater injury by dishonoring him, than he did him good by bringing him into this world, and giving him life."

27. What is this passage mostly about?

    A. The historical origins of duels.

    B. A discussion of the judicial system in early Germany.

    C. A meditation on ways that the criminal justice system has changed in the last two millennia.

    D. A discussion of the definition of war.

    E. A list of reasons why people used to duel.

CONTINUE ON TO THE NEXT PAGE ➡

28. Cauchy defines a duel as:

    F. A "savage state"

    G. A "private war"

    H. Two people fighting to the death.

    J. A method for deciding issues.

    K. A preferred method for conflict resolution.

29. What is one reason provided as to why duels would always have witnesses?

    A. So that participants could show everyone their strength.

    B. Witnesses were needed to make the proceedings legal.

    C. So as to avoid being prosecuted for murder.

    D. Witnesses will be the following contestants.

    E. As a sign of courtesy to the vanquished.

30. Gondebaud is important in the history of the duel because:

    F. He was the first leader to recommend duels as a way of resolving conflict.

    G. He was the first to condemn it as savage

    H. He was the first to practice a duel.

    J. He was the first to introduce a judicial code associated with dueling.

    K. He was the first to ban duels in his country.

31. Duels originated in which country?

    A. France

    B. Britain

    C. Germany

    D. Italy

    E. Greece

32. Dupin is most likely to prefer what modification to dueling practices?

    F. For them to be outlawed.

    G. For them to be modified such that death does not occur.

    H. For them to have stricter judicial codes.

    J. For them to only be used in the most severe cases.

    K. For them to not be usable by those within the same family.

CONTINUE ON TO THE NEXT PAGE ➡

President Andrew Jackson's early opportunities for education were very limited, and the unceasing action of his later years left him little time to remedy this defect. He is said, on very good authority, to have believed that the earth was flat. His familiar letters are disfigured by grammatical and other mistakes. His public papers were always carefully revised, and often entirely written, by trusted subordinates. When forced to rely altogether upon his own pen he was apt to slip. It is an open secret that his nullification proclamation was the work of Edward Livingston, and his bank veto that of Amos Kendall; nevertheless, in all cases, it is equally certain that Jackson allowed his subordinates only the privilege of expressing his ideas and policy, and that he expected from them a certain mechanical skill of expression, not the inception of a policy. Any influence upon him by subordinates was only obtained by indirection or by force of sympathy.

In temper Jackson was arbitrary, forceful, persistent, not at all impulsive but willing to yield to his naturally hot temper. In brief, he was force personified, not aggressive force merely, but the force of self-control as well. According to the necessity of the case, he could either maintain equanimity against any exasperation, or pass into a fit of passion more demoniacal than human. In politics he was the self-anointed successor of Jefferson as the assertor of individual rights against the tendency to class formation, but with this difference, that in Jefferson's time individualism claimed only recognition, while in Jackson's it had advanced to more active life.

Under Madison, Monroe and Adams, features had become powerful in the government which for Jackson seemed evil from the individual point of view: the incorporation of a bank to do government work, the protection of various classes of manufactures by tariff taxation, and the expenditure of public money upon roads and canals. Against all these, Jackson fought as actively as Jefferson did passively. On the other hand, Jackson's individualism did not prevent him, as it did Jefferson, from being a thoroughly national man, for in Jackson's time individualism had taken a place as a co-ordinate factor in the national development.

It is easy to mark the points in Jefferson's teachings from whose unhealthy development arose the Calhoun idea of nullification, but it would be impossible to imagine such a process in Jackson's case. Jefferson and Jackson had the same ultimate goal, but a different immediate object: the former to protect the individual through the states; the latter to protect the individual through the nation. Jefferson would have opposed nullification in 1831-1832, but not with the heat and sense of personal antipathy which Jackson exhibited.

33. What is this passage mostly about?

   A. Biographical details of Andrew Jackson.
   B. Andrew Jackson's upbringing.
   C. Andrew Jackson's opinion on individuality.
   D. Andrew Jackson's differences from Jefferson.
   E. Andrew Jackson's inability to read.

34. The author notes Jackson's belief that the earth was flat as an example of:

   F. Popular opinions of Jackson's time.
   G. Evidence that Jackson was not well learned.
   H. Evidence that Jackson did not believe in science.
   J. Evidence that the Earth was flat.
   K. The example is a superfluous anecdote.

35. Jackson had a naturally ___ temper.

   A. Calm
   B. Arrogant
   C. Capricious
   D. Hot
   E. Mild

36. According to the passage, Jackson was similar to Jefferson in his concern over the ___?

   F. Individual
   G. State
   H. Nation
   G. National bank
   K. Hair style

37. According to the passage, Jackson was more passionately supportive of the ___ than Jefferson?

   A. Individual
   B. Revolution
   C. Nation
   D. Rights of the President
   E. All of the above

38. Which of the following was not, according to Jackson, an assault on individual rights?

   F. A national bank
   G. Industry tariffs
   H. The use of public funds on roads.
   J. The use of public funds on canals.
   K. The use of public funds on the military.

The following is an excerpt of an essay, written by an economist, from 1899.

Even the ablest and most conscientious management is not always able to maintain a balance between the resources and the expenses of a country. No country is insured
5 against accidents which may decrease its income or cause unforeseen expense. An event, a period of scarcity, for instance, or a revolution, may produce both a decrease of income and a great increase of expense.
10 Again, the suddenness of a national want, its extent and its urgent character, are such as to prevent providing for it with a rapidity corresponding to its suddenness: wealthy England herself attempted this in vain
15 during the Crimean war. Finally, enterprises of evident usefulness, but the introduction of which demands time and are very costly, may outweigh the current resources of the state, and necessitate for a longer or shorter
20 period of additional revenue.

In the absence of actual resources furnished by taxation, and those which result from state savings in the past, recourse must be had to the future. The state, like the private
25 man, discounts the future: it borrows. Much has been said of the advantages of credit in private business: its usefulness in public affairs is not less than in private. There is no essential difference between the national
30 demand for credit and the demand for credit made by individuals. In both cases, the borrower appeals to the capitalist and for time within which to return the value he received. These are the two constituent
35 elements of every credit operation. As to the use the loan is put to and the results of the operation, the state which borrows can be compared only to the individual who

borrows for purposes of consumption. In
40 fact, the state rarely asks money for productive investment; it borrows mostly because its disposable or prospective funds are insufficient for the present or the near future.

45 Credit is a marvelous instrument of action, one of the most powerful springs of the material and even moral progress of society. Its development, therefore, should be favored in every way; its uses and the
50 forms it assumes cannot become too numerous. But, in order to be really profitable, they should be in keeping with the very essence and real end of credit. This end is, as all know, in the first place, to keep
55 capital from lying idle for a longer or shorter time, as the case may be, and in the second, always to place capital in the hands of those who, at a given moment, may make the most productive use of it. Credit thus assures the
60 continued circulation and fruitful employment of a nation's capital, and adds to the motive and protective power of this mighty instrument of labor.

39. What is this passage mostly about?

A. The nature of credit.

B. The use of credit by countries.

C. How credit is used.

D. Why credit should be used by individuals.

E. Defining credit.

40. What is not provided as a reason a country may seek credit?

    F. A country may need money to deal with a natural disaster.

    G. A country may need to make a long term investment, but does not have the funds to create the investment.

    H. A country may need to pay its military extra in war time.

    J. To rebuild following a revolution.

    K. In order to purchase goods during a period of scarcity.

41. The economist makes which claim in the second paragraph?

    A. A country will never take on debt so as to make an investment.

    B. A country will normally take on debt to pay for a good as opposed to an investment.

    C. A country will only take on debt if it is for the sake of investing.

    D. A country will never take on debt.

    E. A country should never take on debt.

42. What situation does the author claim to be the second principle by which capital will be used most profitably?

    F. If a country uses it.

    G. If an individual uses it.

    H. If a corporation uses it.

    J. If no one uses it.

    K. If the entity that can make the most use of the capital gains the capital.

43. Does the author believe public debt to be as important as personal debt?

    A. The author is indifferent.

    B. The author clearly favors individual use of debt.

    C. The author clearly favors national use of debt.

    D. The author believes the two uses to be of equal usefulness.

    E. The author makes no distinct claims.

44. What would be an example of an item with "evident usefulness, but the introduction of which demands time and are very costly?"

    F. A bridge connecting two urban centers

    G. Back pay on pensions

    H. A new law

    G. Military expenses

    K. None of the above

CONTINUE ON TO THE NEXT PAGE ➡

Fermiers généraux was the name given in France under the old monarchy to a company which farmed certain branches of the public revenue, that is to say, contracted with the government to pay into the treasury a fixed yearly sum, taking upon itself the collection of certain taxes as an equivalent. The system of farming the taxes was an old custom of the French monarchy. Under Francis I, the revenue arising from the sale of salt was farmed by private individuals in each town. This was, at the time, a monopoly of the government.

The government reserved to itself the power of providing the people with salt, which it collects in its stores, and sells to the retailers at its own price. This monopoly was first assumed by Philippe de Valois in 1350. Other sources of revenue were likewise farmed by several individuals, most of whom were favorites of the court or of the minister of the day. Sully, the able minister of Henry IV., seeing the dilapidation of the public revenue occasioned by this system, by which, out of one hundred and fifty million dollars paid by the people, only thirty millions reached the treasury, opened the contracts for farming the taxes to public auction, given them to the highest bidder, according to the ancient Roman practice. By this means he greatly increased the revenue of the state.

But the practice of private contracts through favor or bribing was renewed under the following reigns. Colbert, the minister of Louis XIV, called the farmers of the revenue to a severe account, and by an act of power deprived them of their enormous gains. In 1728, under the regency, the various individual leases were united into a ferme générale, which was lent to a company, the members of which were henceforth called fermiers généraux.

In 1759, Silhouette, minister of Louis XV., quashed the contracts of the farmers general, and levied the taxes by his own agents. But the system of contracts revived: for the court, the ministers and favorites were all well-disposed to them, as private bargains were made with the farmers general, by which they paid large sums as douceurs. In the time of Necker, the company consisted of forty-four members, who paid a rent of one hundred and eighty-six millions of livres, and Necker calculated their profit at about two millions yearly—no very extraordinary sum, if correct.

But independent of this profit there were the expenses of collection, and a host of subalterns to support: the company had its officers and accountants, receivers, collectors, etc., who, having the public force at their disposal, committed numerous acts of injustice toward the people, especially the poorer class, by distraining their goods, selling their chattels, etc. The "gabelle" or sale of salt, among others, was a fruitful source of oppression.

45. What is this passage mostly about?

A. How salt was extracted for sale in 18th century France.

B. The rights of farmers in France in the 18th century.

C. A history of agricultural farmers in France.

D. Methods of tax collection in monarchal France.

E. Methods monarchs used to oppress the peasants of France.

46. What word and/or phrase would most closely mean Fermiers généraux?

F. General farmers

G. Privatized tax collectors

H. Fermented generals

J. Farmers

K. No English equivalent

47. Based on the passage, what is the most likely reason a farmer would be given his position in 1350?

A. Family history of farming.

B. Merit

C. Farmers were appointed by lottery.

D. The individual was politically aligned with the monarch.

E. Only the monarch farmed.

48. Tax collection is discussed as a means to do all of the following except what?

F. Gain funds for the state

G. Reward those who are favored by the monarch

H. Build roads

J. Oppress the poor

K. None of the above

49. Sully implemented a method for determining tax collectors based on which previous empire?

A. Rome

B. Britain

C. Athens

D. Earlier French empires

E. Ottoman

50. How many members were in the company during the time of Nekter?

F. 1350

G. 1728

H. 44

J. 89

K. 103

ARGO BROTHERS

Select the best answer from the choices given by carefully solving each problem. Bubble the letter of your answer on the answer sheet. Please refrain from making any stray marks on the answer sheet. If you need to erase an answer, please erase thoroughly.

Important Notes:

1. There are no formulas or definitions in the math section that will be provided.
2. Diagrams may or may not be drawn to scale. Do not make assumptions based on the diagram unless it is specifically stated in the diagram or question.
3. Diagrams are not in more than one plane, unless stated otherwise.
4. Graphs are drawn to scale, therefore, you can assume relationships according to the graph. If lines appear parallel, then you can assume the lines to be parallel. This is also true for right angles and so forth.
5. Simplify fractions completely.

Practice Test 2 (Questions 51-100)

51. $(\sqrt{100})(\sqrt{64})$

    A. 8

    B. 10

    C. 18

    D. 80

    E. 164

52.
    7.2 aliens = 1 monster
    1 monster = 15.5 oranges

Using the conversion above, how many oranges are equal to 1 alien?

    F. 0.46

    G. 1.95

    H. 2.15

    J. 22.7

    K. 111.6

CONTINUE ON TO THE NEXT PAGE →

53. What is the greatest common factor of 147 and 98?

- **A.** 2
- **B.** 3
- **C.** 7
- **D.** 14
- **E.** 49

54. If $x = 7$ and $y = 0$, what is the value of $\frac{11x}{x-y}$?

- **F.** 0
- **G.** 7
- **H.** 10
- **J.** 11
- **K.** 77

55. Lucy scored a 85, 64 and 76 on her math exams. What score must Lucy obtain on the next math test to have an average of exactly 80?

- **A.** 93
- **B.** 97
- **C.** 94
- **D.** 95
- **E.** 96

56. Helga has 4 dogs, 3 cats and 2 birds. If she closes her eyes and picks one animal, what is the probability that it does not have 4 legs?

- **F.** $\frac{3}{7}$
- **G.** $\frac{2}{7}$
- **H.** $\frac{7}{9}$
- **J.** $\frac{2}{9}$
- **K.** $\frac{4}{7}$

57. If $y = x^2 \bullet x^x$, what is y when $x = 2$?

- **A.** 16
- **B.** 8
- **C.** 4
- **D.** 32
- **E.** 0

58. Train A, traveling at 200mph, leaves station A at 1P.M. Train B, traveling at 300mph, leaves station B at 3P.M. Both stations are directly across from each other and X miles away. If the trains meet at 4P.M., what is X?

- **F.** 500mi
- **G.** 900mi
- **H.** 700mi
- **J.** 600mi
- **K.** 400mi

CONTINUE ON TO THE NEXT PAGE ➡

59. Bernard is now y years old. Luis is 8 years older than Bernard. In terms of y, how old was Luis 5 years ago?

A. $8y$

B. $8y - 5$

C. $y + 3$

D. $y + 13$

E. $y - 5$

60.

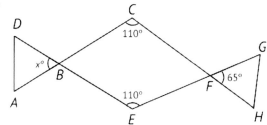

In the figure above, ABC, DBE, EFG and CFH are straight line segments. What is the value of x?

F. $25°$

G. $45°$

H. $65°$

J. $70°$

K. $75°$

61. Which of the following shows the fraction $\frac{13}{3}$, $\frac{37}{8}$ and $\frac{19}{4}$ in order from greatest to least?

A. $\frac{37}{8}$, $\frac{19}{4}$, $\frac{13}{3}$

B. $\frac{37}{8}$, $\frac{13}{3}$, $\frac{19}{4}$

C. $\frac{19}{4}$, $\frac{13}{3}$, $\frac{37}{8}$

D. $\frac{19}{4}$, $\frac{37}{8}$, $\frac{13}{3}$

E. $\frac{13}{3}$, $\frac{19}{4}$, $\frac{37}{8}$

62. If x and y are integers, which is always even?

F. $\frac{x + y}{2}$

G. $2\left(\frac{x + y}{x}\right)$

H. $x - y$

J. $2(x + y)$

K. $x^2 + y^2$

CONTINUE ON TO THE NEXT PAGE ➡

63.

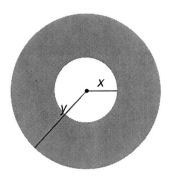

What is the probability that a point chosen will be in the shaded region?

A. $\dfrac{y^2}{x^2}$

B. $\dfrac{(x + y^2)}{y^2}$

C. $\dfrac{x^2}{y^2 - x^2}$

D. $\dfrac{y^2 - x^2}{y^2}$

E. π

64. If $q = x + y$ and $x = y + z$, what is z in terms of y and q?

F. $q - 2x$

G. $q - 2y$

H. $2x - q$

J. $2y + q$

K. $2q + x$

65. What is $\dfrac{(5!)!}{5!}$?

A. 1

B. 5

C. 120

D. 720

E. None of the above

66. What is $\dfrac{a^2 + 2ab + b^2}{(a + b^3)}$?

F. $(a + b)$

G. $a^2 + b^2$

H. $\dfrac{1}{a + b}$

J. $\dfrac{1}{(a + b)^2}$

K. $(a + b^2)$

CONTINUE ON TO THE NEXT PAGE ➡

67. It takes 3 cats 3 minutes to catch 3 mice. How many cats are needed to catch 99 mice in 99 minutes?

A. 3
B. 6
C. 11
D. 33
E. 99

68. The sum of seven consecutive odd integers is 749, what is the largest of the seven integers?

F. 99
G. 103
H. 11
J. 113
K. 115

69. $V = \pi r^2 h$
Using the formula above, if r is doubled and h is divided by 2, what is the ratio of the original volume to the new volume?

A. 1:4
B. 1:2
C. 1:1
D. 2:1
E. 4:1

70. A yellow cab has a base fare of $3.50 per ride plus $0.20 for each $\frac{1}{4}$ of mile ridden. If a yellow cab costs $22.50, how many miles long was the ride?

F. 23.75 miles
G. 42.5 miles
H. 47.5 miles
J. 95 miles
K. 112.5 miles

71. John works 40 hours a week, and his monthly salary in June was $4,000. In the month of July, John got a 4% raise on his monthly salary. In the month of July, what was John's hourly rate?

A. $25
B. $26
C. $40
D. $100
E. $104

CONTINUE ON TO THE NEXT PAGE ➡

72. If $8{,}575 = 5^x \cdot 7^y$, what is $(xy)-5$?

    F. 1

    G. 3

    H. 6

    J. 7

    K. 12

---

73. When d is divided by 8, the remainder is 3. What is the remainder when $d + 3$ is divided by 8?

    A. 1

    B. 3

    C. 4

    D. 6

    E. 7

---

74. Tommy is making a 6 letter password using only the letters A, B, C, D, E and F. How many different codes can Tommy make, if every letter can only be used once in each code?

    F. 1

    G. 6

    H. 120

    J. 720

    K. 46,656

75. $-5(x - 3) \geq 20$

What is the solution to the inequality shown above?

    A. $x \geq -1$

    B. $x \geq 7$

    C. $x \leq -1$

    D. $x \leq 7$

    E. $x \geq 1$

---

76. Which number line below shows the solution to the inequality $-2 < \frac{x}{3} \leq 2$?

CONTINUE ON TO THE NEXT PAGE ➡

77. Favorite Genres of Movies amongst Teens

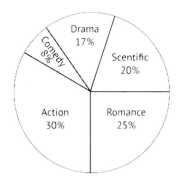

There are 15,000 teens whose favorite genre is comedy. How many teens have a favorite genre of action?

A. 30
B. 41,250
C. 52,500
D. 56,250
E. 70,000

78. A computer originally priced at $550.50 is on sale for 20% off. Jamie used a 5% discount coupon which was applied to the sales price. How much did Jamie pay for the computer? (Assume there is no tax.)

F. $412.88
G. $418.38
H. $440.40
J. $522.98
K. $539.49

79. Given the following value 4,760. Solve the following, $\frac{x^2}{y}$, if x represents the smallest prime factor of the given value, and y represents the greatest prime factor of the given value.

A. $\frac{119}{4}$

B. $\frac{4}{17}$

C. $\frac{2}{119}$

D. $\frac{4}{119}$

E. $\frac{2}{17}$

CONTINUE ON TO THE NEXT PAGE ➡

80. An adult male Diptera has a mass of 11.5 milligrams. What is the Diptera's mass in grams?

F. 0.0115 g

G. 0.115 g

H. 1.15 g

J. 11.5 g

K. 115 g

81. Michael has a project due in exactly 83 hours. It is currently 8:30 on a Monday morning. What time is his project due?

A. 6:30 PM Friday

B. 7:30 PM Friday

C. 7:30 AM Thursday

D. 7:30 PM Thursday

E. 9:30 PM Thursday

82. $\left(\dfrac{2}{3} + \dfrac{1}{4}\right) \div 2 =$

F. $\dfrac{22}{12}$

G. $\dfrac{1}{12}$

H. $\dfrac{11}{24}$

J. $\dfrac{1}{3}$

K. 12

83. Michelle bought a dress that costs $103.00, a pair of shoes that costs $73.00 and a bag that costs $111.00. There is a 7% sales tax on all items priced at $90.00 and higher. There is no sales tax on items under $90.00. How much did Michelle spend on the following items, including tax?

A. $287.00

B. $266.00

C. $295.49

D. $300.60

E. $301.98

84. How many terms are in the sequence, $0, 3, 6, \ldots, 57, 60$?

F. 20

G. 21

H. 23

J. 30

K. 60

CONTINUE ON TO THE NEXT PAGE ➡

85. The larger of two consecutive even integers is two times the smaller. What is their sum?

- A. 2
- B. 3
- C. 4
- D. 6
- E. 8

86. $3^x = 27^{a+b}$ and $\dfrac{a^2-b^2}{(a-b)} = 5$
What is x?

- F. 6
- G. 9
- H. 12
- J. 15
- K. 27

87. In Mr. Farmer's class there are 30 kids. If there are twice as many boys as there are girls in the English club, then what percentage of the English club are boys?

- A. 33.3%
- B. 10%
- C. 30%
- D. 20%
- E. 66.6%

88. $a \star b = a^3 - 3a^2b + 3ab^2 - b^3$
$a \oplus b = (a-b)(a-b)$
What is $\dfrac{a \star b}{a \oplus b}$

- F. $a^2 + b^2$
- G. $(a-b)$
- H. $a^2 + 3b^2 + 3ab$
- J. $a^2 - b^2$
- K. $b^2 + 3a$

89. What is the prime factorization of 752?

- A. $2^3 \cdot 48$
- B. $2^3 \cdot 49$
- C. $3^3 \cdot 49$
- D. $2^4 \cdot 47$
- E. $3^4 \cdot 47$

90. If x can be any integer, what is least possible value of the expression $4x^2 - 10$?

- F. -10
- G. -4
- H. 4
- J. 10
- K. ∞

99

CONTINUE ON TO THE NEXT PAGE ➡

91. There are a total of 5 bicycles and tricycles in a park. There are 12 wheels. How many tricycles are there?

A. 2

B. 3

C. 6

D. 7

E. 8

92. What is least possible value of $\dfrac{x^2-1}{x^2}$ if $x \geq 1$

F. -1

G. 0

H. 3

J. $\dfrac{3}{4}$

K. $\dfrac{2}{3}$

93. What is the maximum number of points in which a circle and triangle can intersect?

A. 3

B. 5

C. 6

D. 8

E. ∞

94.

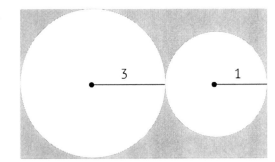

Figure not drawn to scale.

What is the area of the shaded region?

F. 48 - 10π

G. 64 - 22π

H. 10π

J. 48 - 6π

K. 16π

CONTINUE ON TO THE NEXT PAGE ➡

95. There are 45 plastic ducks in a bag. If there are black, green, blue, and purple plastic ducks and $\frac{1}{3}$ of the plastic ducks are black, $\frac{1}{5}$ of the plastic ducks are blue, one third of the number of black plastic ducks are green, then how many purple plastic ducks are in the bag?

A. 6

B. 15

C. 16

D. 21

E. 39

96.

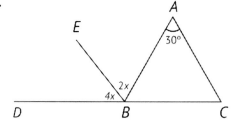

Figure not drawn to scale.

In the figure above, point B is on line segment DC. If $AB = BC$, what is the measure of angle ABE?

F. 20°

G. 40°

H. 80°

J. 90°

K. 100°

97.

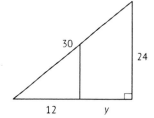

According to the figure above, what is the value of y?

A. 3

B. 6

C. 12

D. 15

E. 18

98. A painter needs 4 gallons of paint to paint each room. If a house has 8 rooms in total, how many quarts of paint is he going to need?

F. 12

G. 32

H. 128

J. 200

K. 512

CONTINUE ON TO THE NEXT PAGE ➡

99. A rectangle is inscribed in a circle. The rectangle is tangent at the points *A, B, C* and *D*. If the diagonal of the rectangle is 20 inches long, what is the area of the circle?

A. 10π

B. 15π

C. 20π

D. 100π

E. 400π

THIS IS THE END OF THE TEST. IF THERE IS TIME REMAINING, YOU MAY CHECK YOUR ANSWERS TO PART 1 OR PART 2.

100.

Gas Prices	
Regular	$2.00
Premium	$2.25
Unloaded	$2.50

The prices in the table above show the different types of gas offered at a gas station and the prices of the gas per gallon. If Emily has $50, what is the least amount of gas, in gallons, she can purchase subtracted from the greatest amount of gas, in gallons, she can purchase?

F. 2 gallons

G. 3 gallons

H. 5 gallons

J. 20 gallons

K. 25 gallons

SHSAT PRACTICE TEST 2
ANSWER KEY

PART 1 (VERBAL)

Scrambled Paragraphs

1. **S, R, U, T, Q**
2. **T, U, S, R, Q**
3. **R, U, T, Q, S**
4. **Q, T, S, U, R**
5. **T, R, Q, S, U**

Logical Reasoning

11. **E**
12. **J**
13. **A**
14. **K**
15. **A**
16. **K**
17. **C**
18. **H**
19. **B**
20. **H**

Reading

21. **A**	44. **F**
22. **J**	45. **D**
23. **B**	46. **G**
24. **J**	47. **D**
25. **A**	48. **H**
26. **J**	49. **A**
27. **A**	50. **H**
28. **G**	
29. **C**	
30. **J**	
31. **C**	
32. **F**	
33. **A**	
34. **G**	
35. **D**	
36. **F**	
37. **C**	
38. **K**	
39. **B**	
40. **H**	
41. **B**	
42. **K**	
43. **D**	

PART 2 (MATHEMATICS)

Math

51. **D**	63. **D**	75. **C**	87. **E**	99. **D**
52. **H**	64. **G**	76. **J**	88. **G**	100. **H**
53. **E**	65. **E**	77. **D**	89. **D**	
54. **J**	66. **H**	78. **G**	90. **F**	
55. **D**	67. **A**	79. **B**	91. **A**	
56. **J**	68. **J**	80. **F**	92. **G**	
57. **A**	69. **B**	81. **D**	93. **C**	
58. **G**	70. **F**	82. **H**	94. **F**	
59. **C**	71. **B**	83. **E**	95. **A**	
60. **K**	72. **F**	84. **G**	96. **F**	
61. **D**	73. **D**	85. **D**	97. **B**	
62. **J**	74. **J**	86. **J**	98. **H**	

To calculate your score visit our web site
and download excel calculator:
www. einstein-academy.com/calc

SCRAMBLED PARAGRAPHS

1. **S, R, U, T, Q**

   S: "This designation" refers to the description of the war as cold, as opposed to hot.

   R: This sentence expands on sentence S, detailing why it is a cold word.

   U: "These previously neutral countries" refers to the neighboring countries referenced in sentence R.

   T: "Gaining influence" expands on the activities discussed in sentence U.

   Q: This sentence concludes the topic, using such cue words as "ended."

2. **T, U, S, R, Q**

   T: All sentences have contrary content to the introductory sentence; thus, however must be in the first sentence.

   U: Sentences S, R, and Q all discuss an example and principle introduced in this sentence.

   S: "This economic paradox" refers to the one introduced in sentence U.

   R: R describes the principle introduced in sentence S.

   Q: Q brings us back to the example introduced in sentence U, and connects it to the principle

discussed in sentence R. Normally, discussions of an example immediately follow the example, but here there are other options which follow better, and Q relies on the topic introduced in R.

3. **R, U, T, Q, S**

   R: U—the sentence with however—designates a break in topics. R coincides with the introductory sentence, and must thus be before U and the three sentences which break in topic.

   U: "This designation" refers to the designation referred to in sentence R. Furthermore, as it has however it must signal the break between the topics in R and the topics in T, Q, and S.

   T: "Firstly" indicates that this is the first reason provided.

   Q: "Secondly" will follow after the first explanation given in sentence T.

   S: "Finally" indicates that this reason comes after the first two reasons.

4. **Q, T, S, U, R**

Q: This sentence utilizes the transition word "however." All sentences besides Q give information on "the man for whom these schools are named" and must thus come after Q.

T: "To do so" refers to being able to "discuss" the man, as noted in sentence Q.

S: "These classes" refer to the classes noted in sentence T.

U: "To the contrary" indicates that the sentence will give a contrary opinion to the opinion noted in the previous sentence. U most closely notes a disagreement with sentence S.

R: This sentence expands on the principle discussed in sentence U, showing why he thought that the idea was "preposterous."

5. **T, R, Q, S, U**

T: T provides an example of the principle introduced in the introductory sentence. S and Q discuss the example introduced in T and must thus come after. U and R both have pronouns that refer to later sentences.

R: "These large sums" refers to the sums referenced in sentence T.

Q: Q expands on the principle introduced in sentence R.

S: S provides a reason why it would take long to show gains, as noted in sentence Q.

U: "As this example illustrates" follows from the example discussed in the previous sentences.

LOGICAL REASONING

11. E This is a sequencing game. First set up the game board. Number the slots 1 through 6. The direction does not matter as long as you stay consistent with the rules. Rules do not dictate which side of Amy Enog and Felicity stand, but Felicity can only be directly in front of Cacey if Enog is infront of Amy and Felicity. Cacey is infront of Derick, and Brady is in front of Deric, so Deric must be last. At this point, there are two potential boards, one in which Brady is first, and one in which he is fifth.

$$\frac{D}{6} \quad \frac{B}{5} \quad \frac{C}{4} \quad \frac{E}{3} \quad \frac{A}{2} \quad \frac{F}{1}$$

$$\frac{D}{6} \quad \frac{C}{5} \quad \frac{F}{4} \quad \frac{A}{3} \quad \frac{E}{2} \quad \frac{B}{1}$$

Enog can be in position 2 or position 3. Thus, the correct answer is E.

12. J Derick is in position 6 in both boards. Thus, the correct answer is J.

13. A These logical statements include bi-conditional statements, but do not make use of them. The written statements should read:

$$[S \leftrightarrow \cancel{B}; B \leftrightarrow \cancel{S}]$$

$$[\cancel{B} \rightarrow ST; \cancel{ST} \rightarrow B]$$

If you are not eligible for the tournament, then you must be playing basketball. Thus, A is the correct answer.

14. K B and store are the only terms prevalent in all rows, thus they must be a pair. A, C, D and Tom, Bat, and Carl occur in three. However, A stands alone with Tom in row one, thus A is paired with Tom. C and D cannot be further determined, thus they can be alternatively Bat or Carl. Once you have these, finish out the pairs.

B = Store
A = Tom, ~~Bat, Carl~~
C = ~~Tom~~, Bat, Carl
D = ~~Tom~~, Bat, Carl
E = Farm
G = Sam
F = Heat
H = Hope

D can be either Bat or Carl. Thus, the correct answer is K.

15. A A is paired with Tom. Thus, the correct answer is A.

16. K G is paired with Sam. Thus, the correct answer is K.

17. C The logical statements should read:

$$[\geq 5'10 \rightarrow I; \cancel{I} \rightarrow < 5'10]$$

Two friends were not invited to try out, thus they must be shorter than 5'10. Since Anna is 5'10, this means that there are students who are shorter than her at her school. Thus, the correct answer is C.

18. H The logical statements should read:

$$[D \rightarrow \cancel{J}; J \rightarrow \cancel{D}]$$

$$[C \rightarrow PF \rightarrow D; \cancel{D} \rightarrow \cancel{PF} \rightarrow \cancel{C}]$$

Due to the logical chain, anyone invited to the Cat party must like Dogs. Thus, the correct answer is H.

19. B This is a pairing game. Devin will not play with Elanor, Fiona, or Heather, so he must play with Biatrice. Fiona must play with Greg or Adam, but refuses to play with Greg. Thus, she must be paired with Adam. Elanor and Greg are the only two players left, thus they must go together, making B the correct answer.

20. H The logical statements should read:

$$[F \to C; \cancel{C} \to \cancel{F}]$$

$$[C \to S \ \& \ B; \cancel{S \ or \ B} \to \cancel{C}]$$

If Jaryd does not go to the carwash, then it cannot be Friday. Thus, the correct answer is H.

READING COMPREHENSION

21. A This answer choice relates to all three paragraphs in the passage. Other answer choices at most relate to one paragraph.

22. J All other answers can be found in the first paragraph.

23. B This answer derives from line 23.

24. J This answer derives from lines 53-59. Watch out for answer F, which includes extreme language.

25. A This answer derives from line 51. A caucus requires members of the same party coming together prior to a vote in a legislative or election setting. No other answer fulfills both of these requirements.

26. J This answer derives from line 36.

27. A This answer choice relates to all three paragraphs. B relates to two paragraphs, which is the second most common answer choice.

28. G This answer derives from line 5.

29. C This answer derives from line 49.

30. J This answer derives from line 30.

31. C This answer derives from line 21.

32. F This answer derives from lines 14-17. He is "severe" in his definition, and would thus mostly likely prefer it to not be legal.

33. A This answer relates to all paragraphs. C relates to multiple paragraphs, but not all.

34. G The statement is made as an example illustrating that he was not well educated.

35. D This answer derives from line 26.

36. F This answer derives from the last two paragraphs. Jefferson was more interested in the state. Jackson was more interested in the nation. Jefferson's opinion on a national bank is not noted within the passage.

37. C This answer derives from line 64.

38. K All other answer choices are noted explicitly to be against the rights of individuals. This answer derives from lines 43-47.

39. B This answer choice occurs in all paragraphs. A is too broad for the specifics discussed in the paragraphs. C can be connected to all paragraphs, but credit generally is not discussed in all paragraphs—only credit as it concerns countries.

40. H All other answers are provided explicitly. Remember that an answer's accuracy outside of the passage is irrelevant to the contents of the passage.

41. B This answer derives from lines 37-39.

42. K This answer derives from lines 56-59.

43. D This answer derives from lines 27.

44. F The appropriate answer requires time to create and high expense. F is the only answer that fulfills this, as a bridge both takes a very long time to build and is very expensive.

45. D D relates to all paragraphs. E may relate, but it is only explicitly stated in one paragraph that taxation and the methods associated with taxation were used as a form of class based oppression. This passage relies very heavily on recognizing what the term "farmer" means.

46. G Lines 1-7 define this term.

47. D This answer derives from lines 20-22.

48. H All other options can be found explicitly within the passage.

49. A This answer derives from line 30.

50. H This answer derives from line 53.

51. D $(\sqrt{100})(\sqrt{64}) = (10)(8) = 80$

52. H 7.2 aliens = 1 monster = 15.5 oranges

$(\frac{1}{7.2})$ monster = 1 alien = $(\frac{15.5}{7.2})$

oranges = 2.15 oranges.

53. E Factor each value, then chose all copies of the factors and multiply.
147: 3 • 7 • 7
98: 2 • 7 • 7
GCF: 7 • 7 = 49

54. J $\frac{11x}{x\text{-}y} = \frac{11(7)}{7\text{-}0} = \frac{77}{7} = 11$

55. D Lucy's average is the sum of all of her test scores divided by the total number of tests which is 4.

$$\frac{85 + 64 + 76 + x}{4} = 80$$

$$\frac{225 + x}{4} = 80$$

$$320 = 225 + x$$
$$x = 95$$

56. J There are 7 animals that have 4 legs out of 9 animals. So, there are 2 animals that do not have 4 legs out of 9.

$\frac{2}{9}$

57. A $y = (x^2)(x^x) = x^{2+x}$
if $x = 2$, then $y = 2^{2+2} = 2^4 = 16$

58. G By 4pm, train A has been traveling at 200 mph for 3 hours. Train A has traveled 600 miles. By 4pm, train B has been traveling 300 mph for 1 hour. Train B traveled 300 miles.

600 miles + 300 miles = 900 miles

59. C

	Present Age	Age 5 years ago
Bernanrd:	y	$y - 5$
Luis:	$y + 8$	$y + 3$

60. K $\angle CBE = \angle DBA$ due to vertical angles.
The sum of the integer angles of $BCFE$ is 360° and $\angle CBE$ can be found as followed.
Knowing that $\angle CFE = \angle GFH$, it follows
$360° - (110° + 110° + 65° + \angle CBE) = 0$
$360° - 285° = \angle CBE = x°$
$x° = 75°$

ARGO BROTHERS

61. D $(\frac{19}{4})(\frac{2}{2}) = \frac{37}{8}$. This means

$$\frac{19}{4} > \frac{37}{8}$$

Using cross multiplication, for $\frac{13}{3}$ and $\frac{37}{8}$, it follows

$(8)(13) < (3)(37)$

$104 < 111$, so $\frac{13}{3} < \frac{37}{8}$

Therefore: $\frac{19}{4} > \frac{37}{8} > \frac{13}{3}$

62. J   Two times any integer is even always. Thus, this leaves our choices to probably **G** or **J**.

Since $(\frac{x+y}{x})$ is not always an integer, and $x + y$ is, the answer is **J**.

63. D   The probability of a point being chosen if the shaded region is

$$\frac{\text{Average of shaded region}}{\text{Total Area}} =$$

$$\frac{\pi y^2 - \pi x^2}{\pi y^2}.$$

This simplifies to $\frac{y^2 - x^2}{y^2}$

64. G $q = x + y$ and $x = y + z$
so, $q = y + z + y = 2y + z$
$q - 2y = z$

65. E   Let $x = 5!$; $\frac{(5!)!}{5!} = \frac{x!}{x} = (x-1)!$
$(x-1)! = (5!-1)!$ This answer is huge relative to the rest of the answers, therefore the answer is none of the above.

66. H $(a+b)(a+b) = a^2 + 2ab + b^2 = (a+b)^2$
$$\frac{a^2 + 2ab + b^2}{(a+b)^3} = \frac{(a+b)^2}{(a+b)^3} = \frac{1}{a+b}$$

67. A   If it takes 3 cats 3 minutes to catch 3 mice, then it will take 3(1) cats $3x$ minutes to catch $3x$ mice, as long as x is an integer.
$3x = 99$
$x = 33$. Since x is an integer, it will take 3(1) = 3 cats

68. J   Seven consecutive odd integers may be expressed as:
1st   2nd   3rd   4th   5th
$x + (x+2) + (x+4) + (x+6) + (x+8) +$
6th   7th
$(x+10) + (x+12) = 7x + 42 = 749$
$7x = 707$
$x = 707$
The largest is $x + 12$ or
$101 + 12 = 113$

69. B
Original Volume = $\pi r^2 h$
New Volume = $\pi(2r)^2 \left(\dfrac{h}{2}\right) = \pi(4r^2)\left(\dfrac{h}{2}\right)$
$= 2\pi r^2 h$

$\cancel{\pi} \cancel{r^2} \cancel{h} : 2\cancel{\pi} \cancel{r^2} \cancel{h}$
1:2

70. F
$\$3.50 + \$0.20(4x) = \$22.50$
Where x is the number of miles ridden.

Solving for x:
$\$0.20(4x) = \$19$
$4x = 95$
$x = 23.75$ miles

71. B
Assuming there are 4 weeks in July, John's hourly rate can be calculated as follows:
$$\dfrac{\$(1.04)(4000)}{4 \text{ weeks}} = \dfrac{\$1040}{\text{week}}$$

$$\dfrac{\$1040}{\cancel{\text{week}}} \cdot \dfrac{1 \cancel{\text{week}}}{40 \text{ hours}} = \dfrac{\$26}{\text{hours}}$$

72. F
$8575 = 5^2 \cdot 7^3$
$x = 2, y = 3; (xy) - 5 = (6) - 5 = 1$

73. D
Since d is not specified, the value can be chosen to be 43.
When 43 is divided by 8, there is a remainder of 3.

$d + 3 = 46$.
When 46 is divided by 8, there is a remainder of 6.

74. J
Permutations can be used. For 6 letters,
$6! = 6 \cdot 5 \cdot 4 \cdot 3 \cdot 2 \cdot 1 = 720$

75. C
$-5(x - 3) \geq 20$
$(x - 3) \leq -4$
$x \leq -1$

76. J
$-2 < \dfrac{x}{3} \leq 2$
$-6 < x \leq 6$

77. D
If there are x teens in total, then
$15{,}000 = 0.08x$
$x = 187{,}500$
Now, to find the number of teens whose favorite genre is action:
$(.30)(187{,}500) = 56{,}250$

78. G
With the 20% sale, the price becomes $(0.8)(\$550.50) = \$440.40$
Applying the 5% coupon:
$(0.95)(\$440.4) = \$418.38$

79. B
$4760 = 2^3 \cdot 5 \cdot 7 \cdot 17$
$x = 2, y = 17$
$\dfrac{x^2}{y} = \dfrac{4}{17}$

80. F
11.5 milligrams = $\left(\dfrac{11.5}{1000}\right)$ grams
= 0.0115 grams

81. D 83 hours = (24 + 24 + 24 + 11) hours
Each 24 hours is a full day. So three days and eleven hours passes.
Thus, this leaves the project due at 7:30 PM Thursday.

82. H $(\frac{2}{3} + \frac{1}{4}) \div 2 = (\frac{8}{12} + \frac{3}{12}) \cdot \frac{1}{2}$

$\frac{11}{12} \cdot \frac{1}{2} = \frac{11}{24}$

83. E The dress and the bag are the only items taxed with 7% sales tax.
All the items cost:
1.07($103 + $111) + ($73)
1.07($214) + ($73) = $301.98

84. G There are $(\frac{60 - 0}{3}) + 1$ numbers.

85. D The two numbers are x and $(x + 2)$.
$x + (x + 2)$. The larger is $(x + 2)$.
So, $(x + 2) = 2x$
$x = 2$
$x + (x + 2) = 2 + (2 + 2) = 6$

86. J $3^x = 27^{a+b} = (3^3)^{a+b} = 3^{3a+3b}$
$x = 3a + 3b$ and $\frac{a^2 - b^2}{(a-b)} = \frac{(a-b)(a+b)}{(a-b)}$

$= a + b = 5$
$x = 3(a+b) = 3(5) = 15$

87. E Let x = # of boys
Let y = # of girls
$x = 2y$; $x + y = 2y + y = 30$
$3y = 30$
$y = 10$

The percentage of boys is
$\frac{x}{30} = \frac{2y}{30} = \frac{2(10)}{30} = \frac{20}{30} = \frac{2}{3} = 66.66\%$

88. G $a \star b = (a - b)^3$
$a \oplus b = (a - b)^2$

$\frac{a \star b}{a \oplus b} = \frac{(a - b)^3}{(a - b)^2} = a - b$

89. D $752 = 2^4 \cdot 47$

90. F Squaring any integer results in a positive integer.

The least value of $4x^2 - 10$ occurs when $4x^2$ is the lowest it can be, which happens at $x = 0$.
Then $4(0)^2 - 10 = -10$

91. A Let x = # of bicycles
Let y = # of tricycles
$x + y = 5$
$2x + 3y = 12$
$x = 5 - y$
$2(5 - y) + 3y = 10 - 2y + 3y = 12$
$10 + y = 12$
$y = 2$.
So, there are 2 tricycles.

92. G x^2 can never be negative for $x \geq 1$
So, the lowest value of x^2 is chosen, to make $\dfrac{x^2-1}{x^2}$ the lowest.

That occurs at $x = 1$

$$\frac{x^2-1}{x^2} = \frac{1^2-1}{1^2} = \frac{1-1}{1} = 0$$

93. C

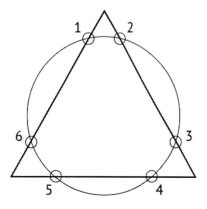

94. F The area of the rectangle is
$(3 + 3 + 1 + 1) \cdot (3 + 3) = 48$
$\qquad$ Length $\qquad$ Width

The area of the two circles is
$9\pi + \pi = 10\pi$

The area of the shaded region is
$48 - 10\pi$

95. A There are $\frac{1}{3}(45) = 15$ black ducks
and $\frac{1}{5}(45) = 9$ blue ducks and
$\frac{1}{3}(15) = 15$ green ducks.
$45 = 15 + 9 + 15 +$ purple, where
purple = # of purple ducks.
purple = 6

96. F $\sphericalangle ABC + 2x + 4x = \sphericalangle ABC + 6x$,
then $6x + \sphericalangle ABC = 180°$.

$\sphericalangle ABC = 180° - 120° = 60°$,
since $\triangle ABC$ is isosceles.
So, $4x + 2x + 120° = 180°$

$6x = 180° - 120°$
Solve for x and you get $x = 10°$
So $2x = 2(10°) = 20°$

97. B This is a triangle with a 3, 4, 5
special right triangle proportion.

$$\frac{30}{6} = 5, \quad \frac{24}{6} = 4$$

$$\frac{12 + y}{6} = 3$$

$12 + y = 18$
$y = 6$

98. H 1 gallon = 4 quarts
The painter needs
(4 gallons)(8 rooms) = 32 gallons
of paint = 32 g̶a̶l̶l̶o̶n̶s̶ • 4 quarts
= 128 quarts. $\qquad$ 1 g̶a̶l̶l̶o̶n̶

99. D

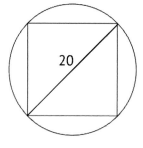

The radius is half of the diagonal length.
Circle Area = $\pi(r)^2 = \pi(10)^2 = 100\pi$

100. H   Divide $50 by the unloaded price and regular price respectively.
Thus, this comes out to 20 gallons and 25 gallons, which gives a difference of 5 gallons.

SHSAT
Practice Test 3

TIME TO FINISH TEST:
VERBAL: 75 minutes
MATH: 75 minutes

— This exam is 2 hours and 30 minutes long. Try to take this full exam in one sitting to simulate real test conditions.

— While taking this exam, refrain from hearing music or watching T.V.

— Please note, calculators are not permitted! You are permitted to answer questions in any order you see fit.

— Not all answers need take the same amount of time. Allocate your test time accordingly.

— Concentrate and GOOD LUCK!

To calculate your score visit our web site and download excel calculator:
www. einstein-academy.com/calc

SHSAT PRACTICE TEST 3
ANSWER SHEET

PART 1 (VERBAL)

SCRAMBLED PARAGRAPHS

Paragraph 1

The first sentence is Ⓠ Ⓡ Ⓢ Ⓣ Ⓤ
The second sentence is Ⓠ Ⓡ Ⓢ Ⓣ Ⓤ
The third sentence is Ⓠ Ⓡ Ⓢ Ⓣ Ⓤ
The fourth sentence is Ⓠ Ⓡ Ⓢ Ⓣ Ⓤ
The fifth sentence is Ⓠ Ⓡ Ⓢ Ⓣ Ⓤ

Paragraph 2

The first sentence is Ⓠ Ⓡ Ⓢ Ⓣ Ⓤ
The second sentence is Ⓠ Ⓡ Ⓢ Ⓣ Ⓤ
The third sentence is Ⓠ Ⓡ Ⓢ Ⓣ Ⓤ
The fourth sentence is Ⓠ Ⓡ Ⓢ Ⓣ Ⓤ
The fifth sentence is Ⓠ Ⓡ Ⓢ Ⓣ Ⓤ

Paragraph 3

The first sentence is Ⓠ Ⓡ Ⓢ Ⓣ Ⓤ
The second sentence is Ⓠ Ⓡ Ⓢ Ⓣ Ⓤ
The third sentence is Ⓠ Ⓡ Ⓢ Ⓣ Ⓤ
The fourth sentence is Ⓠ Ⓡ Ⓢ Ⓣ Ⓤ
The fifth sentence is Ⓠ Ⓡ Ⓢ Ⓣ Ⓤ

Paragraph 4

The first sentence is Ⓠ Ⓡ Ⓢ Ⓣ Ⓤ
The second sentence is Ⓠ Ⓡ Ⓢ Ⓣ Ⓤ
The third sentence is Ⓠ Ⓡ Ⓢ Ⓣ Ⓤ
The fourth sentence is Ⓠ Ⓡ Ⓢ Ⓣ Ⓤ
The fifth sentence is Ⓠ Ⓡ Ⓢ Ⓣ Ⓤ

Paragraph 5

The first sentence is Ⓠ Ⓡ Ⓢ Ⓣ Ⓤ
The second sentence is Ⓠ Ⓡ Ⓢ Ⓣ Ⓤ
The third sentence is Ⓠ Ⓡ Ⓢ Ⓣ Ⓤ
The fourth sentence is Ⓠ Ⓡ Ⓢ Ⓣ Ⓤ
The fifth sentence is Ⓠ Ⓡ Ⓢ Ⓣ Ⓤ

LOGICAL REASONING

11 Ⓐ Ⓑ Ⓒ Ⓓ Ⓔ
12 Ⓕ Ⓖ Ⓗ Ⓙ Ⓚ
13 Ⓐ Ⓑ Ⓒ Ⓓ Ⓔ
14 Ⓕ Ⓖ Ⓗ Ⓙ Ⓚ
15 Ⓐ Ⓑ Ⓒ Ⓓ Ⓔ
16 Ⓕ Ⓖ Ⓗ Ⓙ Ⓚ
17 Ⓐ Ⓑ Ⓒ Ⓓ Ⓔ
18 Ⓕ Ⓖ Ⓗ Ⓙ Ⓚ
19 Ⓐ Ⓑ Ⓒ Ⓓ Ⓔ
20 Ⓕ Ⓖ Ⓗ Ⓙ Ⓚ

READING

21 Ⓐ Ⓑ Ⓒ Ⓓ Ⓔ
22 Ⓕ Ⓖ Ⓗ Ⓙ Ⓚ
23 Ⓐ Ⓑ Ⓒ Ⓓ Ⓔ
24 Ⓕ Ⓖ Ⓗ Ⓙ Ⓚ
25 Ⓐ Ⓑ Ⓒ Ⓓ Ⓔ
26 Ⓕ Ⓖ Ⓗ Ⓙ Ⓚ
27 Ⓐ Ⓑ Ⓒ Ⓓ Ⓔ
28 Ⓕ Ⓖ Ⓗ Ⓙ Ⓚ
29 Ⓐ Ⓑ Ⓒ Ⓓ Ⓔ
30 Ⓕ Ⓖ Ⓗ Ⓙ Ⓚ
31 Ⓐ Ⓑ Ⓒ Ⓓ Ⓔ
32 Ⓕ Ⓖ Ⓗ Ⓙ Ⓚ

33 Ⓐ Ⓑ Ⓒ Ⓓ Ⓔ
34 Ⓕ Ⓖ Ⓗ Ⓙ Ⓚ
35 Ⓐ Ⓑ Ⓒ Ⓓ Ⓔ
36 Ⓕ Ⓖ Ⓗ Ⓙ Ⓚ
37 Ⓐ Ⓑ Ⓒ Ⓓ Ⓔ
38 Ⓕ Ⓖ Ⓗ Ⓙ Ⓚ
39 Ⓐ Ⓑ Ⓒ Ⓓ Ⓔ
40 Ⓕ Ⓖ Ⓗ Ⓙ Ⓚ
41 Ⓐ Ⓑ Ⓒ Ⓓ Ⓔ
42 Ⓕ Ⓖ Ⓗ Ⓙ Ⓚ
43 Ⓐ Ⓑ Ⓒ Ⓓ Ⓔ
44 Ⓕ Ⓖ Ⓗ Ⓙ Ⓚ
45 Ⓐ Ⓑ Ⓒ Ⓓ Ⓔ
46 Ⓕ Ⓖ Ⓗ Ⓙ Ⓚ
47 Ⓐ Ⓑ Ⓒ Ⓓ Ⓔ
48 Ⓕ Ⓖ Ⓗ Ⓙ Ⓚ
49 Ⓐ Ⓑ Ⓒ Ⓓ Ⓔ
50 Ⓕ Ⓖ Ⓗ Ⓙ Ⓚ

PART 2 (MATHEMATICS)

MATHEMATICS PROBLEMS

51 Ⓐ Ⓑ Ⓒ Ⓓ Ⓔ
52 Ⓕ Ⓖ Ⓗ Ⓙ Ⓚ
53 Ⓐ Ⓑ Ⓒ Ⓓ Ⓔ
54 Ⓕ Ⓖ Ⓗ Ⓙ Ⓚ
55 Ⓐ Ⓑ Ⓒ Ⓓ Ⓔ

56 Ⓕ Ⓖ Ⓗ Ⓙ Ⓚ
57 Ⓐ Ⓑ Ⓒ Ⓓ Ⓔ
58 Ⓕ Ⓖ Ⓗ Ⓙ Ⓚ
59 Ⓐ Ⓑ Ⓒ Ⓓ Ⓔ
60 Ⓕ Ⓖ Ⓗ Ⓙ Ⓚ

61 Ⓐ Ⓑ Ⓒ Ⓓ Ⓔ
62 Ⓕ Ⓖ Ⓗ Ⓙ Ⓚ
63 Ⓐ Ⓑ Ⓒ Ⓓ Ⓔ
64 Ⓕ Ⓖ Ⓗ Ⓙ Ⓚ
65 Ⓐ Ⓑ Ⓒ Ⓓ Ⓔ

66 Ⓕ Ⓖ Ⓗ Ⓙ Ⓚ
67 Ⓐ Ⓑ Ⓒ Ⓓ Ⓔ
68 Ⓕ Ⓖ Ⓗ Ⓙ Ⓚ
69 Ⓐ Ⓑ Ⓒ Ⓓ Ⓔ
70 Ⓕ Ⓖ Ⓗ Ⓙ Ⓚ

71 Ⓐ Ⓑ Ⓒ Ⓓ Ⓔ
72 Ⓕ Ⓖ Ⓗ Ⓙ Ⓚ
73 Ⓐ Ⓑ Ⓒ Ⓓ Ⓔ
74 Ⓕ Ⓖ Ⓗ Ⓙ Ⓚ
75 Ⓐ Ⓑ Ⓒ Ⓓ Ⓔ

76 Ⓕ Ⓖ Ⓗ Ⓙ Ⓚ
77 Ⓐ Ⓑ Ⓒ Ⓓ Ⓔ
78 Ⓕ Ⓖ Ⓗ Ⓙ Ⓚ
79 Ⓐ Ⓑ Ⓒ Ⓓ Ⓔ
80 Ⓕ Ⓖ Ⓗ Ⓙ Ⓚ

81 Ⓐ Ⓑ Ⓒ Ⓓ Ⓔ
82 Ⓕ Ⓖ Ⓗ Ⓙ Ⓚ
83 Ⓐ Ⓑ Ⓒ Ⓓ Ⓔ
84 Ⓕ Ⓖ Ⓗ Ⓙ Ⓚ
85 Ⓐ Ⓑ Ⓒ Ⓓ Ⓔ

86 Ⓕ Ⓖ Ⓗ Ⓙ Ⓚ
87 Ⓐ Ⓑ Ⓒ Ⓓ Ⓔ
88 Ⓕ Ⓖ Ⓗ Ⓙ Ⓚ
89 Ⓐ Ⓑ Ⓒ Ⓓ Ⓔ
90 Ⓕ Ⓖ Ⓗ Ⓙ Ⓚ

91 Ⓐ Ⓑ Ⓒ Ⓓ Ⓔ
92 Ⓕ Ⓖ Ⓗ Ⓙ Ⓚ
93 Ⓐ Ⓑ Ⓒ Ⓓ Ⓔ
94 Ⓕ Ⓖ Ⓗ Ⓙ Ⓚ
95 Ⓐ Ⓑ Ⓒ Ⓓ Ⓔ

96 Ⓕ Ⓖ Ⓗ Ⓙ Ⓚ
97 Ⓐ Ⓑ Ⓒ Ⓓ Ⓔ
98 Ⓕ Ⓖ Ⓗ Ⓙ Ⓚ
99 Ⓐ Ⓑ Ⓒ Ⓓ Ⓔ
100 Ⓕ Ⓖ Ⓗ Ⓙ Ⓚ

ARGO BROTHERS

DIRECTIONS: This section requires you to rearrange five given sentences, such that they form a proper paragraph. The introductory sentence for each paragraph will be given. An appropriate answer will order sentences so that they are logical and grammatically sound. Credit is exclusively given for answers perfectly correct. There are no partially correct answers.

Scrambled Paragraphs
Practice Test 3 (Paragraphs 1-5)

Paragraph 1

It is often said that fiction can be less terrifying than the reality it represents.

_____ **Q.** Many of the stories about his life are likely exaggerated by foreign powers, but all agree that under his reign torture, public execution, and the public display of severed heads was commonplace.

_____ **R.** These other countries, such as Germany, would go on to use him as an example of political tyranny for centuries after his death.

_____ **S.** Known posthumously as Vlad the Impaler, Vlad would become world famous when fictionalized as the vampire named Count Dracula.

_____ **T.** Like the famous character, Vlad was a count from Transylvania who terrorized the population, although not by turning into a bat or growing fangs.

_____ **U.** This is certainly true in the case of Vlad Dracula.

CONTINUE ON TO THE NEXT PAGE ➡

Paragraph 2

The influence of lobbies is a hot topic throughout academic and political circles.

_____ **Q.** Most pundits analyze how money donated by these lobbying firms impact the way that politicians vote.

_____ **R.** When analyzing the most influential lobby in the United States, American Association for Retired Persons, political scientists found that while money did help candidates gain name recognition during campaigns, by far the largest influence came from their large membership base.

_____ **S.** While the circulation of money throughout the political realm is important, the true power of lobbying firms exists elsewhere.

_____ **T.** Financial donations largely matter insofar as they help a candidate to reach out to their constituents, and lobby firms with large memberships are able to reach out to constituents more powerfully than any advertisement.

_____ **U.** Lobbying firms are powerful entities within U.S. politics, but analysts should continue to explore the diverse ways that they contribute to the political sphere.

Paragraph 3

Grammar laws associated with the English language are far more fluid than many are taught to believe.

_____ **Q.** More recently, authors of the twentieth century had no issue ending sentences with a preposition or starting sentences with a conjunction.

_____ **R.** If one were to look at literature from past eras, they would find a plethora of examples in which today's grammatical laws are not upheld.

_____ **S.** When reading English texts from the nineteenth century, for example, it is rare to see citations of any kind.

_____ **T.** Even today, there is little consensus over proper use of implied subjects and objects.

_____ **U.** As teaching practices become standardized through national curriculums, it will be interesting to see if these transitions begin to be derived from more centralized forces.

CONTINUE ON TO THE NEXT PAGE ➡

Paragraph 4

The Tower of Babel, as told in the stories, pales in comparison to the skyscrapers of today.

_____ **Q.** Burgeoning cities continue to spend far larger amounts than necessary so as to have impressive skylines capable of being seen as modern and industrious.

_____ **R.** In the titular myth, the tower collapsed largely due to the hubris of the creators.

_____ **S.** Today, the towering heights of skyscrapers are no longer dedicated to the heavens, but are instead driven by the forces of population density.

_____ **T.** However, while these considerations largely address the impetus for building contemporary urban landscapes, prestige is still important.

_____ **U.** The builders built the tower higher and higher so that they would be closer to the heavens, and this lack of utilitarian purpose led to its demise.

Paragraph 5

Until recently, use of lottery was viewed as critical to democratic governance.

_____ **Q.** In the philosophy of Aristotle, the use of lottery in the selection of leadership was the single most important requirement for any democratic regime.

_____ **R.** Lottery, he postulated, ensured that a person truly from the general populous, or _demos_, would eventually come to rule the population.

_____ **S.** Throughout medieval times and the Renaissance, lottery continued to be a critical component to all democratic regimes.

_____ **T.** This is partially because most adults in contemporary society already partake in lottery selection when enlisted for jury duty.

_____ **U.** Theorists debate over how well lottery scales as a mechanism for selecting political leaders in contemporary times, but we should be careful about dismissing it outright.

CONTINUE ON TO THE NEXT PAGE ➡

Logical Reasoning
Practice Test 3 (Paragraphs 11-20)

DIRECTIONS: This section requires you to closely analyze the problems and choose the correct answer choice. Exclusively use premises provided within the text. Pay close attention to the rules, setups, and wording.

11. Players A, B, C and D receive their batting order. After the last batter hits, the first batter will be next. C will be the last batter in order. B will not bat before or after C. A will be immediately before C.

Who will be batting in the number one position?

A. Player A
B. Player B
C. Player C
D. Player D
E. None of the above

Questions 12 and 13 refer to the following information.

Five students — Anne, Bob, Cindy, Deborah, and Eliza — are standing in line for a movie. Anne and Bob have exactly one person between them. Eliza is standing directly before Anne. Cindy and Bob are friends, so are standing next to each other. Anne is very punctual, so is in front of Bob. Deborah raced Eliza and arrived early enough to stand in front of her.

12. What position is Eliza?

F. First
G. Second
H. Third
J. Fourth
K. Fifth

CONTINUE ON TO THE NEXT PAGE ➡

13. Who can not be behind Eliza?

   A. Cindy

   B. Deborah

   C. Anne

   D. Bob

   E. Cannot be determined

14. June is 20 years old. Annette is either older than Thomas or younger than June. If Annette is older than Thomas, then Annette is 28. If Annette is younger than Thomas, then Annette is twenty-one. Thomas is younger than June. How old is Annette?

   F. 21

   G. 28

   H. Less than twenty

   J. More than thirty

   K. Not enough information to know

Questions 15, 16 and 17 refer to the following information.

Uncover the code below. Each letter corresponds to a word in the line directly below it. A letter **may** or **may not** be directly above its corresponding word.

A	C	B	D	F	means...
Cat	Hat	Bat	Sat	Stew	

A	D	E	B		means...
Sat	Cat	Hat	Crew		

H	G	C	B	D	means...
Two	Few	Hat	Bat	Sat	

A	D	C	E	B	means...
Bat	Hat	Cat	Crew	Sat	

15. Which word corresponds to A?

   A. Few

   B. Sat

   C Stew

   D. Cat or Bat

   E. Cat

16. Which word corresponds to H?

   F. Crew

   G. Two

   H. Stew

   J. Bat

   K. Few or Two

CONTINUE ON TO THE NEXT PAGE ➡

17. Which word corresponds to D?

A. Hat or Cat

B. Hat

C. Crew

D. Sat or Hat

E. Cat

18. Jamie does not go swimming if it is cold or raining. Last week it rained Monday through Thursday. Jamie did not go swimming on Friday. What must be true?

F. It was cold on Friday.

G. Jamie went swimming on either Saturday or Sunday.

H. Jamie went swimming on either Saturday or Sunday, as long as it wasn't raining or cold.

J. If it rained on Saturday, then Jamie did not go swimming on that day.

K. Jamie goes to an outdoor pool.

Questions 19 and 20 relate to the following scenario:

A group of six and seventh graders are going on a field trip. In order to stay safe, each sixth grader will be paired with one seventh grader and one teacher. There are four six graders, four seventh graders, and four teachers. The six graders are Anne, Barthe, Chad, and Dan. The seventh graders are Eric, Felice, Gabrielle, and Heather. The teachers are Jared, Kimberly, Loraine, and Margareta. Anne, Felice, and Loraine are in a group together. Barthe is not with Jared or Kimberly. Chad is also not with Kimberly. Dan is paired with Heather. Margareta is not paired with Gabrielle.

19. Who is in a group with Eric?

A. Jared

B. Kimberly

C. Loraine

D. Margareta

E. Cannot be determined

20. Who is in a group with Dan and Heather?

F. Jared

G. Kimberly

H. Loraine

J. Margareta

E. Either Jared or Kimberly

CONTINUE ON TO THE NEXT PAGE ➡

Reading
Practice Test 3 (Questions 21-50)

DIRECTIONS: Analyze the passages below, and answer the commensurate questions. Only use information provided within the passage for your answers. There is only one answer for each question.

More than twenty-eight million school-age children have parents who are employed, and between seven and fifteen million children go home to an empty house on any
5 given day. According to research conducted by the Urban Institute, "an estimated 4 million 6- to 12-year-olds with employed mothers are regularly without adult supervision when not at school."

10 There are many risks associated with leaving children and youth without supervision during afterschool hours. When children are in "self-care" rather than supervised, their personal safety as well as their emotional
15 security can be compromised. For older youth, being unsupervised after school increases the likelihood that they will become involved in criminal activity, develop a substance-abuse problem, or
20 engage in early sexual activity or other high-risk behaviors. Both juvenile crime and victimization of children and youth peak between the hours of 3 and 6 p.m..

The younger children are when they are left
25 alone, and the more hours they are unsupervised, the greater the probability they will be adversely affected.

In one study, sixth-graders who had been unsupervised regularly between first and
30 third grade were less socially competent and had lower grades than a control group. A study of nearly 5,000 eighth-graders found that those who took care of themselves for eleven or more hours a week were twice as
35 likely to smoke, drink, or use marijuana than those who were not in self-care after school.

21. What is the main idea of the passage?

A. Staying home increases an adolescent's chance of taking drugs.

B. Adolescents should participate in afterschool programs.

C. Being left self-monitored for extended periods of time can lead to adverse effects in adolescents.

D. It is never good for an adolescent to be left home alone.

E. The longer an adolescent is left home, the more likely they are to become criminals.

CONTINUE ON TO THE NEXT PAGE ➡

22. The study in paragraph 4 is used to illustrate:

    F. The impacts of being self-monitored at home for extended periods of time.

    G. How likely sixth graders are to smoke or drink.

    H. What is necessary to get good grades in school.

    J. Fourth and Fifth grade is not important in adolescent development.

    K. All adolescents who go to afterschool programs have superior social skills to those who are self-monitored frequently.

23. According to the passage, which eighth grader is at greatest risk of criminal behavior.

    A. A student who was self-monitored from kindergarten through third grade, but who has been in afterschool programs since that time.

    B. Students who were in after-school programs regularly until sixth grade, but have been self-monitored for 20 hours a week since then.

    C. Students who are home-schooled.

    D. A student who's sibling was self-monitored growing up.

    E. A student who was has no social skills.

24. Which of the following is not listed as an issue associated with frequent self-monitoring amongst adolescents?

    F. Higher drug use

    G. Worse grades

    H. Higher crime rate

    J. Decreased intelligence

    K. Less safety

25. What may also be considered "high-risk behavior" according to its usage in the passage?

    A. Robbing a convenience store.

    B. Not studying for a test.

    C. Not eating vegetables.

    D. Playing the game, "Risk."

    E. Not preparing for a job interview.

26. Lines 21-23 is most likely used as an example of:

    F. Why afterschool programs are useful.

    G. A reason why cops should be on patrol between 3 and 6pm.

    H. Why school should start later and end after 6pm.

    J. Prove that being supervised is only critical during the hours of 3pm and 6pm.

    K. This sentence is irrelevant to the passage.

CONTINUE ON TO THE NEXT PAGE ➡

There is a broad international agreement today on a minimal or threshold standard by which to judge whether or not a regime is a democracy. This minimal criterion is the regular occurrence of free, open, fair, and contested elections by which an inclusive citizenry selects its representatives in government. Thus, there is government by consent of the governed in which the people's representatives are accountable to the people.

In 2002, 121 of the world's 192 sovereign states could be recognized as democracies in terms of the minimal global standard for an electoral democracy. The collective populations of these electoral democracies accounted for 64.6% of the world's population. By contrast, in 1900 there was not even one country in the world that met today's minimal global standard for democracy. In 1950, there were only 22 authentic democracies comprising 14.3% of the world's population. By the end of the twentieth century, however, there was a dramatic global trend toward electoral democracy as communist regimes and other types of autocratic or authoritarian systems withered and died.

There is more to the content and process of democracy than is entailed by the minimal electoral standard. An advanced or more fully developed conceptualization of democracy in today's world includes electoral democracy in concert with such core concepts as representational government, constitutionalism, human rights, citizenship, civil society, and market economy. The idea of constitutionalism is the key to comprehending an advanced conceptualization of democracy. Constitutionalism means limited government and the rule of law to prevent the arbitrary use of power, to protect human rights, to regulate democratic procedures in elections and public policymaking, and to achieve a community's shared purposes.

Constitutionalism in a democracy, therefore, both limits and empowers the government of, by, and for the people. Through a constitution to which they have consented, the people grant power to the government to act effectively for the common good. The people also set constitutional limits on the power of their democratic government in order to prevent tyranny and to protect their rights. So, in an authentic constitutional democracy, the people's elected representatives in government are limited by the supreme law of the people's constitution for the primary purposes of protecting equally the rights of everyone in the polity and thereby promoting the common good of the community.

27. This passage mostly serves to:

   A. Explain constitutionalism.

   B. Show that democracy is more prevalent today than in the past.

   C. Admonish non-democratic regimes.

   D. Provide analysis of democratic regimes.

   E. Outline the defining features of contemporary democracy.

28. What change to a country's election standards, since 1900, may have allowed it to now be considered democratic?

F. Woman and minorities were granted enfranchisement.

G. A single ruler was elected multiple times.

H. Control changed from a Republican Party to a Democratic Party.

J. A country enforced compulsory participation in elections.

K. Nothing short of revolution is capable of changing a regime from non-democratic to democratic.

29. What element of a democracy establishes election procedure, according to the passage?

A. Whatever the ruler states

B. International precedent

C. Constitution

D. Human rights

E. Law developed since 1900

30. According to the passage, what would be covered by a constitution?

F. Street parking regulations

G. Human rights

H. The Gross Domestic Product

J. Education policy

K. The name of the country

31. What is true about democracies since 1950, according to the passage?

A. On average, they are more democratic.

B. On average, they possess more human rights.

C. They are no more nor less democratic than democracies existing before 1950.

D. On average, individual democratic countries in 1950 made up a larger percent of the global population than today.

E. On average, individual democratic countries in 1950 had a larger population than today.

32. What about constitutionalism, compared to basic election procedure, is necessary "to comprehending an advanced conceptualization of democracy?"

F. Elections need to be free and open.

G. Constitutionalism ensures that there will be multiple candidates in an election.

H. Constitutionalism limits the power of the people, but ensures the democratic rights of all.

J. Constitutions exclusively deal with election procedure.

K. Constitutions did not exist prior to 1900.

CONTINUE ON TO THE NEXT PAGE ➡

The year 1000 was a turning point in the fortunes of western Europe. Within a decade of that date, Olaf had converted most of the Scandinavians to Christianity, and the Viking threat came to an end. King Stephen accepted Christianity for himself and the Hungarian people, and the Magyars joined Christendom. The Muslim Caliphate of Cordoba collapsed into civil war, and the armed merchant vessels of the Italian city-states wrested control of the western Mediterranean from the Muslim fleets of north Africa.

The Muslims who controlled the mountain passes between France and Italy made the mistake of capturing Majolus, abbot of Cluny, and holding him for ransom. After obtaining his freedom, the Burgundian warrior class drove the Muslims from their fortresses and restored secure land communication between France and Italy.

Otto I, the German emperor, entered Rome and freed the papacy from the control of local Roman political factions. He turned the papacy over to Gerbert of Aurillac, a learned and reform-minded monk and teacher, and the Cluniac reform movement finally reached the highest levels of the western Church. Meanwhile, the Guiscards and Hautevilles, a family of adventurers from Normandy, began the reconquest of southern Italy and the establishment of the Norman Kingdom of Naples and Sicily.

Western Europe's economic fortunes began to change just as quickly. The rulers of Kiev had destroyed the Khazar state to the east of them and, by so doing, removed a buffer that had protected the Varangian Route of Russian rivers from the peoples of central Asia. One of these peoples, the Patchinaks (there are various spellings of this name), settled around 1000 in those lands where the

Varangian rivers entered the Black Sea. The Varangian route was blocked, and merchants began once again to carry goods from the Baltic to Mediterranean markets by way of the Seine-Loire-Garonne/Rhone river routes of France. In turn, Eastern merchants in appreciable numbers began to appear once again in the West.

33. What is this passage mostly about?

    A. How trade influenced Europe and Asia

    B. The rise of the Medieval Christian Church.

    C. The political, economic, and religious developments during 1000 AD.

    D. The developments of the Vikings and Germans during 1000 AD.

    E. The passage is an overview of important developments in Western European history.

34. What is implied in the passage concerning Scandinavians prior to the actions of Olaf?

    F. Christianity was not the dominant religion.

    G. Scandinavians were Vikings.

    H. Scandinavia was not an important part of Western Europe.

    J. Scandinavia had more territory.

    K. Olaf was not considered an important rule.

CONTINUE ON TO THE NEXT PAGE ➡

35. Otto I was responsible for assisting which reform movement in gaining power?

    A. Catholic reform movement

    B. Protestant reform movement

    C. Gerbert reform movement

    D. Cluniac reform movement

    E. Guiscards

36. What does the author cite as a reason for economic success during the year 1000?

    F. Political reform

    G. Social reform

    H. Religious reform

    J. Change in trading routes

    K. The frequency of wars

37. The "eastern merchants" were responsible for what development in the year 1000 AD?

    A. Economic prosperity

    B. Religious migration

    C. Population migration

    D. Linguistic migration

    E. All of the above

38. According to the passage, what was true of King Stephan prior to the year 1000 AD?

    F. He was not a king.

    G. He was Christian, but not catholic.

    H. He practiced a pagan religion.

    J. He conquered Hungary.

    K. He was not Christian.

CONTINUE ON TO THE NEXT PAGE ➡

Let's first define heresy. The technical definition is "error, obdurately held," which meant, in the Middle Ages, that a person believed something that was contrary to the "revealed truth" offered
5 by God to humanity through the Church, and that the person continued to hold that belief even after it had been pointed out to him or her how that belief was contrary to "revealed truth." Heresy was both hated and feared.

10 People believed in physical Hell, in which sinners would suffer the most excruciating pain imaginable forever and would be aware that their agony would never end. You would do well to think about that for a moment.
15 The Church taught, and most people believed, that the only way to avoid such a fate was by following the teachings and being protected by the rituals (sacraments) of the Church.

20 A heretic was doomed to Hell, but could also convince others of his or her wrong belief and so lead them to Hell as well. So, a heretic was regarded as we might regard someone carrying a highly contagious and incurable
25 disease. We would lock such a person up where they would not come in contact with anyone; the people of the Middle Ages killed them. Moreover, they often killed them in public and horrible ways as a warning to
30 everyone of how dangerous heretics were.

39. What is this passage mostly about?

A. Contagious diseases in the middle ages.
B. The judicial system in the middle ages.
C. Reasons for execution in the middle ages.
D. Defining heresy and explaining why it was publicly feared.
E. Describing the origin of heresy.

40. Why did people consider heresy a public, as opposed to purely private, concern?

F. All people are connected religiously.
G. Incorrect beliefs spread, corrupting others.
H. Heresy was a contagious disease.
J. People would discuss their heresy in public.
K. Someone wrong in their beliefs could bring about demons and bad luck.

41. Based on the word's context, what is the meaning of "obdurate" as used in the passage?

A. Refusing to change opinion, regardless of argumentation.
B. Non-religious
C. Heretical
D. Confident
E. Strongly

CONTINUE ON TO THE NEXT PAGE ➡

42. According to the passage, what was a common penalty for heresy in the Middle Ages?

   F. Life in prison
   G. Torture
   H. Exile
   J. Required to repent
   K. Execution

43. According to the passage, who offered the "revealed truth?"

   A. The Church
   B. Priests
   C. Heretics
   D. Christians
   E. God

44. Gruesome execution standards were used as a means to both remove a heretic and ___?

   F. Provide disincentive to potential future heretics.
   G. Illustrate the Churches ultimate authority.
   H. Instill fear in the heart of believers.
   J. More humane standards were not available.
   K. Heretics could be purified through pain.

CONTINUE ON TO THE NEXT PAGE →

You're probably surprised that I think that a stratified and status-ridden society like medieval Europe was the origin of the concept of equality. As I said, we often fall
5 short of our ideals, but our ideal of the integrity of the individual was born in medieval Europe.

The Greek Stoics, whose philosophy had a great effect on the early Christian Church,
10 held that there was a Brotherhood of Man and that the highest calling of every person was to treat others justly and compassionately. In the minds of the Stoics, however, this meant that people should be
15 kind to their slaves, not that there shouldn't be any slaves at all.

Under the best of conditions, such as in a well-run Benedictine monastery, medieval Europeans strove to achieve this ideal of
20 equality. A tightly-run organization such as a monastery required some hierarchy, but the Benedictines based theirs solely upon seniority. Whoever had entered the monastery first held precedence over all
25 those who had entered afterwards, regardless of what rank or status they might have held in secular life.

There is a neat story about this. A nobleman had decided to abandon secular life and
30 enter a monastery that he had endowed with considerable wealth. When he rode up to the gate of the monastery, with his slave trotting along behind him and carrying his luggage, the abbot had the gates opened wide and
35 greeted the noble with deference. When he was asked to step inside, the noble told his slave to take in his baggage. The slave did so and entered the monastery a couple of paces in front of his master.

40 For the rest of his life, the noble had to defer to his former slave since the slave had entered monastic life before he had.

45. What is this passage mostly about?

    A. Medieval society may not have practiced ideals such as equality perfectly, but this ideals were important to the society.

    B. The stoics preached equality.

    C. Nobles and slaves were considered equals.

    D. Nobles and slaves were treated the same by the church.

    E. Medieval society took monastic life seriously.

46. Based on the passage, the nobleman in paragraph four was most likely joining what kind of monastery?

    F. Benedict

    G. Stoic

    H. Medieval

    J. Church

    K. Noblesville

CONTINUE ON TO THE NEXT PAGE ➡

47. Which group believed that there was a "Brotherhood of Man," according to the passage?

    A. Benedict

    B. Nobleman

    C. Churches

    D. Medieval prophets

    E. Stoics

48. What is implied about medieval society?

    F. Medieval society was more advanced than contemporary society.

    G. Society was heavily stratified.

    H. There were no kings.

    J. Nobles owned slaves, but not by choice.

    K. Benedicts were the most equal people of the time.

49. What is the purpose of the story in paragraph four?

    A. To illustrate that not everyone agreed with slavery.

    B. To illustrate how high-minded the benedicts were.

    C. To illustrate how concepts of equality were enacted in medieval society.

    D. To illustrate how a slave could become free.

    E. To illustrate how concepts of freedom were enacted in medieval society.

50. What would the author most likely agree with?

    F. Medieval society was more enlightened than contemporary society.

    G. An individual can have an ideal without necessarily following the ideal perfectly.

    H. The medieval period was the most important moment in the development of individualism as a concept.

    J. The nobleman in the story made the right choice to join the monastery.

    K. Slavery cannot occur in a place where individual rights are considered important.

CONTINUE ON TO THE NEXT PAGE ➡

ARGO BROTHERS

Select the best answer from the choices given by carefully solving each problem. Bubble the letter of your answer on the answer sheet. Please refrain from making any stray marks on the answer sheet. If you need to erase an answer, please erase thoroughly.

Important Notes:

1. There are no formulas or definitions in the math section that will be provided.
2. Diagrams may or may not be drawn to scale. Do not make assumptions based on the diagram unless it is specifically stated in the diagram or question.
3. Diagrams are not in more than one plane, unless stated otherwise.
4. Graphs are drawn to scale, therefore, you can assume relationships according to the graph. If lines appear parallel, then you can assume the lines to be parallel. This is also true for right angles and so forth.
5. Simplify fractions completely.

Practice Test 3 (Questions 51-100)

51. $3[9 \div (-3)] + [-3 - (-8)] =$

   A. -20
   B. -4
   C. -2
   D. 2
   E. 14

52. If $\dfrac{2,000}{2x} = 10$, then what is $\sqrt{x}$?

   F. $\sqrt{10}$
   G. 10
   H. $\sqrt{1,000}$
   J. 100
   K. 1,000

CONTINUE ON TO THE NEXT PAGE ➡

53. If $x = 9$, $y = -9$ and $z = -1$, what is the value of $yz + \sqrt{x} + yz - \sqrt{x}$?

- **A.** -24
- **B.** -18
- **C.** 0
- **D.** 18
- **E.** 24

54.

1 dollar = 0.5 pillets
4 coss = 1 dollar

Lindsey has $20 to spend. She needs to buy exactly 2 pillets. She spends the remaining amount buying coss. How many coss does Lindsey purchase?

- **F.** 4
- **G.** 5
- **H.** 64
- **J.** 72
- **K.** 76

55. $\sqrt{100} \div \sqrt{25} =$

- **A.** $\sqrt{2}$
- **B.** 2
- **C.** 4
- **D.** 10
- **E.** $\frac{1}{2}$

56. If $x = -8$, what is the value of $\frac{1}{2}|4x-4|$?

- **F.** -18
- **G.** -14
- **H.** -8
- **J.** 14
- **K.** 18

57.

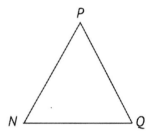

Triangle NPQ is an equilateral triangle. If its perimeter is 27, what is the length of $NP + NQ$?

- **A.** 16
- **B.** 18
- **C.** 4
- **D.** 32
- **E.** 0

58. If 40% of x is 160, what is x?

- **F.** .0025
- **G.** 4
- **H.** 64
- **J.** 360
- **K.** 400

138

CONTINUE ON TO THE NEXT PAGE ➡

59. When *d* is divided by 7, the remainder is 5. What is the remainder when *d* + 1 is divided by 7?

A. 0
B. 1
C. 4
D. 5
E. 6

60.

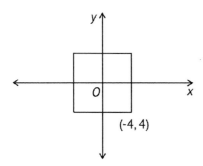

(-4, 4)

In the figure above, *O* is the center of the square. What is the area of the square?

F. 8
G. 16
H. 32
J. 64
K. 256

61.

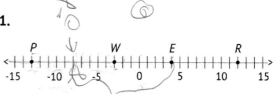

If O is the midpoint of $\overline{PW}$, then what is the distance of $\overline{OE}$?

A. 10
B. 11
C. 12
D. 13
E. 17

62. The average of 7 consecutive even integers is 20. What is the median?

F. 18
G. 20
H. 20.5
J. 22
K. 24

63. What is 0.003815 in scientific notation?

A. 3815×10^{-2}
B. 3.815×10^{-3}
C. 0.03815×10
D. 0.003815×10^{2}
E. 3.815×10^{3}

64.

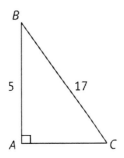

In the figure above, what is the length of $\overline{AC}$?

F. 8
G. 12
H. $2\sqrt{66}$
J. $2\sqrt{289}$
K. $\sqrt{314}$

65. What time will it be 53 hours after 3:30 P.M. on Thursday?

A. 7:30 A.M. Saturday
B. 8:30 A.M. Saturday
C. 7:30 P.M. Saturday
D. 8:30 P.M. Saturday
E. 8:30 P.M. Sunday

66.

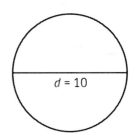

If x represents the circumference of the above figure, and y represents the area, what is $\frac{x}{y}$?

Note: d is the diameter of the circle above.

F. $\frac{10}{25}\pi$

G. $\frac{5}{2}$

H. $\frac{2}{5}$

J. $\frac{25}{10}\pi$

K. $\frac{5\pi}{25}$

67. A certain substance has a mass of 98 milligrams. What is the mass of this substance in kilograms?

  A. 9.8×10^5 kg

  B. 9.8×10^3 kg

  C. 9.8 kg

  D. 9.8×10^{-3} kg

  E. 9.8×10^{-5} kg

---

68. Samuel scored a 72, 92 and 80 on his first three exams. What is the minimum score he needs to get an average of 85?

  F. 85

  G. 90

  H. 93

  J. 96

  K. 100

---

69. Five out of 10 marbles in a bag are red. What percentage of the marbles is **not** red?

  A. 50%

  B. 55%

  C. 60%

  D. 75%

  E. 80%

70.

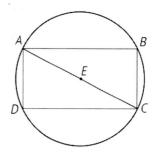

Figure not drawn to scale.

In the figure above, the rectangle *ABCD* is inscribed in the circle. Where *E* is the center and the radius is 5. If the length of *AD* is 6, what is the area of rectangle *ABCD*?

  F. 30

  G. 48

  H. 60

  J. 25π

  K. 180

---

71. $(\sqrt{81})(\sqrt{25}) + \sqrt{16} =$

  A. 5

  B. 40

  C. 49

  D. 56

  E. 64

72. It takes George 3 minutes to read 300 words. If each page in a book that he is reading has 750 words, how long will it take George to read 6 pages?

F.   30 minutes

G.   45 minutes

H.   60 minutes

J.   90 minutes

K.   250 minutes

3 m = 300
1 min = 100 works
⇒ time = $\frac{6 \times 750}{100}$
= 45

73. $(\frac{1}{2} - \frac{3}{4})^2 + \frac{5}{10} =$

A. $\frac{9}{16}$

B. $\frac{1}{2}$

C. $\frac{1}{16}$

D. $\frac{3}{4}$

E. $\frac{1}{4}$

74. If $x = 2^5 \cdot 3^2 \cdot 7$, then what is the value of x?

F.   1150

G.   2000

H.   2015

J.   2016

K.   3050

75.

A right cylindrical can is being filled with water. At 1 P.M. it is half full. At 2 P.M. it is $\frac{3}{4}$ th full. At this rate, when was it empty?

A.   11:00 A.M.

B.   11:30 A.M.

C.   12:00 P.M.

D.   12:30 P.M.

E.   3:00 P.M.

76. If $x^8 = 2^{2^{2^4}}$, what is x^2?

F.   2

G.   4

H.   8

J.   64

K.   128

CONTINUE ON TO THE NEXT PAGE ➡

77. James has yard work to finish. He finishes $\frac{1}{8}$ of the total work on the first day. What fraction of the work is left?

A. $\frac{1}{8}$

B. $\frac{3}{8}$

C. $\frac{7}{8}$

D. $\frac{3}{4}$

E. $\frac{1}{4}$

78.

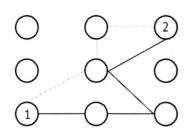

There are two different pathways connecting ① and ②. How many fewer steps is the solid-line path than the dotted-line path. (A step is defined as a line segment connecting 2 circles)?

F. -4

G. -1

H. 1

J. 4

K. 7

79. Jackie and Jesse each solve the same problem a different way.

Problem: $\sqrt{a + b}$ = ?

Jackie's way: $\sqrt{a + b} = \sqrt{a} + \sqrt{b}$

Jesse's way: $\sqrt{a + b} = \sqrt{a + b}$

If $a = 9$ and $b = 25$, how much bigger is Jackie's way than Jesse's way?

A. -2

B. 0

C. 2

D. $\sqrt{36}$

E. $8 - \sqrt{34}$

80. If $\Theta\,(a, b, c, d, e, f, g, h, i) =$

$$\frac{(a)(b) - (c)(d) + (ef)^2\,(gh)^2}{i}$$

which cannot be a value of Θ?

F. $\Theta\,(0, 0, 0, 0, 0, 0, 0, 0, 1)$

G. $\Theta\,(1, 1, 1, 1, 1, 1, 1, 1, 0)$

H. $\Theta\,(2, 2, 2, 2, 2, 2, 2, 2, 10)$

J. $\Theta\,(2, 3, 1, 4, 5, 6, 7, 0, 10)$

K. 0

81. If James grows by 20 inches every day starting Monday, what is the difference in his height between Wednesday and Monday?

- **A.** 0 inches
- **B.** 20 inches
- **C.** 30 inches
- **D.** 40 inches
- **E.** 60 inches

82. $(\frac{1}{2} - \frac{3}{4}) \div \frac{1}{2} =$

- **F.** $\frac{1}{2}$
- **G.** $\frac{3}{2}$
- **H.** $\frac{-1}{2}$
- **J.** $\frac{-3}{4}$
- **K.** 1

83.

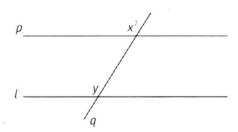

Line q intersects the parallel lines p and l. What is $\frac{y^3}{3}$?

- **A.** $\frac{x^4}{3}$
- **B.** x^6
- **C.** x^9
- **D.** $\frac{x^4}{9}$
- **E.** $\frac{x^6}{3}$

84. Given the arithmetic sequence $x, y, 30, z, f$ find $x + y + z + f$?

- **F.** 60
- **G.** 80
- **H.** 120
- **J.** 130
- **K.** 140

$x, x+n, x+2n, x+3$
$x+4$
$\Rightarrow x+2n = 50$
$x+y+z+f$
$= 4x+8n$
$= 4(x+2n)$
$x = 4 \cdot 30$
$= 120$

144   CONTINUE ON TO THE NEXT PAGE ➡

85. If $(-1)^2 = 1$, then the value of $(-1)^{2023}$ is

    A. -2023
    B. -1
    C. 0
    D. 1
    E. 2023

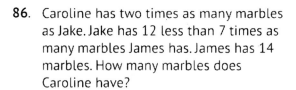

86. Caroline has two times as many marbles as Jake. Jake has 12 less than 7 times as many marbles James has. James has 14 marbles. How many marbles does Caroline have?

    F. 32
    G. 54
    H. 86
    J. 98
    K. 172

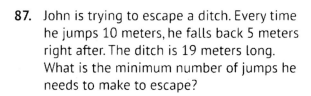

87. John is trying to escape a ditch. Every time he jumps 10 meters, he falls back 5 meters right after. The ditch is 19 meters long. What is the minimum number of jumps he needs to make to escape?

    A. 3
    B. 4
    C. 5
    D. 7
    E. 8

88. What is the largest number of digits the product of a 3 digit and a 2 digit number has?

    F. 4 digits
    G. 5 digits
    H. 6 digits
    J. 7 digits
    K. 8 digits

89. If $F_n = 2F_{n-1} + 3F_{n-2}$, then what is F_3 if $F_1 = F_2 = 1$?

    A. 2
    B. 3
    C. 4
    D. 5
    E. 10

90. Sam walks 3m to the West, then 4m South, then 4m North. How far is he from his original location?

    F. 3m
    G. 5m
    H. 7m
    J. 8m
    K. 12m

CONTINUE ON TO THE NEXT PAGE ➡

91. If $a = 3$, and $b = 5$, what is the value of

$$\frac{9a}{b-a} \ ?$$

A. 9

B. 27

C. $\frac{13}{5}$

D. $\frac{27}{2}$

E. $\frac{26}{5}$

---

92. The perimeter of a square is **four** times the circumference of a circle with radius of 1m. What is the area of the square?

F. 4π

G. 8π

H. $4\pi^2$

J. $8\pi^2$

K. $16\pi^2$

---

93. If means $bc + ad$, then

what is the value of ?

A. 24

B. 66

C. 67

D. 68

E. 1120

---

94. Convert $\frac{3}{40}$ to a decimal.

F. 0.0075

G. 0.075

H. 0.06

J. .75

K. 7.5

95. For what value of q is
$6(q + 3) = 2(q + 4)$?

A. $\dfrac{-1}{2}$

B. $\dfrac{-4}{9}$

C. $\dfrac{-5}{2}$

D. -3

E. $\dfrac{-2}{5}$

96.

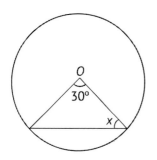

What is ∢ x of circle O?

F. $45°$

G. $60°$

H. $75°$

J. $150°$

K. $\dfrac{\pi}{2}$

97. For how many values of x is, $\dfrac{-3x^2}{4} > 0$?

A. 0

B. 1

C. 3

D. 5

E. 6

98. x is 40% of y and y is the square of x. Which is x?

F. $\sqrt{x}$

G. $0.4\sqrt{x}$

H. $0.4x^2$

J. x^2

K. $0.4x$

CONTINUE ON TO THE NEXT PAGE ➡

99. If $x = 7$; and $4x(3y - 2x) = 112$; what is the value of y?

A. 4

B. 6

C. 7

D. 28

E. 84

THIS IS THE END OF THE TEST. IF THERE IS TIME REMAINING, YOU MAY CHECK YOUR ANSWERS TO PART 1 OR PART 2.

100. If $x \, \partial \, y = \dfrac{x + y}{x - y}$, what is $a \, \partial \, (a-b)$?

F. $\dfrac{2a}{b}$

G. $\dfrac{2a-b}{2a}$

H. $\dfrac{2a-b}{b}$

J. $\dfrac{2a-b}{2b}$

K. $\dfrac{a+b}{a-2b}$

SHSAT PRACTICE TEST 3
ANSWER KEY

Scrambled Paragraphs

1. U, S, T, Q, R
2. Q, S, R, T, U
3. R, S, Q, T, U
4. R, U, S, T, Q
5. Q, R, S, U, T

Logical Reasoning

11. D
12. G
13. B
14. G
15. E
16. K
17. D
18. J
19. D
20. G

Reading

21. C	44. F
22. F	45. A
23. A	46. F
24. J	47. E
25. A	48. G
26. F	49. C
27. E	50. G
28. F	
29. C	
30. G	
31. D	
32. H	
33. C	
34. F	
35. D	
36. J	
37. A	
38. K	
39. D	
40. H	
41. A	
42. K	
43. E	

Math

51. B	63. B	75. A	87. A	99. B
52. G	64. H	76. G	88. G	100. H
53. D	65. D	77. C	89. D	
54. H	66. H	78. G	90. F	
55. B	67. E	79. E	91. D	
56. K	68. J	80. G	92. H	
57. B	69. A	81. D	93. C	
58. K	70. G	82. H	94. G	
59. E	71. C	83. E	95. C	
60. J	72. G	84. H	96. H	
61. C	73. A	85. B	97. A	
62. G	74. J	86. K	98. H	

To calculate your score visit our web site
and download excel calculator:
www. einstein-academy.com/calc

Practice Test 3 (Answers and Explanations)

SCRAMBLED PARAGRAPHS

1.   U, S, T, Q, R

U: "This" refers to the saying in the introductory sentence.

S: Continues discussion of Vlad.

T: "The famous character" is a reference to sentence S.

Q: This sentence gives examples of the way Vlad terrorized Transylvania, as discussed in sentence T.

R: "These other countries" refers to the foreign powers noted in sentence Q.

2.   Q, S, R, T, U

Q: "These lobbying firms" is a reference to the introductory sentence.

S: "Circulation of money" is a continuation of sentence Q.

R: This sentence gives an alternative source of power from money, and thus follows from sentence S.

T: "The study concluded" follows from the work performed by the political scientists in sentence R.

U: U does not follow succinctly from any previous sentence, and eloquently concludes the paragraphs thoughts.

3.   R, S, Q, T, U

R: S must follow from R, since S provides an example for R. R must come before Q, S, or U; thus, R must come first.

S: S provides an example from a "past era" as noted in sentence R.

Q: "More recently" cannot follow from "even today"(T).

T: "Even today" comes chronologically after Q, but is not discussing the future like U.

U: U references the future, and is thus chronologically after T.

4.   R, U, S, T, Q

R: "Titular myth" refers to the story mentioned in the introductory sentence.

U: "The tower" refers to the tower as discussed in sentence R.

S: S provides a break from the myth to contemporary building. This is the topic of the other two sentences and so must follow S.

T: "These considerations" refers to the dictates of population density. "However" indicates that the following sentence will be different from the considerations discussed in S.

Q: Q provides the example indicated in T.

5.   **Q, R, S, U, T**

Q: Q introduces the earliest reasoning for lottery. It provides a strong example of the topic introduced in the introductory sentence.

R: "He" refers to Aristotle. The content of the sentence also follows from the general point discussed in sentence Q.

S: "Continued" must follow from an earlier example; thus, S must follow Q and R.

U: T must follow from U, as the "this" refers to the statement at the end of U.

T: "This" refers to the statement at the end of U. T provides an example of the general claim provided in the previous sentence.

LOGICAL REASONING

11. D This is a sequencing game. First set up the board:

$$\overline{}\ \overline{}\ \overline{}\ \overline{}$$
$$4\quad 3\quad 2\quad 1$$

Player 1 can be on the far right or far left, depenfing on which space is numbered 1, but make sure that the rules adhere to the board's setup. C bats last, so place it directly in the position 4:

$$\frac{C}{4}\ \overline{3}\ \overline{2}\ \overline{1}$$

The next rule should be written as:

This rule indicates that B cannot be in position 3 or 1, so fill in the game accordingly:

$$\frac{C}{4}\ \frac{\cancel{B}}{3}\ \overline{2}\ \frac{\cancel{B}}{1}$$

A will be immediately before C. Write this rule as:

$$\boxed{C\ A}$$

and then fill A into the board:

$$\overset{A}{\frac{C}{4}}\ \frac{\cancel{B}}{3}\ \overline{2}\ \frac{\cancel{B}}{1}$$

B must go in 2, thus D must go in position 1. Fill out game, then find appropriate answer.

12. G This is a sequencing game. First set up the board:

$$\overline{5} \quad \overline{4} \quad \overline{3} \quad \overline{2} \quad \overline{1}$$

The first rule should be written as:

$$A\overset{\wedge}{\_}B$$

Write the next rule directly into the previous rule, creating both possibilities:

$$\boxed{AEB}$$
$$\boxed{B\_AE}$$

The next rule creates 3 possible boards:

1. $\boxed{AEBC}$ 2. $\boxed{CB\_AE}$ 3. $\boxed{BCAE}$

The next rule eliminates board 1. D can only be ahead of E in board 3, eliminating board 2. The final board looks as follows:

$$\frac{B}{5} \quad \frac{C}{4} \quad \frac{A}{3} \quad \frac{E}{2} \quad \frac{D}{1}$$

13. B Only Deborah can be in front of Eliza.

14. G These logical statements should be written as follows:

$$[J \to 20; \cancel{20} \to \cancel{J}]$$

$$[A > T \to \cancel{A<J}; A < J \to \cancel{A>T}]$$

$$[A > T \to A = 28; \cancel{A < 28} \to \cancel{A>T}]$$

$$[A < T \to A = 21; A = 21 \to A < T]$$

$$[T < J]$$

If Annette is younger than Thomas, and thus 21, then she is older than June, who is 20. However, Thomas must be younger than June, and so cannot be older than 21. If Annette is 28, then Thomas can be any age under 20. Thus, Annette must be 28.

15. E
16. K
17. D

For 15, 16, and 17, first solve the full game, finding what all letters stand for.

First, look for any letters that occur in all four rows. B and D both occur in all four rows, and thus should be written down first.

Next, look for the two words that occur in all four rows. Both Hat and Sat occur in all four rows. At this point, your game should look like this:

$$B = Hat/Sat$$
$$D = Hat/Sat$$

As there are no further rules that could determine which words are

ARGO BROTHERS

associated with B or D, simple cross out B, D, Hat, and Sat from all instances in the game.

Once those are removed, look for all letters that occur three times in the game. A and C occur in three games.

Now find the two words that occur in three games. Bat and Cat each occur in three games.

However, Cat occurs in the second group, while C does not; thus, a must equal Cat and C must equal Bat. Cross off all instances of A, C, Cat, and Bat from the game.

Find the remaining codes. The final board should look as follows:

B = Hat/Sat

D = Hat/Sat

A = Cat/B̶a̶t̶

C = C̶a̶t̶/Bat

F = Stew

E = Crew

H = Two/Few

G = Two/Few

18. J These logical statements should be written as follows:

[C → S̶; S → C̶]

[R → S̶; S → R̶]

[M, T, W or Th → R̶; R → M, T, W or Th]

[F → S; S̶ → F̶]

We know that he did not swim on Friday, but not why. Thus, F is incorrect.

No rules dictate that Jamie goes swimming on either Saturday or Sunday. Thus, G is incorrect.

If it is raining or cold then he will not go swimming; however, the rules do not indicate the inverse. Thus, H is incorrect.

If it rains, then Jamie does not go swimming. J indicates that it rains on Saturday, thus he would not go swimming on that day. J is correct.

K contains irrelevant information.

19. D Questions 19 and 20 refer to a pairing game. There will be four groups total, so set up the game and players like this:

1	2	3	4	6 = A̶, B, C, D
A				7 = E, F̶, G, H
F				T = J, K, L̶, M
L				

A, F and L are in a group together, so put those players directly into the board, and cross them out from your

154

list. B is not with J or K, so must be with M. Put this rule like this:

1	2	3	4
A	B		
F	M		
L			

Chad is not with Kimberly, and M/L are both taken; thus, chad must be with J. D and K are the only players left in the 6 and T columns; thus, they must also go together. Add H to the group that D is in. M is not with G, thus G must be with C and J.

1	2	3	4
A	B	C	D
F	M	J	K
L			

As you fill out the board, cross out the players from the list, leaving only E. The final board should look as follows:

1	2	3	4
A	B	C	D
F	M	J	K
L	E	G	H

According to the board, E is with B and M; thus, answer choice D is the correct answer.

20. **G** According to the board, D and H are paired with K; thus, answer choice G is correct.

READING COMPREHENSION

21. **C** Three out of four paragraphs explicitly discusses this answer choice. B may seem appropriate, but connotes a proscriptive tone, while this passage is largely descriptive.

22. **F** The study shows adverse consequences of long periods of self-monitoring.

23. **A** As paragraph three notes, age is a critical factor. The younger a child is when left alone, the more impactful self-care will be for that child. C, D, and E are not situations explicitly noted within the passage.

24. **J** All other answer choices can be found directly in the passage. While the student may suffer in grades, this does not necessarily mean that they have less intelligence.

25. **A** B and E have some risk, but are not of the same level as A. "Criminal activity" is mentioned explicitly as a high-risk behavior.

26. **F** This evidence shows that students are at their greatest risk from 3-6. This is the same time frame as after school programs. The role of police is not discussed in the passage, thus G is not correct. H is an interesting policy derived from the fact mentioned in these lines, but it is not one that is discussed within the passage.

27. E This passage alludes to contemporary democracy in all paragraphs. A is the topic of only two paragraphs. B is the topic of only one paragraph. C is not discussed.

28. F One criteria noted in the first paragraph is that an "inclusive citizenry selects its representatives." If minorities and women are not able to vote, then the country would not be considered democratic. Gaining these rights would in turn potentially allow it to be considered democratic.

29. C This answer derives from line 44.

30. G This answer derives from line 43.

31. D This answer derives from paragraph 2. In 1950, 22 democracies comprised 14.3% of the world's population, whereas today 121 countries comprise 64.6%. This means that in 1950 an average democracy accounted for .65% of the world population, while today a single democratic country on average only accounts for .53% of the world population.

32. H This answer derives from the final paragraph.

33. C This passage relates to all three developments during this time and the answer choice is prevalent in all paragraphs.

34. F As noted in line 3, Olaf converted most of Scandinavia to Christianity. This implies that prior to Olaf, much of Scandinavia was not Christian.

35. D This answer derives from line 26.

36. J This answer derives from lines 42-49.

37. A The passage notes how changes in trade barriers allowed eastern merchants to frequent Europe, leading to economic growth.

38. K Line 5 notes that King Stephen accepted Christianity in the year 1000. This implies that he was not Christian prior to this date.

39. D This is the only answer that occurs in every paragraph. Other answer choices are only in one paragraph.

40. H This answer derives from the third paragraph.

41. A The passage notes that people believed heresy to be an incorrect belief that went against the "revealed truth." As such, obdurate should mean an unwillingness to change one's opinion regardless of whether or not is can be proven false.

42. K This answer derives from line 28.

43. E This answer derives from line 5.

44. F The passage notes that gruesome execution methods were used as a way of "warning" people as to how dangerous it was to be a heretic. Warnings exist to dissuade people from doing an action and thus act as a disincentive.

45. A This passage shows the importance of equality to medieval society, even while showing where it sometimes fell short of this ideal. All other answer choices appear in fewer paragraphs.

46. F The story indicates that it is "about this." "This" refers to the form of equality performed by the Benedictine monastery.

47. E This answer choice derives from line 10.

48. G The author notes that medieval society was stratified and status-ridden.

49. C This story illustrated a way that equality occurred in a medieval monastery.

50. G This answer follows from his statement made in lines 4-7.

Practice Test 3 (Answers and Explanations)

51. B   We must perform the operations inside the parentheses first and follow the order of operations:

Parentheses
Exponentiation
Multiplication
Division
Addition
Subtraction

3[-3] + [5] = -9 +5 = -4 , which is answer choice B.

52. G   Simplify the expression to $\frac{1000}{x}$ = 10, which when we solve, gives us, x = 100. If x = 100, then, $\sqrt{100}$ = 10, which is the answer choice G.

53. D   Plug in the values for x, y and z:
$9 + \sqrt{9} + 9 - \sqrt{9}$ = 18, which is answer choice D.

54. H   If she needs to buy 2 pillets, that will cost $(\frac{2}{0.5})$ dollars = 4 dollars

So, she will have $20-$4 left, or $16. With 16 dollars, she can buy (16 • 4) coss , or 64 coss, which is answer choice H.

55. B   Simplifying gives us:
$\frac{\sqrt{100}}{\sqrt{25}}$ = $\frac{10}{5}$ = 2, which is answer choice B.

56. K   If x = -8, then 4 • -4 = -36. Since we have an absolute value sign, we must take the positive of whatever number we have inside, which in this case, is -36.

So we have:
$(\frac{1}{2})$(36) = 18, which is answer choice K.

57. B   Triangle NPQ is an equilateral triangle, which means all sides are equal. If the perimeter is 27, then the length of each side must be a third of the perimeter, or 9. Side lengths NP and NQ must add to 2(9) = 18, which is answer choice B.

58. K   40% is equivalent to $(\frac{2}{5})$, so our expression is
$(\frac{2}{5})(x)$ = 160, and solving for x gives us 400, which is answer choice K.

59. E

We know that the statement must hold for all numbers. We can substitute a number of our choosing such as 40. When 40 is divided by 7, we get a remainder of 5. Adding 1 to 40, we get 41, which when divided by 7, gives us a remainder of 6, which is answer choice E.

60. J

The vertical distance (parallel to the y-axis) from the origin to a point on the square must be 4. Doubling that would give us the side length of the square, which is 8. The area of the square is just the side length squared. $8^2 = 64$, which is answer choice J.

61. C

The points we are concerned with here are P, W, O and E. It is helpful to state the coordinates of those points. O is the midpoint of P and W. To find the midpoint, all we need to do is take the difference between points P and W, divide by 2, and subtract it from point P.

$P(-13)$
$W(-3)$
$O(-8)$
$E(4)$

So, therefore, the distance between O and E is $|-8 - 4| = 12$, which is answer choice C.

62. G

The median of an odd number of even consecutive integers is actually just the average of those numbers. For example:

$\{2,4,6\}$

The mean of those numbers is 4, and the median is 4. So the answer here is 20, which is answer choice G.

63. B

3.815×10^{-3} is the answer since we moved the decimal point three places to the right.

64. H

Applying the Pythagorean Theorem, we get that the length of AC is:
$(-17^2 - 5^5)^{\frac{1}{2}} = 2\sqrt{66}$,
which is answer choice H.

65. D

53 hours from 3:30PM on a Thursday is composed of 2 sets of 24 hour days and 5 extra hours. This gives us Saturday at 8:30PM, which is answer choice D.

66. H

The ratio of the circumference to the area of any circle is $(\frac{2}{r})$, where r is the radius. The radius of this circle is half of the diameter, which gives us 5.
The answer is $(\frac{2}{5})$, which is answer choice H.

67. E To convert from milligrams to grams, we must divide by 1000. To convert from grams to kilograms, we must divide by 1000. So, to convert between milligrams to kilograms, we must divide by 1,000,000, which would give us, 9.8×10^{5}, which is answer choice E.

68. J Let x be the minimum score he must get to get the desired average. The average equation can be expressed as:

$$\frac{244 + x}{4} = 85,$$

and solving for x, we get $x = 96$, which is answer choice J.

69. A If 5 out of 10 marbles in a bag are red, then 5 are not red, making the percentage 50%, which is answer choice A.

70. G If the radius is 5, then the diameter or length AC is 10 units. We know that length AD is 6, so then we must also know that length DC is 8 (3, 4 ,5 special right triangle), which gives the rectangle an area of $6 \cdot 8 = 48$, which is answer choice G.

71. C $(9 \cdot 5) + (4) = 49$

72. G If it takes him 3 minutes to read 300 words, then it will take him 7.5 minutes to read 750 words. If there are 6 pages, each with 750 words, then it will take him $(6 \cdot 7.5)$ minutes to read the 6 pages.
$(7.5 \cdot 6) = 45$ minutes, which is answer choice G.

73. A If we simplify what is in the parentheses first, we get $(-\frac{1}{4})$.

$$(-\frac{1}{4})^{2} + (\frac{5}{10}) = (\frac{1}{16}) + (\frac{1}{2}) =$$
$$(\frac{1}{16}) + (\frac{8}{16}) = (\frac{9}{16}), \text{which is}$$

answer choice A.

74. J The only answer choice that is divisible by 7, is 2016, which is answer choice J.

75. A We can tell that each consecutive hour adds $\frac{1}{4}^{th}$ to the amount. Let's say the units is gallons. So, if we work backwards, we can tell that the cylinder was empty 2 hours ago. So, the answer is 11AM, which is answer choice A.

76. G After simplifying, we get $x^8 = 2^8$, so we know that $x = 2$ and therefore $x^2 = 4$, which is answer choice G.

77. C

78. G The solid line path takes 4 steps. The dotted line path takes 3 steps. So the solid line path is -1 steps fewer than the dotted line path, which is answer choice G.

79. E Jackie's way: $\sqrt{34}\sqrt{9} + \sqrt{25} = 8$
Jesse's way: $= \sqrt{9} + 25 = \sqrt{34}$

$8 - \sqrt{34}$, the answer choice is E.

80. G We need theta to be a real value. Since i, is in the denominator, if i ever equals to 0, it will make the value undefined. Answer choice G gives i the value of 0, and therefore using the values in answer choice G cannot give us a value for theta. Therefore, the answer choice is G.

81. D Every day, James grows by 20 inches. There is a difference of 2 days between Monday and Wednesday, which means the answer is $2(20) = 40$ inches, which is answer choice D.

82. H Simplify and you will get $(-\frac{1}{2})$, which is answer choice H.

83. E We can tell that $x^2 = y$ since they are corresponding angles. So, $y^5 = x^5$, and x^2 and y are corresponding angles, meaning that they are equal.

*Note: Make sure you know the difference between corresponding, alternate interior, alternate exterior, and consecutive interior angles to help you with these types of problems.

Since x^2 and y are equal, and the question asks what is $\frac{y^5}{3}$, replace the y is x^2.
This gives you $\frac{x^{3^{(3)}}}{3}$, simplify to get $\frac{x^6}{3}$, which is answer choice E.

84. H Let, d, be the difference between consecutive terms. Each consecutive term differs by d. The values of x, y, z and f in terms of the difference d, is:

$x = 30 - 2d$
$y = 30 - d$
$z = 30 + d$
$f = 30 + 2d$

so when we add x, y, z and f, we get, 120, which is answer choice H.

85. B   If a negative number in parentheses is raised to an even exponent, then the answer will always be positive. However, 2023 is an odd exponent, making the value of this expression -1, which is answer choice B.

86. K   If Jake has X marbles, then Caroline has $2X$ marbles. If James has Y marbles, then:

$X = 7Y - 12$.

We know that James has 14 marbles, so $Y = 14$, so $X = 86$. Therefore, Caroline has $2X$ marbles or 172, which is answer choice K.

87. A   The first jump he makes, he goes up 10 meters. Then he falls back 5 meters. Then he jumps again, reaching the 15 meter mark, then falls back 5 meters to the 10 meter mark. He only has to jump one last time to reach the 20 meter mark, which is past the 19 meter mark.
In total, he jumped 3 times, so the answer is A.

88. G   We can take the highest 3 digit number, 999, and the highest 2 digit number, which is 99. When we multiply them, we get a 5 digit number, 98901.
The answer is G.

89. D   We can plug in the initial values into the formula to get F_3.

$F_3 = 2 \cdot F_2 + 3 \cdot F_1 = 2 \cdot 1 + 3 \cdot 1 = 5$.
The answer is D.

90. F   Sam moves 3 meters to the West. Since Sam walked 4 meters North after walking 4 meters South, he undid his vertical movement, making him end up 3 meters from his original location.
The answer is F.

91. D   Plugging in for the values of a and b, we get:
$$\frac{9(3)}{5 - 3} = \frac{27}{2},$$
which is answer choice D

ARGO BROTHERS

92. H The circumference of a circle with a radius of 1m is 2π, which equals 4 times the perimeter of the square. The perimeter of a square is 4 times the length of one of its sides. If s is the side length of the square, then we can write:
$4s = 8\pi$, which means $s = 2\pi$ and the area is $s^2 = 4\pi^2$.
The answer is H.

93. C Following the pattern in the question, we know that $a = 4, b = 5, c = 7$ and $d = 8$. The question is asking what is the value of $bc + ad$. Plug in the values, and you get $(4)(8) + (7)(5) = 32 + 35 = 67$, which is answer choice C.

94. G We know that $(\frac{3}{4})$ equates to 0.75 as a decimal. We simply multiply the denominator by 10 to get $(\frac{3}{40})$, which gives us 0.075 as a decimal, which is answer choice G.

95. C This requires us to solve for q.
$6(q + 3) = 2(q + 4)$
$3(q + 3) = (q + 4)$
$3q + 9 = q + 4$
$2q = -5$
$q = -\frac{5}{2}$
The answer is C.

96. H The two sides of the triangle that are adjacent to the angle of 30 degrees are equal since they make up two radii of the circle. All radii are equal.
Therefore, the remaining two angles must be equal and must add up to 150° (180° - 30°).
This means that angle x is 75°, which is answer choice H.

97. A For this expression to be true, we must find a value of x that makes $\frac{-3x^2}{4}$ positive, which is impossible for real values of x since we are squaring x. When we square x, we return a positive value. So the answer is 0, which is answer choice A.

98. H We must equate the sentence into mathematical terms. We know that,
$x = 0.4y$ and
$y = x^2$ so,
$x = 0.4x^2$
which is answer choice H.

99. B   Plugging in 7 for x in the equation, we get,
$4(7)(3y - 2(7)) = 112$, which gives us
$28(3y - 14) = 112$ and solving for y, we get,
$(3y - 14) = 4$
$3y = 18$ so,
$y = 6$, which is answer choice B.

100. H   Using the formula, we get,
$$\frac{a + (a - b)}{a - (a - b)} = \frac{2a - b}{b}$$
which is answer choice H.

TIME TO FINISH TEST:
VERBAL: 75 minutes
MATH: 75 minutes

— This exam is 2 hours and 30 minutes long. Try to take this full exam in one sitting to simulate real test conditions.

— While taking this exam, refrain from hearing music or watching T.V.

— Please note, calculators are not permitted! You are permitted to answer questions in any order you see fit.

— Not all answers need take the same amount of time. Allocate your test time accordingly.

— Concentrate and GOOD LUCK!

To calculate your score visit our web site and download excel calculator:
www. einstein-academy.com/calc

SHSAT PRACTICE TEST 4
ANSWER SHEET

PART 1 (VERBAL)

SCRAMBLED PARAGRAPHS

Paragraph 1

The first sentence is ⓠ ⓡ ⓢ ⓣ ⓤ
The second sentence is ⓠ ⓡ ⓢ ⓣ ⓤ
The third sentence is ⓠ ⓡ ⓢ ⓣ ⓤ
The fourth sentence is ⓠ ⓡ ⓢ ⓣ ⓤ
The fifth sentence is ⓠ ⓡ ⓢ ⓣ ⓤ

Paragraph 2

The first sentence is ⓠ ⓡ ⓢ ⓣ ⓤ
The second sentence is ⓠ ⓡ ⓢ ⓣ ⓤ
The third sentence is ⓠ ⓡ ⓢ ⓣ ⓤ
The fourth sentence is ⓠ ⓡ ⓢ ⓣ ⓤ
The fifth sentence is ⓠ ⓡ ⓢ ⓣ ⓤ

Paragraph 3

The first sentence is ⓠ ⓡ ⓢ ⓣ ⓤ
The second sentence is ⓠ ⓡ ⓢ ⓣ ⓤ
The third sentence is ⓠ ⓡ ⓢ ⓣ ⓤ
The fourth sentence is ⓠ ⓡ ⓢ ⓣ ⓤ
The fifth sentence is ⓠ ⓡ ⓢ ⓣ ⓤ

Paragraph 4

The first sentence is ⓠ ⓡ ⓢ ⓣ ⓤ
The second sentence is ⓠ ⓡ ⓢ ⓣ ⓤ
The third sentence is ⓠ ⓡ ⓢ ⓣ ⓤ
The fourth sentence is ⓠ ⓡ ⓢ ⓣ ⓤ
The fifth sentence is ⓠ ⓡ ⓢ ⓣ ⓤ

Paragraph 5

The first sentence is ⓠ ⓡ ⓢ ⓣ ⓤ
The second sentence is ⓠ ⓡ ⓢ ⓣ ⓤ
The third sentence is ⓠ ⓡ ⓢ ⓣ ⓤ
The fourth sentence is ⓠ ⓡ ⓢ ⓣ ⓤ
The fifth sentence is ⓠ ⓡ ⓢ ⓣ ⓤ

LOGICAL REASONING

11 Ⓐ Ⓑ Ⓒ Ⓓ Ⓔ
12 Ⓕ Ⓖ Ⓗ Ⓙ Ⓚ
13 Ⓐ Ⓑ Ⓒ Ⓓ Ⓔ
14 Ⓕ Ⓖ Ⓗ Ⓙ Ⓚ
15 Ⓐ Ⓑ Ⓒ Ⓓ Ⓔ
16 Ⓕ Ⓖ Ⓗ Ⓙ Ⓚ
17 Ⓐ Ⓑ Ⓒ Ⓓ Ⓔ
18 Ⓕ Ⓖ Ⓗ Ⓙ Ⓚ
19 Ⓐ Ⓑ Ⓒ Ⓓ Ⓔ
20 Ⓕ Ⓖ Ⓗ Ⓙ Ⓚ

READING

21 Ⓐ Ⓑ Ⓒ Ⓓ Ⓔ
22 Ⓕ Ⓖ Ⓗ Ⓙ Ⓚ
23 Ⓐ Ⓑ Ⓒ Ⓓ Ⓔ
24 Ⓕ Ⓖ Ⓗ Ⓙ Ⓚ
25 Ⓐ Ⓑ Ⓒ Ⓓ Ⓔ
26 Ⓕ Ⓖ Ⓗ Ⓙ Ⓚ

27 Ⓐ Ⓑ Ⓒ Ⓓ Ⓔ
28 Ⓕ Ⓖ Ⓗ Ⓙ Ⓚ
29 Ⓐ Ⓑ Ⓒ Ⓓ Ⓔ
30 Ⓕ Ⓖ Ⓗ Ⓙ Ⓚ
31 Ⓐ Ⓑ Ⓒ Ⓓ Ⓔ
32 Ⓕ Ⓖ Ⓗ Ⓙ Ⓚ

33 Ⓐ Ⓑ Ⓒ Ⓓ Ⓔ
34 Ⓕ Ⓖ Ⓗ Ⓙ Ⓚ
35 Ⓐ Ⓑ Ⓒ Ⓓ Ⓔ
36 Ⓕ Ⓖ Ⓗ Ⓙ Ⓚ
37 Ⓐ Ⓑ Ⓒ Ⓓ Ⓔ
38 Ⓕ Ⓖ Ⓗ Ⓙ Ⓚ

39 Ⓐ Ⓑ Ⓒ Ⓓ Ⓔ
40 Ⓕ Ⓖ Ⓗ Ⓙ Ⓚ
41 Ⓐ Ⓑ Ⓒ Ⓓ Ⓔ
42 Ⓕ Ⓖ Ⓗ Ⓙ Ⓚ
43 Ⓐ Ⓑ Ⓒ Ⓓ Ⓔ
44 Ⓕ Ⓖ Ⓗ Ⓙ Ⓚ

45 Ⓐ Ⓑ Ⓒ Ⓓ Ⓔ
46 Ⓕ Ⓖ Ⓗ Ⓙ Ⓚ
47 Ⓐ Ⓑ Ⓒ Ⓓ Ⓔ
48 Ⓕ Ⓖ Ⓗ Ⓙ Ⓚ
49 Ⓐ Ⓑ Ⓒ Ⓓ Ⓔ
50 Ⓕ Ⓖ Ⓗ Ⓙ Ⓚ

PART 2 (MATHEMATICS)

MATHEMATICS PROBLEMS

51 Ⓐ Ⓑ Ⓒ Ⓓ Ⓔ
52 Ⓕ Ⓖ Ⓗ Ⓙ Ⓚ
53 Ⓐ Ⓑ Ⓒ Ⓓ Ⓔ
54 Ⓕ Ⓖ Ⓗ Ⓙ Ⓚ
55 Ⓐ Ⓑ Ⓒ Ⓓ Ⓔ

56 Ⓕ Ⓖ Ⓗ Ⓙ Ⓚ
57 Ⓐ Ⓑ Ⓒ Ⓓ Ⓔ
58 Ⓕ Ⓖ Ⓗ Ⓙ Ⓚ
59 Ⓐ Ⓑ Ⓒ Ⓓ Ⓔ
60 Ⓕ Ⓖ Ⓗ Ⓙ Ⓚ

61 Ⓐ Ⓑ Ⓒ Ⓓ Ⓔ
62 Ⓕ Ⓖ Ⓗ Ⓙ Ⓚ
63 Ⓐ Ⓑ Ⓒ Ⓓ Ⓔ
64 Ⓕ Ⓖ Ⓗ Ⓙ Ⓚ
65 Ⓐ Ⓑ Ⓒ Ⓓ Ⓔ

66 Ⓕ Ⓖ Ⓗ Ⓙ Ⓚ
67 Ⓐ Ⓑ Ⓒ Ⓓ Ⓔ
68 Ⓕ Ⓖ Ⓗ Ⓙ Ⓚ
69 Ⓐ Ⓑ Ⓒ Ⓓ Ⓔ
70 Ⓕ Ⓖ Ⓗ Ⓙ Ⓚ

71 Ⓐ Ⓑ Ⓒ Ⓓ Ⓔ
72 Ⓕ Ⓖ Ⓗ Ⓙ Ⓚ
73 Ⓐ Ⓑ Ⓒ Ⓓ Ⓔ
74 Ⓕ Ⓖ Ⓗ Ⓙ Ⓚ
75 Ⓐ Ⓑ Ⓒ Ⓓ Ⓔ

76 Ⓕ Ⓖ Ⓗ Ⓙ Ⓚ
77 Ⓐ Ⓑ Ⓒ Ⓓ Ⓔ
78 Ⓕ Ⓖ Ⓗ Ⓙ Ⓚ
79 Ⓐ Ⓑ Ⓒ Ⓓ Ⓔ
80 Ⓕ Ⓖ Ⓗ Ⓙ Ⓚ

81 Ⓐ Ⓑ Ⓒ Ⓓ Ⓔ
82 Ⓕ Ⓖ Ⓗ Ⓙ Ⓚ
83 Ⓐ Ⓑ Ⓒ Ⓓ Ⓔ
84 Ⓕ Ⓖ Ⓗ Ⓙ Ⓚ
85 Ⓐ Ⓑ Ⓒ Ⓓ Ⓔ

86 Ⓕ Ⓖ Ⓗ Ⓙ Ⓚ
87 Ⓐ Ⓑ Ⓒ Ⓓ Ⓔ
88 Ⓕ Ⓖ Ⓗ Ⓙ Ⓚ
89 Ⓐ Ⓑ Ⓒ Ⓓ Ⓔ
90 Ⓕ Ⓖ Ⓗ Ⓙ Ⓚ

91 Ⓐ Ⓑ Ⓒ Ⓓ Ⓔ
92 Ⓕ Ⓖ Ⓗ Ⓙ Ⓚ
93 Ⓐ Ⓑ Ⓒ Ⓓ Ⓔ
94 Ⓕ Ⓖ Ⓗ Ⓙ Ⓚ
95 Ⓐ Ⓑ Ⓒ Ⓓ Ⓔ

96 Ⓕ Ⓖ Ⓗ Ⓙ Ⓚ
97 Ⓐ Ⓑ Ⓒ Ⓓ Ⓔ
98 Ⓕ Ⓖ Ⓗ Ⓙ Ⓚ
99 Ⓐ Ⓑ Ⓒ Ⓓ Ⓔ
100 Ⓕ Ⓖ Ⓗ Ⓙ Ⓚ

ARGO BROTHERS

DIRECTIONS: This section requires you to rearrange five given sentences, such that they form a proper paragraph. The introductory sentence for each paragraph will be given.
An appropriate answer will order sentences so that they are logical and grammatically sound.
Credit is exclusively given for answers perfectly correct. There are no partially correct answers.

Scrambled Paragraphs
Practice Test 4 (Paragraphs 1-5)

Paragraph 1

Modern artists and art historians have proliferated an unusual interpretation of Plato's discussion on art.

_____ **Q.** In his "Republic," Plato notes that art is a shadow of reality and is thus inferior to its ontologically richer alternatives, such as math and reason.

_____ **R.** For the aforementioned contemporary practitioners; however, they instead read this text to state that while art may at base level be a fabrication, it nonetheless has the ability to possess a richer meaning.

_____ **S.** Using this reasoning, artists and curators argue that works which are more conceptual than representational align more properly with Plato's ideal.

_____ **T.** Similarly, these same artists claim that Hegel's End of Art thesis operates in the same manner.

_____ **U.** Rather than simply meaning art no longer has value, they interpret this thesis as meaning that art no longer has value as mere representation.

CONTINUE ON TO THE NEXT PAGE ➡

Paragraph 2

The role of domesticated animals has changed radically over the last few centuries.

_____ **Q.** Merely by existing, domesticated animals can teach children empathy and radically decrease levels of anxiety and depression for people of all ages.

_____ **R.** Some dogs were capable of increasing hunting yields.

_____ **S.** In earlier times, domesticated animals, such as dogs, were members of the family insofar as they provided utility to the household.

_____ **T.** As the necessity for these services have waned, domesticated animals have fulfilled psychic, rather than physical, needs.

_____ **U.** Others could assist with the shepherding of herd animals.

Paragraph 3

Students who learned the names of the planets through the phrase, "My Very Educated Mother Just Served Us Nine Pizzas," may be confused following recent astronomical developments.

_____ **Q.** Pluto, or "pizzas" in the mnemonic device, was recently taken off the list of planets.

_____ **R.** Recently, this learning tool has come under assault, leaving students curious about what their mothers have served them in groups of nine.

_____ **S.** As scientists explored the solar system more, it came to their attention that many large objects orbiting the sun within the asteroid belt would need to be considered planets if Pluto fit the criteria.

_____ **T.** This serves as an important reminder that the universe as we know it only exists within the conceptualization deemed fit by the scientific community.

_____ **U.** Rather than expand the definition of planets, they instead limited the criteria.

CONTINUE ON TO THE NEXT PAGE ➡

Paragraph 4

The game of professional basketball has seen many changes over the course of its history.

_____ **Q.** A rule created in the 1990s banning hand-checking, for instance, allowed perimeter shooters to become more valuable.

_____ **R.** Many of these changes have developed either from alterations in rules or the application of rules.

_____ **S.** For example, while traveling has always been against the rules, the rule is seldom enforced during the course of the game.

_____ **T.** While rule changes can be explicit, other changes have come from more implicit alterations in how referees choose to adjudicate the rules.

_____ **U.** Consequently, players can stay on the perimeter where they would normally shoot, and still successfully slash to the basket regardless of the amount of steps taken.

Paragraph 5

A form of dumpling can be found in nearly every culinary culture of the world.

_____ **Q.** Perhaps dumplings are as central to human development as fertility goddesses.

_____ **R.** Pierogis, momos, and ravioli are only a few of the many kinds.

_____ **S.** Carl Jung discusses the presence of archetypes throughout human history which seem to exist regardless of the culture, such as the fertility goddess.

_____ **T.** Consistent in all of these alternative styles is a starch based wrapper with filling inside.

_____ **U.** While this generality of the dumpling is such that it may be unsurprising to see them developed in different parts of the world, it is still surprising, given that other seemingly simple culinary inventions are not found nearly universally.

Logical Reasoning
Practice Test 4 (Paragraphs 11-20)

DIRECTIONS: This section requires you to closely analyze the problems and choose the correct answer choice. Exclusively use premises provided within the text. Pay close attention to the rules, setups, and wording.

11. If Jared goes to the store, then he will not go out for dinner. If Jared does go out for dinner, then he will not get home until after 8:00 P.M.

    What must be true?

    A. If Jared goes to the store, then he will be home before 8:00 P.M.

    B. If Jared does not go to the store, then he will go to dinner.

    C. Jared is not going to the movies after his dinner.

    D. If Jared gets home at 7:00 P.M., then he must have not gone out for dinner.

    E. If Jared gets home at 9:00 P.M., then he did not go to the store.

12. At Thorough Middle School, students on the cross country team are also on the indoor track team. Thomas went to running camp. Everyone who went to running camp is on the indoor track team.

    What must be true?

    F. Thomas is on the cross country team.

    G. Thomas is not on the cross country team.

    H. Thomas is on the same team as some students who are on the cross country team.

    J. Thomas likes running.

    K. Thomas is on a team with all members of the cross country team.

CONTINUE ON TO THE NEXT PAGE ➡

13. Four students are standing in a line: Anne, Bob, Carl, and Dom. Bob and Dom are standing next to each other. Carl is standing second in line.

Where is Anne standing?

A. First
B. Second
C. Third
D. Fourth
E. Undetermined

14. For college tours, there are six students (Arthur, Ben, Colton, Derick, Ethan, and Francine), and three tour guides (Grant, Henry, and Kate). Arthur and Derick are in the same group. Colton is not with Ethan. Ben is not with Colton. If every group has equal numbers of students, then who is Ethan with?

F. Ben
G. Derick
H. Either Francine or Ben
J. Arthur
K. Undeterminable

Questions 15 and 16 refer to the following information.

Uncover the code below. Each letter corresponds to a word in the line directly below it. A letter **may** or **may not** be directly above its corresponding word.

D	B	A	E	means...
!	$	@	%	
F	E	C	B	means...
^	#	%	@	
F	G	A	B	means...
&	^	!	@	
A	B	C		means...
!	@	#		

15. Which symbol corresponds to F?

A. ^
B. !
C. #
D. &
E. % or @

16. Which word corresponds to E?

F. %
G. ^ or &
H. @
J. !
K. #

CONTINUE ON TO THE NEXT PAGE ➡

17. If Pam goes to the concert, then her parents will yell at her. If her parents yell at her, they will not let her sleep at her friend's house. If she cannot sleep at her friend's house, then she will have to babysit her sister.
Pam decided to not go to the concert.

What must be true?

A. She will not have to babysit her sister.

B. Her parents will laud her exemplary behavior.

C. She will sleep at her friend's house.

D. Undetermined based on evidence.

E. Pam will listen to the band on her IPod.

Questions 18, 19 and 20 all relate to the following scenario:

The knights of the round table are sitting for a council. The present knights are Arthur, Gawain, Percival, Kay, Lancelot, Tristan, and Bedivere. Bedivere and Gawain are sitting across from each other, with two people sitting in-between them to one side. Kay is sitting to the right of Percival. Tristan is not sitting next to Lancelote or Kay, but is sitting next to Bedivere. There is only one knight in between Tristan and Gawain.

18. Which knight must be sitting in between the same people?

F. Gawain

G. Lancelot

H. Arthur

J. Percival

K. Berdivere

19. Who is sitting to the right of Arthur?

A. Lancelot

B. Tristan

C. Gawain or Tristan

D. Kay

E. Percival

20. Who cannot be sitting next to Percival?

F. Lancelot

G. Gawain

H. Kay

J. Bedivere

K. Arthur

CONTINUE ON TO THE NEXT PAGE ➡

Reading
Practice Test 4 (Questions 21-50)

DIRECTIONS: Analyze the passages below, and answer the commensurate questions. Only use information provided within the passage for your answers. There is only one answer for each question.

Those enactments were called agrarian laws by the Romans which related to the public lands. The objects of these agrarian laws were various. A law (*lex*) for the establishment of a colony and the assignment of tracts of land to the colonists was an agrarian law. The laws which regulated the use and enjoyment of the public lands, and gave the ownership of portions of them to the commonalty (*plebes*), were also agrarian laws. Those agrarian laws indeed which assigned small allotments to the plebeians, varying in amount from two jugera to seven jugera (a jugerum is about three-fourths of an acre), were among the most important; but the agrarian laws, or those clauses of agrarian laws which limited the amount of public land which a man could use and enjoy, are usually meant when the term agrarian laws is now used.

The origin of the Roman public land, or of the greater part of it, was this: Rome had originally a small territory, but by a series of conquests carried on for many centuries she finally obtained the dominion of the whole Italian peninsula. When the Romans conquered an Italian state, they seized a part of the lands of the conquered people; for it was a Roman principle that the conquered people lost everything with the loss of their political independence; and what they enjoyed after the conquest was a gift from the generosity of the conqueror.

A state which submitted got better terms than one which made an obstinate resistance. Sometimes a third of their land was taken from the conquered state, and sometimes two-thirds. It is not said how this arrangement was effected; whether each landholder lost a third, or whether an entire third was taken in the lump, and the conquered people were left to equalize the loss among themselves. But there were probably in all parts of Italy large tracts of uncultivated ground which were under pasture, and these tracts would form a part of the Roman share, for we find that pasture land was a considerable portion of the Roman public land. The ravages of war also often left many of the conquered tracts in a desolate condition, and these tracts formed part of the conqueror's share. The lands thus acquired could not always be carefully measured at the time of the conquest, and they were not always immediately sold or assigned to the citizens. The Roman state retained the ownership of such public lands as were not sold or given in allotments, but allowed them to be occupied and enjoyed by any Roman citizen.

CONTINUE ON TO THE NEXT PAGE ➡

21. What is this passage mostly about?

    A. Roman conquest
    B. Roman imperial tactics
    C. The origin of agrarian laws and the public laws they created
    D. How Rome got so big
    E. The fall of Rome

22. *Lex* is a Latin word for:

    F. Lawn
    G. Lord
    H. Lexicon
    J. Law
    K. Land

23. According to the passage, how did Rome acquire its public land?

    A. Laws turned private Rome into public land.
    B. Rome aquired land through conquest.
    C. Nobles gave up land to the *plebes*.
    D. Rome had public land since its inception.
    E. The *plebes* claimed land from nobles.

24. According to the passage, what was one benefit to not defending yourself against an invading Roman army?

    F. You would not lose any of your land.
    G. You would not need to have war.
    H. You would not need to give up as much land to the Roman public.
    J. You would gain seats in the Roman Senate.
    K. You would gain all the rights afforded to *plebes*.

25. What kind of land was most likely to be Roman Agrarian land?

    A. Farms
    B. Cities
    C. Roads
    D. Pasture
    E. Aqueducts

26. All land not under Roman control, but in a state conquered by Rome, was:

    F. At one point controlled by Rome.
    G. Not inhabited by Romans.
    H. Off limits to Roman *plebes*.
    J. The less valuable land in a country.
    K. Of high value.

It has been observed that the shortest man, standing on the shoulders of a giant, will see farther than the giant himself; and the moderns, standing as they do on the vantage ground of former discoveries, and uniting all the fruits of the experience of their forefathers with their own actual observation, may be admitted to enjoy a more enlarged and comprehensive view of things than the ancients themselves. But by whom is antiquity enjoyed? Not by the ancients who did live in the infancy, but by the moderns who do live in the maturity of things. Therefore, as regards the age of the world, we may lay a juster claim to the title of being the ancients, even than our forefathers themselves; for they inhabited the world when it was young, but we occupy it now that it is old.

Therefore, that precedent may not exert too despotic a rule over experience, and that the dead may not too strictly govern the living, may I be pardoned in taking a brief and cursory view of the claims of the ancients to our veneration, so far as they are built on the only proper foundation—superiority of mind? But it is by no means my object to lessen our esteem for those great men who have lived before us, and who have accomplished such wonders, considering the scantiness of their means; my intention is merely to suggest that the veneration due to times that are past is a hind-sight focused veneration, the moment it is paid at the expense of times that are present; for as these very ancients themselves were once the moderns, so we moderns must also become the ancients in our turn.

What I would principally contend for is that the moderns enjoy a much more extended and comprehensive view of science than the ancients; not because we have greater capacities, but simply because we enjoy far greater capabilities. For that which is perfect in science, is most commonly the elaborate result of successive improvements, and of various judgments exercised in the rejection of what was wrong, no less than in the adoption of what was right. We, therefore, are profiting not only by the knowledge, but also by the ignorance, not only by the discoveries, but also by the errors, of our forefathers. The march of science, like that of time, has been progressing in the darkness, no less than in the light.

27. What is this passage mostly about?

A. Why past civilizations were ignorant.

B. Why future societies will never surpass modern society.

C. Why contemporary civilization is more knowledgeable than ancient civilization.

D. The scientific beliefs of the ancients.

E. The nature of science.

CONTINUE ON TO THE NEXT PAGE ➡

28. The author uses the metaphor of a short man and a giant to illustrate that:

    F. A giant is capable of holding up a smaller man.

    G. All of the past can be considered one entity.

    H. Contemporary civilization cannot help being more advanced in science than ancient civilizations.

    J. Contemporary civilizations are higher-minded than ancient civilizations.

    K. The metaphor is used as a way to introduce an undisclosed topic.

29. Why does the author claim that contemporaries have a greater claim to being called ancient?

    A. They live in a more ancient world than the ancients.

    B. Because in the far future, they will be the ancient past.

    C. The author believes contemporary civilization will invent time travel.

    D. The phrase is used to indicate that all civilizations become ancient over time.

    E. The statement is used rhetorically, so that its absurdity can be utilized in the subsequent paragraphs.

30. What would be an example of a "hind-sight focused" opinion?

    F. Past cartographers were bad at making maps.

    G. The first high jumper to jump laterally was a better jumper than current record-holders.

    H. The inventor of an old technology was a genius.

    J. A past movie was important to the development of cinema.

    K. Nothing in the future will be as great as things are today.

31. The author notes explicitly that contemporary civilization is better at _____ than ancient civilizations.

    A. Everything

    B. Nothing

    C. Reading

    D. Language acquisition

    E. Science

CONTINUE ON TO THE NEXT PAGE ➡

32. What does the author mean by
"The march of science, like that of time,
has been progressing in the darkness, no
less than in the light?"

    F. It was not until modern times that
science made real discoveries.

    G. Past science was done poorly.

    H. Science was not always conducted
during day time.

    J. Mistakes are as valuable to the
furthering of science as discoveries.

    K. Science is an imperialist force.

CONTINUE ON TO THE NEXT PAGE ➡

Ralph Waldo Emerson

Some years ago, in company with an agreeable party, I spent a long summer day in exploring the Mammoth Cave in Kentucky. We traversed, through spacious galleries
5 affording a solid masonry foundation for the town and county overhead, the six or eight black miles from the mouth of the cavern to the innermost recess which tourists visit—a niche or grotto made of one seamless
10 stalactite, and called, I believe, Serena's Bower. I lost the light of one day. I saw high domes, and bottomless pits; heard the voice of unseen waterfalls; paddled three quarters of a mile in the deep Echo River, whose
15 waters are peopled with the blind fish; crossed the streams "Lethe" and "Styx;" plied with music and guns the echoes in these alarming galleries; saw every form of stalagmite and stalactite in the sculptured
20 and fretted chambers,—icicle, orange-flower, acanthus, grapes, and snowball. We shot Bengal lights into the vaults and groins of the sparry cathedrals, and examined all the masterpieces which the four combined
25 engineers, water, limestone, gravitation, and time, could make in the dark.

The mysteries and scenery of the cave had the same dignity that belongs to all natural objects, and which shames the fine things to
30 which we foppishly compare them. I remarked, especially, the mimetic habit, with which Nature, on new instruments, hums her old tunes, making night to mimic day, and chemistry to ape vegetation. But I then took
35 notice, and still chiefly remember, that the best thing which the cave had to offer was an illusion. On arriving at what is called the "Star-Chamber," our lamps were taken from us by the guide, and extinguished or put
40 aside, and, on looking upwards, I saw or seemed to see the night heaven thick with stars glimmering more or less brightly over our heads, and even what seemed a comet flaming among them. All the party were
45 touched with astonishment and pleasure. Our musical friends sung with much feeling a pretty song, "The stars are in the quiet sky," etc., and I sat down on the rocky floor to enjoy the serene picture. Some crystal
50 specks in the black ceiling high overhead, reflecting the light of a half-hid lamp, yielded this magnificent effect.

I own, I did not like the cave so well for eking out its sublimities with this theatrical
55 trick. But I have had many experiences like it, before and since; and we must be content to be pleased without too curiously analyzing the occasions. Our conversation with Nature is not just what it seems. The
60 cloud-rack, the sunrise and sunset glories, rainbows, and northern lights are not quite so absolute as our childhood thought them; and the part our organization plays in them is too large. The senses interfere
65 everywhere, and mix their own structure with all they report of. Once, we fancied the earth a plane, and stationary. In admiring the sunset, we do not yet deduct the rounding, coordinating, pictorial powers of the eye.

33. What is this passage mostly about?

    A. The beauty of nature.

    B. The curiosity of man.

    C. The ignorance of man concerning nature.

    D. The importance of nature to man.

    E. The way human senses interact with our understanding of nature.

CONTINUE ON TO THE NEXT PAGE →

34. What is implied about the "star-chamber?"

    F. It was the only natural phenomenon of its kind.

    G. The stars were very bright.

    H. There was a comet.

    J. There were no actual stars on display.

    K. It was his favorite view of the visit to Kentucky.

35. Why does Emerson describe water as an engineer?

    A. Water is necessary for engineering.

    B. Water is one of the forces that created the cave.

    C. Water is the only force that created the cave.

    D. Water is the most important force in the creation of the cave.

    E. He knew an engineer whose name was water.

36. Why did the party start singing under the "star-chamber?"

    F. They were tired after a long day of hiking.

    G. It is tradition to sing under the "star-chamber."

    H. They were moved by the beauty of the "star-chamber."

    J. They were always singing.

    K. They were memebers of a choir.

37. Why does Emerson note that we once believed the earth was flat?

    A. It is an example of when the senses led us to an incorrect belief.

    B. To show that humans are not capable of understanding nature.

    C. To show that nature is never understood.

    D. To show that it is best to avoid deeply considering the nature of the world.

    E. It is an example of people analyzing the world using technological instruments.

38. In what state did Emerson's adventure take place?

    F. Maine

    G. North Dakota

    H. South Dakota

    J. Kentucky

    K. Florida

CONTINUE ON TO THE NEXT PAGE ➡

There is a current impression that it is unpleasant to have to run after one's hat. Why should it be unpleasant to the well-ordered and pious mind? Not merely because it is running, and running exhausts one. The same people run much faster in games and sports. The same people run much more eagerly after an uninteresting, little leather ball than they will after a nice silk hat.

There is an idea that it is humiliating to run after one's hat; when people say it is humiliating they mean that it is comic. It certainly is comic; but man is a very comic creature, and most of the things he does are comic—eating, for instance. And the most comic things of all are exactly the things that are most worth doing. A man running after a hat is not half so ridiculous as a man running after a job.

Now a man could, if he felt rightly in the matter, run after his hat with the manliest ardor and the most sacred joy. He might regard himself as a jolly huntsman pursuing a wild animal, for certainly no animal could be wilder. In fact, I am inclined to believe that hat-hunting on windy days will be the sport of the upper classes in the future. There will be a meet of ladies and gentlemen on some high ground on a gusty morning. They will be told that the professional attendants have started a hat in such-and-such a thicket, or whatever be the technical term.

Notice that this employment will in the fullest degree combine sport with humanitarianism. The hunters would feel that they were not inflicting pain. Nay, they would feel that they were inflicting pleasure, rich, almost riotous pleasure, upon the people who were looking on. When last I saw an old gentleman running after his hat in Hyde Park, I told him that a heart so benevolent as his

ought to be filled with peace and thanks at the thought of how much unaffected pleasure his every gesture and bodily attitude were at that moment giving to the crowd.

The same principle can be applied to every other typical domestic worry. A gentleman trying to get a fly out of the milk or a piece of cork out of his glass of wine often imagines himself to be irritated. Let him think for a moment of the patience of anglers sitting by dark pools, and let his soul be immediately irradiated with gratification and repose. Again, I have known some people of very modern views driven by their distress to the use of theological terms to which they attached no doctrinal significance, merely because a drawer was jammed tight and they could not pull it out.

39. How best could this passage be described?

A. A study of the aerodynamic tendencies of hats.

B. An analysis as to why there persists a preference for traditional sports over futuristic sports.

C. A list of ways that irritancies can give amusement.

D. A satirical analysis of modern irritation.

E. A guide to Victorian-era design preferences.

CONTINUE ON TO THE NEXT PAGE ➡

40. Why does the author mention running for sport?

    F. To show that running alone is not a sufficient cause to be irritated.

    G. To assert the irritation associated with sports.

    H. To show that sports are as ridiculous as running after one's hat.

    J. To show that running after one's hat is already a sport.

    K. The comment is inconsequential.

41. Why did the author claim that the old man should be thanked?

    A. Because he was illustrating the athletic prowess of the elderly.

    B. Because he was not irritated, despite the situation.

    C. Because he was providing amusement to onlookers.

    D. Because he served in the past wars.

    E. Because one should always thank the elderly.

42. What "principle" does the author refer to in his final paragraph?

    F. Do not run after that which you cannot reach.

    G. Do not take mundane occurrences too seriously.

    H. Do not participate in sports that you do not enjoy.

    J. Do not swear.

    K. Do not take objects out of your beverages.

43. What is not explicitly mentioned as a situation that makes people unnecessarily annoyed?

    A. Having your hat fly away in the wind.

    B. Chasing after a job.

    C. Having your desk drawer jam.

    D. Not doing well in school.

    E. Dropping something in your milk.

44. What does the author imply when he mentions that one could view chasing his or her hat as a hunt?

    F. Our irritation over mundane activities is rightfully placed.

    G. People are not overly irritated while hunting.

    H. Hunting in the woods makes even mundane tasks pleasurable.

    J. Only the wealthy hunt.

    K. We should take finding one's hat more seriously.

CONTINUE ON TO THE NEXT PAGE ➡

The attorney general of the United States, although his office was created by congress as early as Sept. 24, 1789, was not made the head of a department until June 22, 1870, when the department of justice was created. By this act, the various law officers of the government, whose functions under previously existing laws were to interpret and apply the statutes governing the business of the various departments and bureaus, and to prosecute violations of United States laws in certain cases, were placed under the supervision of the attorney general. One leading reason for creating a department of justice was to bring about uniformity in the construction and application of the laws, which had not been realized under the previously existing system, with half a dozen independent law officers, responsible to no common head.

The attorney general is made the head of the department of justice, being the chief law officer of the executive branch of government. He is one of the members of the presidential cabinet, advising the president on questions of law, and, when required, renders opinions to the heads of any of the executive departments upon legal questions arising as to the administration of any one of them. He is the representative of the United States in all matters involving legal questions. He has supervision of the United States district attorneys and marshals in the United States courts of the states and territories. He sometimes appears in the supreme court of the United States to argue causes in which the government is a party, and even sometimes in a subordinate court of the United States. In all other cases, the attorney general directs what officer is to appear and argue cases in which the United States is interested, in the Supreme Court, the court of claims, or any other court, providing special counsel for the United States when in his judgment it is required.

Besides the conduct of law cases involving the interests or authority of the government, the department of justice is charged with the extensive and complicated business connected with the judicial establishment, including some appointment (or recommendation for appointment) of judges, attorneys and marshals of the circuit and district courts of the United States. He or she is also in charge of paying these various people, and adjusting the salaries competitively.

45. What is this passage mostly about?

    A. The history and roll of the attorney general.

    B. The origin of the first attorney general.

    C. The nature of law in federal government

    D. Moments where the federal government needs to be represented in court.

    E. The different jobs of an attorney general.

46. According to the passage, the attorney general is the lead legal counsel to the president and___?

    F. Appoints all judges.

    G. Has the final say in all lower court decisions.

    H. Is the head official of the department of justice.

    J. Is the lead legal counsel to the house and senate.

    K. Is in charge of representing individual states.

CONTINUE ON TO THE NEXT PAGE ➡

47. What is one reason provided in the passage for why the department of justice was created?

    A. To give the president more power.

    B. To streamline the legal system.

    C. To add a cabinet post.

    D. To enlarge government.

    E. It was mandated by the constitution.

48. What does the author imply was true prior to 1870?

    F. There was a simpler legal system.

    G. There was no attorney general.

    H. The attorney general was not a part of the federal government.

    J. The attorney general was not the ultimate legal officer.

    K. No one had considering creating a department of justice.

49. What is not listed as a duty of an Attorney General?

    A. Provide legal advice to the president.

    B. Prosecute cases at the supreme court.

    C. Manage the salaries of those working under the control of the department of justice.

    D. To represent the united states legally.

    E. To train judges.

50. Based on the passage, a successful attorney general must be outstanding at both ____?

    F. Law and management

    G. Law and politics

    H. Politics and governing

    J. School and law

    K. Management and school

CONTINUE ON TO THE NEXT PAGE ➡

MATHEMATICS
INSTRUCTIONS

75 MINUTES • 50 QUESTIONS

Select the best answer from the choices given by carefully solving each problem. Bubble the letter of your answer on the answer sheet. Please refrain from making any stray marks on the answer sheet. If you need to erase an answer, please erase thoroughly.

Important Notes:

1. There are no formulas or definitions in the math section that will be provided.
2. Diagrams may or may not be drawn to scale. Do not make assumptions based on the diagram unless it is specifically stated in the diagram or question.
3. Diagrams are not in more than one plane, unless stated otherwise.
4. Graphs are drawn to scale, therefore, you can assume relationships according to the graph. If lines appear parallel, then you can assume the lines to be parallel. This is also true for right angles and so forth.
5. Simplify fractions completely.

Practice Test 4 (Questions 51-100)

51. What is the value of, $\sqrt{25} + \sqrt{64}$?

   A. 10
   B. 13
   C. 14
   D. 89
   E. 100

52. What is the value of r in the equation:
$2r = 10^2$

   F. 5
   G. 10
   H. 25
   J. 50
   K. 100

CONTINUE ON TO THE NEXT PAGE ➡

53. What is the area of a square with a perimeter of 16?

    A. 4

    B. 8

    C. 12

    D. 16

    E. 24

54. What is 10% of a number whose square is 81?

    F. 0.81

    G. 0.9

    H. 8.1

    J. 9

    K. 10

55. What is the range of the set $\{1, 2, 5, 10, 6, 12\}$?

    A. -16

    B. -11

    C. 3

    D. 11

    E. 22

56. Nancy found a formula for the area of a square in terms of its perimeter. Let A stand for the area and P for perimeter. What is the formula Nancy found?

    F. P^2

    G. $\dfrac{P^2}{8}$

    H. $\dfrac{P^2}{4}$

    J. $\dfrac{P^2}{16}$

    K. $4P$

57. Anayet is driving to work from home and realizes he left his wallet at home when he is at his workplace. He turns back to retrieve his wallet. His workplace and home are 45 miles apart and it takes him twice as long to get to workplace from his home than the other way around. It is a 30 minute drive from his workplace to home. What is the average speed for the round trip in miles per minute?

    A. 0.75

    B. 1.5

    C. 1

    D. 2

    E. 0.5

CONTINUE ON TO THE NEXT PAGE ➡

58. Given that, $\overleftrightarrow{a} = a^2 + a$, what is $\overleftrightarrow{a} \div a$?

   F. a

   G. $a + 2$

   H. 1

   J. $a + 1$

   K. $2a$

59. Sarah has a trick coin that has heads on both sides. She asks her friend John, who believes the coin is fair, to guess what face it will land on. If they flip the coin 100 times, how many times bigger is Sarah's expected probability of the coin landing on heads than John's expected probability of the coin landing on heads?

   A. 0.25

   B. 0.5

   C. 1

   D. 2

   E. 4

60. What is the square of a number that when added to any number does not change that number's value?

   F. 0

   G. 0.5

   H. 1

   J. 4

   K. undefined

61. How many nonzero numbers are between 3 and 5?

   A. 0

   B. 2

   C. 8

   D. 9

   E. ∞

62. The circle that is inscribed in the square below has a radius of 2. What is the length of the diagonal of the square?

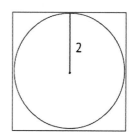

   F. 2

   G. 4

   H. 16

   J. $4\sqrt{2}$

   K. $2\sqrt{2}$

CONTINUE ON TO THE NEXT PAGE ➡

63. What is the absolute value of the difference between the number of integers between 0 and 5 inclusive and the number of integers between 1 and 6 exclusive?

A. 0

B. 1

C. 2

D. 3

E. 5

64. Corey is walking on a path. Every three steps he takes, he makes a 30 degree rotation to counterclockwise. If he took 18 steps in total, how many full revolutions was he able to make all together?

F. 0.25

G. 0.5

H. 1

J. 2

K. 5

65. What is 20% of 20% of 20?

A. 0.2

B. 0.8

C. 2

D. 8

E. 8000

66. What is the difference between the largest and lowest integer in the sequence of consecutive odd integers whose sum is 15?

F. 2

G. 4

H. 5

J. 9

K. 12

CONTINUE ON TO THE NEXT PAGE ➡

ARGO BROTHERS

67. The half life of a substance is the time it takes for a substance to decrease to half its initial amount. John has a pile of goo that decreases in amount at a constant rate. If John initially had 100 pounds of goo, and ten days later, he only had 25 pounds of goo, what is the half life of the goo?

A. 10 days
B. 5 days
C. 7.5 days
D. 20 days
E. 25 days

68. What is the value of $\dfrac{9^4 - 8^4}{9^2 + 8^2}$?

F. 1
G. 16
H. 17
J. 18
K. 155

69. Jackie fills a jug with water continuously. It takes her 2 minutes to fill up 50% of the empty space in the jug with water. After every 2 minutes, she puts a penny into a jar to celebrate. How many pennies will she have in the jar at the instant the jug has less than 30% empty space left?

A. 0
B. 1
C. 2
D. 3
E. 4

70.

In the figure above, there are two balance beams that have triangles, circles and squares on them. Both beams are fully balanced. How many circles are needed to balance 70 squares?

F. 10
G. 12
H. 35
J. 70
K. 140

71. $.\overline{7} + \dfrac{2}{9} = .\overline{6} + \underline{\quad}$

A. $\dfrac{1}{2}$
B. $\dfrac{1}{3}$
C. $\dfrac{2}{9}$
D. $\dfrac{4}{9}$
E. 1

CONTINUE ON TO THE NEXT PAGE ➡

72. The distinct prime factors of 232 are

   F. $2, 2, 2, 29$

   G. $116, 2$

   H. $2, 29$

   J. $2, 2, 58$

   K. $2, 58$

73. If the pattern continues, what will be the 438th symbol?

□ ↻ ← ↑ → ↖ □ ↻ ← ↑ → ↖ □ ↻

   A. □

   B. ↑

   C. ↖

   D. ↻

   E. →

74. Find the value of t. $\dfrac{t}{32} = \dfrac{x}{p}$

   F. $\dfrac{32p}{x}$

   G. $\dfrac{xp}{32}$

   H. $\dfrac{32}{px}$

   J. $\dfrac{32x}{p}$

   K. $32px$

75. What is the least integer greater than $\dfrac{52}{3}$?

   A. 16

   B. 17

   C. 18

   D. 19

   E. 20

76. If $5^5 + 5^5 + 5^5 + 5^5 + 5^5 = 5^{a+1}$, what is a?

   F. 3

   G. 4

   H. 5

   J. 6

   K. 7

CONTINUE ON TO THE NEXT PAGE ➡

77. If $(x + y)^2 = x^2 + y^2$ then what condition must be true?

    A. $x = y = 0$

    B. $x + y = 0$

    C. $2x = 0$

    D. $2y = 0$

    E. $xy = 0$

78. What is the maximum number points that two distinct circles can intersect at?

    F.   1

    G.   2

    H.   3

    J.   4

    K. ∞

79. A cumulative product of a set $\{a, b, c,...\}$ is the sequence, $a, ab, abc,...$ What is the mean of the terms in the cumulative product of $\{1, 2, 3, 0\}$?

    A.   0

    B.   2

    C.   2.25

    D.   3.5

    E.   6

80. How many integers are in the set of nonpositive, nonnegative integers?

    F.   0

    G.   1

    H.   2

    J.   3

    K. ∞

81. How many chords are in the circle below?

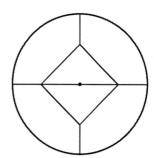

    A.   0

    B.   1

    C.   2

    D.   3

    E.   7

CONTINUE ON TO THE NEXT PAGE ➡

82. In the figure below, there is a function plotted and there are 5 points labeled *A* through *E* drawn. For how many points is *y*(*x*) equal to 0?

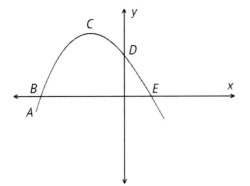

F. 0

G. 1

H. 2

J. 3

K. ∞

83. At what time on a clock will the hands form an acute angle formed of 60°?

A. 1:00 PM

B. 1:15 PM

C. 2:00 PM

D. 2:30 PM

E. 3:00 PM

84. A jar contains only red and blue marbles. The probability of picking a red marble is 20%. One blue marble is added to the jar. What is the probability of picking a blue marble?

F. $\dfrac{1}{3}$

G. $\dfrac{1}{2}$

H. $\dfrac{4}{5}$

J. $\dfrac{1}{6}$

K. Cannot be determined from the information given.

85. If *a* = 35, what is, (-6)(-6)(-6) + 6(-6) in terms of *a*?

A. $a + 1$

B. a^2

C. $a^2 + 1$

D. $a^2 + a$

E. $35a$

CONTINUE ON TO THE NEXT PAGE ➡

86. A circle and an octagon share the same perimeter (circumference for the circle). If the side length of the octagon is, a, and the radius of the circle is, r, then what is the radius in terms of the side length of the octagon?

F. $4a$

G. $\dfrac{a}{\pi}$

H. $\dfrac{4}{\pi}$

J. $\dfrac{4a}{\pi}$

K. 4π

87. What is the least integer greater than the greatest integer less than 1.5?

A. 2

B. 1.5

C. 0.5

D. 1

E. 0

88. What is the area of a semicircle in terms of tau (τ) with a radius of r. Tau is double the value of π.

F. $\tau^2 r$

G. τr^2

H. $\dfrac{\tau r^2}{4}$

J. $\dfrac{\tau r}{2}$

K. $\dfrac{\tau r^2}{2}$

89. If $F = -kx$ and greater than 0, then what happens to the value of k if F triples in value and x remains constant

A. Increases

B. Doubles

C. Decreases

D. Remains Constant

E. Cannot be determined from the information given.

CONTINUE ON TO THE NEXT PAGE ➡

90. If the length of the side of a square is, 7^a, what is the area?

F. 7^a

G. $2 \cdot 7^a$

H. 49^a

J. 7^{2a}

K. $7a^a$

91. What is the circumference of the dotted section of the circle whose center is O below?

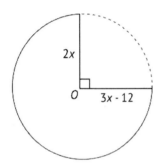

2x

O 3x - 12

A. 6π

B. 12π

C. 24π

D. 48π

E. 64π

92. Given that $0 < x < 1$, and set $A = \{x, x^2, x^3, x^4\}$, what is the smallest value in set A?

F. x

G. x^2

H. x^3

J. x^4

K. Cannot be determined from the information given.

93. Sammy has a faulty clock. Every 15 degrees that one of the hands moves, 5 minutes passes. If a hand is initially 5:35 PM, in how long will the hand be at that same position?

A. 65 minutes

B. 2 hours

C. 1 hour

D. 45 minutes

E. 1 hour and 15 minutes

94. If $(x - 2)(x + 2) = ax^2 + bx + c$, what is the sum of a, b and c?

    F.   -4

    G.   -3

    H.   0

    J.   1

    K.   5

95. Natalie walks in a special way. After every 2 steps she takes, she takes 1 step in the opposite direction. She starts at point A and walks forward. When she is 7 steps away from point A, she has reached her destination, point B. How many steps in total did she take to get from point A to B?

    A.   7

    B.   8

    C.   17

    D.   15

    E.   18

96. If, $C_{m,n} = C(m + n)$, for what value of n is $C_{m,n}$ neither positive nor negative?

    F. $-C$

    G. $-m$

    H. $2m$

    J.   0

    K. $\dfrac{1}{m}$

97. Two sides of a triangle at 6 and 8. What is the length of the third side?

    A.   2

    B.   4

    C.   5

    D.   10

    E.   Cannot be uniquely determined

98. $2 + \dfrac{1}{3} = \dfrac{14}{b}$, What is b?

    F.   3

    G.   6

    H.   7

    J.   9

    K.   28

CONTINUE ON TO THE NEXT PAGE ➡

99. In the formula $V = r^2h$, if h is doubled and r triples, then V is multiplied by?

A. 6

B. 9

C. 12

D. 18

E. 36

THIS IS THE END OF THE TEST. IF THERE IS TIME REMAINING, YOU MAY CHECK YOUR ANSWERS TO PART 1 OR PART 2.

100. Max A returns the largest value in the set A.
Min A returns the lowest value in the set A.
For example, $\max\{1, 2, 3\} = 3$ and
$\min\{0, 4, 5\} = 0$.
What is $\max\{\min\{x, 2x, 3x\}, \max\{\frac{x}{2}, \frac{x}{4}, \frac{x}{8}\}\}$?

F. x

G. $2x$

H. $\frac{x}{2}$

J. $3x$

K. Cannot be uniquely determined.

PART 1 (VERBAL)

Scrambled Paragraphs

1. Q, R, S, T, U
2. S, R, U, T, Q
3. R, Q, S, U, T
4. R, Q, T, S, U
5. R, T, U, S, Q

Logical Reasoning

11. **D**
12. **K**
13. **A**
14. **F**
15. **A**
16. **F**
17. **D**
18. **H**
19. **C**
20. **K**

Reading

21. **C**	44. **G**
22. **J**	45. **A**
23. **B**	46. **H**
24. **H**	47. **A**
25. **D**	48. **J**
26. **F**	49. **E**
27. **C**	50. **F**
28. **H**	
29. **A**	
30. **G**	
31. **E**	
32. **J**	
33. **E**	
34. **J**	
35. **B**	
36. **H**	
37. **A**	
38. **J**	
39. **D**	
40. **F**	
41. **C**	
42. **G**	
43. **D**	

PART 2 (MATHEMATICS)

Math

51. **B**	63. **A**	75. **C**	87. **A**	99. **D**
52. **J**	64. **G**	76. **H**	88. **H**	100. **K**
53. **D**	65. **B**	77. **E**	89. **E**	
54. **G**	66. **G**	78. **G**	90. **J**	
55. **D**	67. **B**	79. **C**	91. **A**	
56. **J**	68. **H**	80. **G**	92. **J**	
57. **C**	69. **B**	81. **B**	93. **B**	
58. **J**	70. **J**	82. **H**	94. **G**	
59. **D**	71. **B**	83. **C**	95. **C**	
60. **F**	72. **F**	84. **K**	96. **G**	
61. **E**	73. **C**	85. **D**	97. **E**	
62. **J**	74. **J**	86. **J**	98. **G**	

To calculate your score visit our web site
and download excel calculator:
www. einstein-academy.com/calc

Practice Test 4 (Answers and Explanations)

SCRAMBLED PARAGRAPHS

1. **Q, R, S, T, U**

   Q: Q provides the source from which artists and art historians noted in the introductory sentence, pull their material.

   R: "This text" refers to the "Republic" noted in sentence Q.

   S: "This reasoning" refers to the argument noted in sentence R.

   T: "Similarly" indicates that the sentence will bring an alternative, but similar, case to that discussed the sentence prior. Sentence S posits the first claim.

   U: "This thesis" refers to the "End of Art" thesis noted in sentence T.

2. **S, R, U, T, Q**

   S: "Earlier times" is the first chronological cue. This follows from the introductory sentence which indicates that there will be a historical trajectory in the sentences.

   R: R provides an example of the types of utility noted in sentence S.

   U: U provides an example of the content introduced in sentence S; however, "other" indicates that it will occur after a first example. Thus, it must come after R.

   T: "These services" refers to the services noted in sentences R and U.

   Q: Q provides the argument concerning "psychic" benefit introduced in sentence T.

3. **R, Q, S, U, T**

   R: "This learning tool" refers to the sentence noted in the introductory sentence.

   Q: Q provides the reason why sentence R stated the sentence to be "under assault."

   S: S provides the reason why Pluto would be taken off the list, as discussed in sentence Q.

   U: U references the criteria noted in sentence S.

   T: "This" refers to the anecdote discussed over the previous sentences.

4. **R, Q, T, S, U**

R: "These changes" refers to the changes noted in the introductory sentence.

Q: Q gives an "instance" of a rule as discussed in sentence R.

T: The explicit rule change is a reference to sentence Q.

S: S provides an example of the topic introduced in sentence T.

U: U discusses a "consequence" of a topic discussed in S.

5. **R, T, U, S, Q**

R: "Many kinds" refers to the forms of dumplings discussed in the introductory sentence.

T: "These alternative styles" refers to the kinds listed in sentence R.

U: The "generality" is the general principle noted in sentence T.

S: Q must follow S, as it refers to the topic introduced in S. Thus, S must come fourth.

Q: Brings together all of the previous sentences when it notes both dumplings and the fertility goddess introduced in sentence S.

LOGICAL REASONING

11. D The logical statements should read:

$$[S \rightarrow \emptyset; D \rightarrow \cancel{S}] [D \rightarrow >8; < 8 \rightarrow \emptyset]$$

Going to the store does not lead to any statement concerning time, thus A is incorrect.

Not going to the store does not lead to subsequent truths, thus b is incorrect. C is irrelevant.

If Jared gets home at 7, then he is home before 8. If he is home before 8, then he must have not gone out for dinner. Thus D is correct.

The only time related rule that leads to a further truth concerns Jared getting home before 8. 9 is after 8, and thus does not lead to subsequent truths.

12. K Thomas is on the Indoor track team, but is not necessarily on the cross country team. Thus, F is incorrect.

There is no indication of whether or not Thomas is on the cross country team. Thus, G is incorrect

All cross country team members are on the indoor track team, thus Thomas is on a team with all members of the cross country team, not only some. Thus, H is incorrect.

J is irrelevant.

All cross country team members are on the indoor track team, thus Thomas is on a team with all members of the cross country team. Thus, K is correct.

13. A B/D can only fit in slots 3 or 4. Since C is in slot 2, A must be in slot 1. Thus, A is correct.

14. F This is a pairing game. The teachers are superfluous information, as one need only find the pairs of students. C cannot be with E, B, A, or D. Thus, C must be with F. This leaves Ethan and Ben as the final group.

15. A B is the only letter occurring in all row groups. Thus, it must be paired with @. A is the only letter occurring in three groups, thus must be paired with !. C is the only letter left in the last row, thus C must be #. E occurs in rows 1 and 2. % is the only sign left in rows 1 and 2, thus must be paired with E. D and $ are alone in row 1, and must thus be paired. F is the only letter left in row two, and ^ is the only symbol left in row 2. Thus, F and ^ must be paired. Finally, G and & are the last available letters/symbols, thus must be paired. The final grouping should look like:

B = @
A = !
E = %
D = $
F = ^
G = &

F is paired with ^, thus the answer is A.

16. F E is paired with %, thus the answer is F.

17. D These logical statements create a logical chain:

$$[C \rightarrow Y \rightarrow \cancel{F} \rightarrow B; \cancel{B} \rightarrow F \rightarrow \cancel{Y} \rightarrow \cancel{C}]$$

Not going to the concert is at the end of a causal chain, thus it does not necessarily lead to any further truths. Thus, D is the answer.

ARGO BROTHERS

18. H There are four possible boards, based on the given rules:

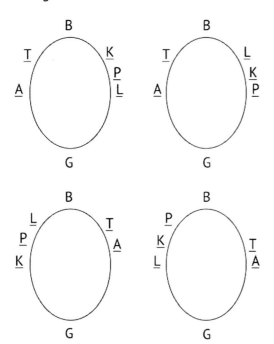

When there can be multiple possibilities, draw them all out. Arthur is in between Tristan and Gawain on all four boards.

19. C Arthur is to the left of Tristan or Gawain in all four games.

20. K Kay, Lancelot, Gawain, and Bedivere all sit next to Percival, depending on the game. Arthur will never sit next to Percival.

READING COMPREHENSION

21. C This answer choice occurs in all paragraphs.

22. J This answer derives from line 4.

23. B This answer derives from line 24.

24. H This answer derives from lines 33-36.

25. D This answer derives from lines 47.

26. F It is stated that, according to Roman tradition, all conquered lands were entirely ruled by Rome, and only then gifted back to the original owners. Thus, F is true.

27. C This answer choice relates more closely to the largest amount of paragraphs.

28. H This answer choice relates more closely to the largest amount of paragraphs.

29. A To the ancients, their world was modern. Yet we have lived in the shadow of their world for millennia, making our world far more ancient than theirs. According to this logic, the far future will be more ancient (B); however, the author is making claims as to contemporary society and not future societies.

30. G Based on the passage, "high-sight focused" opinions require one to think a past achievement is greater than a current achievement, even though based on similar metrics it is inferior. Current record-holders have higher records than the initial jumper.

31. E This is the focus of the final paragraph.

32. J This follows from the line: "We, therefore, are profiting not only by the knowledge, but also by the ignorance..."

33. E Answer choice A occurs in two paragraphs, but E occurs in all three.

34. J It was an illusion, thus there were no actual stars.

35. B Water, along with the other noted "engineers," create caves.

36. H The passage notes that the part was touched with "astonishment and pleasure." It was this feeling that led to the singing.

37. A This example is presented within a discussion of how the senses mislead in relationship to our understanding of nature.

38. J This answer derives from line 3.

39. D The "hat" is an analogy to all mundane irritants that people take overly seriously in modern society.

40. F As noted in the passage, the issue people have with running after their hat is "not merely because it is running, and running exhausts one."

41. C This answer derives from lines 41-45.

42. G The author is discussing the principle noted throughout the passage. G is the best representation of this principle.

43. D All other answer choices can be explicitly found within the passage.

44. G Running after hats irritates people. He offers this frame as a way for chasing hats to no longer irritate. Thus, we can infer that people are not overly irritated when hunting.

45. A This answer occurs in all three paragraphs. E occurs in one paragraph. B occurs in one paragraph.

46. H This answer derives from line 20. J may seem appropriate, but it only states that he is the lead counsel to the executive government, which does not include the house and senate.

47. A This answer derives from lines 14-20.

48. J Prior to 1870, the attorney general was not in charge of a department. This answer has some extreme language, as it includes "ultimate" making it even more of a clear answer.

49. E According to the passage, the attorney general has the power to appoint judges. However, it does not state that he trains judges. All other answer choices can be found explicitly stated within the passage.

50. F The attorney general is not only in charge of many legal duties, but also must run an agency. As such, he must both be an expert at law and management.

Practice Test 4 (Answers and Explanations)

51. B $\sqrt{25} + \sqrt{64} = 5 + 8 = 13$

52. J Simplifying this equation gives

$2r = 100$
$r = 50$
The answer is J.

53. D A square with a perimeter of 16 has a side length of a fourth of the perimeter. So the side length is 4. To find the area of that square, we must square the side length, giving us 16 again.
The answer is D.

54. G A number whose square is 81 is 9. 10% of 9 is 0.9 or answer G.

55. D The range is just the difference between the largest and smallest number. This is just 12 - 1 or 11.
The answer is D.

56. J If P is the perimeter, and A is the area, we must find A in terms of P. We must divide P by 4 to get the side length of the square. Then we must square that value. This gives us $\frac{P^2}{16}$ or answer J.

57. C It takes Anayet 30 minutes to travel from his workplace to home. So it takes him 60 minutes to travel from his home to his workplace. In total, he spends 90 minutes traveling, and since the distance between his home to his workplace is 45 miles, the total distance for the round trip is 90 miles.
His average speed is 1mi/min.
The answer is C.

58. J Dividing by a gives us answer choice J.
$\frac{(a^2 + a)}{a} = a + 1$

59. D Sarah knows that the coin is a trick coin with only heads on both sides. So her expected probability of the coin landing on heads is 1. John's expected probability is 0.5. 1 is two times bigger than 0.5
The answer is D.

60. F 0 is the number that when added to any number, doesn't change that number's value. Squaring 0 gives 0 still.
The answer is F.

61. E Be careful. The question asks for how many nonzero numbers are between 3 and 5. There are an infinite number of numbers between those two integers.
The answer is E.

62. J We know that the diameter of the circle must be 4. So, the side length of the square is also 4. We can use the Pythagorean Theorem to find the length of the diagonal of the square. This gives us $4\sqrt{2}$ or answer J.

63. A There are 6 integers between 0 and 5 inclusive and 6 integers between 1 and 6 inclusive. The absolute value of the difference between 6 and 6 is simply, 0. The answer is A.

64. G If every three steps he takes, he rotates 30°, then if he took 18 steps, he rotated 30° 6 times. 6 times 30° is 180 degrees, which is a half of a full revolution. The answer is G.

65. B We must find 20% of 20 first. That is 4. Then we must take 20% of 4, which is 0.8. The answer is B.

66. G The sequence, 3, 5, 7 adds up to 15. The difference between 7 and 3 is 4. The answer is G.

67. B In 10 days, the goo decreased by 2 half lives. So each half life is 5 days. The answer is B.

68. H Here, we must realize that the numerator is a difference of perfect squares. That allows us to write,

$$\frac{(9^2-8^2)(9^2+8^2)}{9^2+8^2} = 9^2-8^2 = 81-64 = 17$$

The answer is H.

69. B Jackie puts a penny away every 2 minutes. Right after the first 2 minutes, 50% of the jug is filled. She puts 1 penny in the jar at that moment. Then she starts to fill 50% of the empty space left. Well, there is 50% of empty space left, so she starts to reach the filling of 75% of the jug. But before she fills 75% of the jug, the jug already has less than 30% of empty space left. So, she is just left with 1 penny at that instant.
The answer is B.

70. J We see that for every 4 triangles, we need 2 circles to balance it. In other words, we need 2 triangles for every circle. We also need 1 square for every 2 triangles. Therefore, there is a one to one ratio between the number of circles and squares. So we need 70 circles to balance 70 squares. The answer is J.

71. B $(\frac{2}{9})$ is the same as $.\overline{2}$. Solving for the missing number gives us $.\overline{3} = \frac{1}{3}$
The answer is B.

72. F Factoring 232, gives us $2^3 \cdot 29$.
The answer is F.

73. C We can take note of the sequence that each symbol takes. The 6th symbol is also the 12th symbol and the 18th symbol and so on. The 438th symbol will be divisible by 6 as well. This means that the 6th symbol is also the 432nd symbol and therefore the 438th symbol as well.
The answer is C.

74. J Cross multiplying gives,
$32x = pt$ and solving for t gives,

$$t = \frac{32x}{p}$$

The answer is J.

75. C $(\frac{52}{3})$ equates to $17.\overline{3}$ and the least integer greater than that is 18. The answer is C.

76. H $5^5 + 5^5 + 5^5 + 5^5 + 5^5 = 5(5^5) = 5^{a+1}$
so then:
$a + 1 = 6$ and $a = 5$.
The answer is H.

77. E We know that,
$(x + y) = x + 2xy + y$ and if this is to equal $x + y$, then $2xy$ must be equal to 0. In other words, $xy = 0$.
The answer is E.

78. G Two circles can intersect at 2 points at maximum.

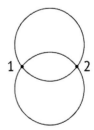

MATHEMATICS
ANSWERS & EXPLANATIONS

ARGO BROTHERS

79. C The cumulative product of the set $\{1, 2, 3, 0\}$ is the sequence, $1, 2, 6, 0$. The mean of this sequence is the sum of the terms divided by the number of terms in the sequence. This equates to $(\frac{9}{2})$ or 2.25. The answer is C.

80. G The only nonpositive, nonnegative integer is 0. So the answer is 1. The answer is G.

81. B A chord must touch the circle at two points. The only segment that does this is the diameter. The answer is B

82. H $y(x)= 0$ at only 2 points, B and E, which are at the roots of the function. The answer is H.

83. C Using the fact that there is 30° between every two consecutive ticks on the clock, we can see that at 2:00, 60 ° is formed between the hands. The answer is C.

84. K The answer to this question depends on the number of marbles in the bag. The answer is K.

85. D The expression can be rewritten as, $(36)(36)-36 = 36(36 - 1) = 36(35)$ and since $a = 35$, then we have, $(a + 1)(a) = a^2 + a$. The answer is D.

86. J Equating the two perimeters for the octagon and circle respectively gives, $8a = 2\pi r$ and solving for r gives, $r = \dfrac{4a}{\pi}$ The answer is J.

87. A The greatest integer less than 1.5 is 1 and the least integer greater than 1 is 2. The answer is A.

88. H We know that, $\tau = 2\pi$ and the area of the semicircle is, $\dfrac{\pi r^2}{2}$ Solving for π and plugging in the area gives, $\dfrac{\tau r^2}{2}$ The answer is H.

89. E If $F = -kx$, then either k or x must be negative since F is greater than 0. We do not know which is negative, so we cannot determine a definite answer. The answer is E.

90. J   We must square the side length to get the area.
$(7^n)^2 = 7^{2n}$
The answer is J.

91. A   Equating the two radii gives and solving for x gives, $x = 12$.
The dotted section represents a fourth of the whole circumference which is $2\pi(12) = 24\pi$.
The answer is 6π or answer choice A.

92. J   The value of x must be a positive fraction, so the smallest value in the set would be the one that takes x to the highest power. The answer is J.

93. B   There are 360° that the hands must move to complete a full revolution and to be at the same time of 5:35. If every 15°, 5 minutes passes, then $(24 \cdot 5)$ minutes will have passed by the time it is 5:35 again. This is 2 hours.
The answer is B.

94. G   This equation simplifies to,
$x^2 - 4 = ax^2 + bx - c$ and,
$a = 1$
$b = 0$
$c = -4$
so the sum of a, b and c is -3.
The answer is G.

95. C   This question requires to count the steps. It is only after 17 steps does Natalie reach the 7 step distance from point A.
The answer is C.

96. G   We must pick a value of n that makes the expression 0, since 0 is neither positive nor negative. This occurs when n is the negative of m. The answer is G.

$C(m + - m) = 0$

97. E   The third side cannot be uniquely determined since we do not know if these two sides are legs of the hypotenuse or if one of the sides is a hypotenuse. The answer is E.

98. G $2 + (\frac{1}{3}) = (\frac{7}{3})$ and multiplying the numerator and denominator of $(\frac{7}{3})$ by 2 gives $(\frac{14}{6})$. Equating this with $(\frac{14}{b})$ gives that $b = 6$. The answer is G.

99. D   If h doubles, then V gets multiplied by a factor of 2. If r triples, then V gets multiplied by a factor of 9 since we are squaring r. We multiply 2 and 9 to get 18. The answer is D.

100. K   The answer cannot be uniquely determined since we do not know if x is negative or positive.

TIME TO FINISH TEST:
VERBAL: 75 minutes
MATH: 75 minutes

— This exam is 2 hours and 30 minutes long. Try to take this full exam in one sitting to simulate real test conditions.

— While taking this exam, refrain from hearing music or watching T.V.

— Please note, calculators are not permitted! You are permitted to answer questions in any order you see fit.

— Not all answers need take the same amount of time. Allocate your test time accordingly.

— Concentrate and GOOD LUCK!

To calculate your score visit our web site and download excel calculator:
www. einstein-academy.com/calc

SHSAT PRACTICE TEST 5
ANSWER SHEET

PART 1 (VERBAL)

SCRAMBLED PARAGRAPHS

Paragraph 1

The first sentence is   Ⓠ Ⓡ Ⓢ Ⓣ Ⓤ
The second sentence is Ⓠ Ⓡ Ⓢ Ⓣ Ⓤ
The third sentence is   Ⓠ Ⓡ Ⓢ Ⓣ Ⓤ
The fourth sentence is Ⓠ Ⓡ Ⓢ Ⓣ Ⓤ
The fifth sentence is   Ⓠ Ⓡ Ⓢ Ⓣ Ⓤ

Paragraph 2

The first sentence is   Ⓠ Ⓡ Ⓢ Ⓣ Ⓤ
The second sentence is Ⓠ Ⓡ Ⓢ Ⓣ Ⓤ
The third sentence is   Ⓠ Ⓡ Ⓢ Ⓣ Ⓤ
The fourth sentence is Ⓠ Ⓡ Ⓢ Ⓣ Ⓤ
The fifth sentence is   Ⓠ Ⓡ Ⓢ Ⓣ Ⓤ

Paragraph 3

The first sentence is   Ⓠ Ⓡ Ⓢ Ⓣ Ⓤ
The second sentence is Ⓠ Ⓡ Ⓢ Ⓣ Ⓤ
The third sentence is   Ⓠ Ⓡ Ⓢ Ⓣ Ⓤ
The fourth sentence is Ⓠ Ⓡ Ⓢ Ⓣ Ⓤ
The fifth sentence is   Ⓠ Ⓡ Ⓢ Ⓣ Ⓤ

Paragraph 4

The first sentence is   Ⓠ Ⓡ Ⓢ Ⓣ Ⓤ
The second sentence is Ⓠ Ⓡ Ⓢ Ⓣ Ⓤ
The third sentence is   Ⓠ Ⓡ Ⓢ Ⓣ Ⓤ
The fourth sentence is Ⓠ Ⓡ Ⓢ Ⓣ Ⓤ
The fifth sentence is   Ⓠ Ⓡ Ⓢ Ⓣ Ⓤ

Paragraph 5

The first sentence is   Ⓠ Ⓡ Ⓢ Ⓣ Ⓤ
The second sentence is Ⓠ Ⓡ Ⓢ Ⓣ Ⓤ
The third sentence is   Ⓠ Ⓡ Ⓢ Ⓣ Ⓤ
The fourth sentence is Ⓠ Ⓡ Ⓢ Ⓣ Ⓤ
The fifth sentence is   Ⓠ Ⓡ Ⓢ Ⓣ Ⓤ

LOGICAL REASONING

11 Ⓐ Ⓑ Ⓒ Ⓓ Ⓔ
12 Ⓕ Ⓖ Ⓗ Ⓙ Ⓚ
13 Ⓐ Ⓑ Ⓒ Ⓓ Ⓔ
14 Ⓕ Ⓖ Ⓗ Ⓙ Ⓚ
15 Ⓐ Ⓑ Ⓒ Ⓓ Ⓔ

16 Ⓕ Ⓖ Ⓗ Ⓙ Ⓚ
17 Ⓐ Ⓑ Ⓒ Ⓓ Ⓔ
18 Ⓕ Ⓖ Ⓗ Ⓙ Ⓚ
19 Ⓐ Ⓑ Ⓒ Ⓓ Ⓔ
20 Ⓕ Ⓖ Ⓗ Ⓙ Ⓚ

READING

21 Ⓐ Ⓑ Ⓒ Ⓓ Ⓔ
22 Ⓕ Ⓖ Ⓗ Ⓙ Ⓚ
23 Ⓐ Ⓑ Ⓒ Ⓓ Ⓔ
24 Ⓕ Ⓖ Ⓗ Ⓙ Ⓚ
25 Ⓐ Ⓑ Ⓒ Ⓓ Ⓔ
26 Ⓕ Ⓖ Ⓗ Ⓙ Ⓚ

27 Ⓐ Ⓑ Ⓒ Ⓓ Ⓔ
28 Ⓕ Ⓖ Ⓗ Ⓙ Ⓚ
29 Ⓐ Ⓑ Ⓒ Ⓓ Ⓔ
30 Ⓕ Ⓖ Ⓗ Ⓙ Ⓚ
31 Ⓐ Ⓑ Ⓒ Ⓓ Ⓔ
32 Ⓕ Ⓖ Ⓗ Ⓙ Ⓚ

33 Ⓐ Ⓑ Ⓒ Ⓓ Ⓔ
34 Ⓕ Ⓖ Ⓗ Ⓙ Ⓚ
35 Ⓐ Ⓑ Ⓒ Ⓓ Ⓔ
36 Ⓕ Ⓖ Ⓗ Ⓙ Ⓚ
37 Ⓐ Ⓑ Ⓒ Ⓓ Ⓔ
38 Ⓕ Ⓖ Ⓗ Ⓙ Ⓚ

39 Ⓐ Ⓑ Ⓒ Ⓓ Ⓔ
40 Ⓕ Ⓖ Ⓗ Ⓙ Ⓚ
41 Ⓐ Ⓑ Ⓒ Ⓓ Ⓔ
42 Ⓕ Ⓖ Ⓗ Ⓙ Ⓚ
43 Ⓐ Ⓑ Ⓒ Ⓓ Ⓔ
44 Ⓕ Ⓖ Ⓗ Ⓙ Ⓚ

45 Ⓐ Ⓑ Ⓒ Ⓓ Ⓔ
46 Ⓕ Ⓖ Ⓗ Ⓙ Ⓚ
47 Ⓐ Ⓑ Ⓒ Ⓓ Ⓔ
48 Ⓕ Ⓖ Ⓗ Ⓙ Ⓚ
49 Ⓐ Ⓑ Ⓒ Ⓓ Ⓔ
50 Ⓕ Ⓖ Ⓗ Ⓙ Ⓚ

PART 2 (MATHEMATICS)

MATHEMATICS PROBLEMS

51 Ⓐ Ⓑ Ⓒ Ⓓ Ⓔ
52 Ⓕ Ⓖ Ⓗ Ⓙ Ⓚ
53 Ⓐ Ⓑ Ⓒ Ⓓ Ⓔ
54 Ⓕ Ⓖ Ⓗ Ⓙ Ⓚ
55 Ⓐ Ⓑ Ⓒ Ⓓ Ⓔ

56 Ⓕ Ⓖ Ⓗ Ⓙ Ⓚ
57 Ⓐ Ⓑ Ⓒ Ⓓ Ⓔ
58 Ⓕ Ⓖ Ⓗ Ⓙ Ⓚ
59 Ⓐ Ⓑ Ⓒ Ⓓ Ⓔ
60 Ⓕ Ⓖ Ⓗ Ⓙ Ⓚ

61 Ⓐ Ⓑ Ⓒ Ⓓ Ⓔ
62 Ⓕ Ⓖ Ⓗ Ⓙ Ⓚ
63 Ⓐ Ⓑ Ⓒ Ⓓ Ⓔ
64 Ⓕ Ⓖ Ⓗ Ⓙ Ⓚ
65 Ⓐ Ⓑ Ⓒ Ⓓ Ⓔ

66 Ⓕ Ⓖ Ⓗ Ⓙ Ⓚ
67 Ⓐ Ⓑ Ⓒ Ⓓ Ⓔ
68 Ⓕ Ⓖ Ⓗ Ⓙ Ⓚ
69 Ⓐ Ⓑ Ⓒ Ⓓ Ⓔ
70 Ⓕ Ⓖ Ⓗ Ⓙ Ⓚ

71 Ⓐ Ⓑ Ⓒ Ⓓ Ⓔ
72 Ⓕ Ⓖ Ⓗ Ⓙ Ⓚ
73 Ⓐ Ⓑ Ⓒ Ⓓ Ⓔ
74 Ⓕ Ⓖ Ⓗ Ⓙ Ⓚ
75 Ⓐ Ⓑ Ⓒ Ⓓ Ⓔ

76 Ⓕ Ⓖ Ⓗ Ⓙ Ⓚ
77 Ⓐ Ⓑ Ⓒ Ⓓ Ⓔ
78 Ⓕ Ⓖ Ⓗ Ⓙ Ⓚ
79 Ⓐ Ⓑ Ⓒ Ⓓ Ⓔ
80 Ⓕ Ⓖ Ⓗ Ⓙ Ⓚ

81 Ⓐ Ⓑ Ⓒ Ⓓ Ⓔ
82 Ⓕ Ⓖ Ⓗ Ⓙ Ⓚ
83 Ⓐ Ⓑ Ⓒ Ⓓ Ⓔ
84 Ⓕ Ⓖ Ⓗ Ⓙ Ⓚ
85 Ⓐ Ⓑ Ⓒ Ⓓ Ⓔ

86 Ⓕ Ⓖ Ⓗ Ⓙ Ⓚ
87 Ⓐ Ⓑ Ⓒ Ⓓ Ⓔ
88 Ⓕ Ⓖ Ⓗ Ⓙ Ⓚ
89 Ⓐ Ⓑ Ⓒ Ⓓ Ⓔ
90 Ⓕ Ⓖ Ⓗ Ⓙ Ⓚ

91 Ⓐ Ⓑ Ⓒ Ⓓ Ⓔ
92 Ⓕ Ⓖ Ⓗ Ⓙ Ⓚ
93 Ⓐ Ⓑ Ⓒ Ⓓ Ⓔ
94 Ⓕ Ⓖ Ⓗ Ⓙ Ⓚ
95 Ⓐ Ⓑ Ⓒ Ⓓ Ⓔ

96 Ⓕ Ⓖ Ⓗ Ⓙ Ⓚ
97 Ⓐ Ⓑ Ⓒ Ⓓ Ⓔ
98 Ⓕ Ⓖ Ⓗ Ⓙ Ⓚ
99 Ⓐ Ⓑ Ⓒ Ⓓ Ⓔ
100 Ⓕ Ⓖ Ⓗ Ⓙ Ⓚ

ARGO BROTHERS

DIRECTIONS: This section requires you to rearrange five given sentences, such that they form a proper paragraph. The introductory sentence for each paragraph will be given.
An appropriate answer will order sentences so that they are logical and grammatically sound.
Credit is exclusively given for answers perfectly correct. There are no partially correct answers.

Scrambled Paragraphs
Practice Test 5 (Paragraphs 1-5)

Paragraph 1

Today, Noam Chomsky is world-renown as a public intellectual, frequently commenting on political and social issues.

_____ **Q.** The concept of internal grammars continues to be wildly influential in countless sectors of academia.

_____ **R.** Chomsky analyzed the different ways in which humans perceive the world and came to the conclusion that without a basis upon which humans organized the world conceptually, there would be no way for people to communicate the existence of shared objects.

_____ **S.** For example, a leaf is only a leaf insofar as the structure of a leaf is viewed as a solitary object.

_____ **T.** His original rise to fame, however, came from a breakthrough in the philosophy of knowledge.

_____ **U.** This primordial mode of perception became labeled in his work as internal grammars.

CONTINUE ON TO THE NEXT PAGE ➡

Paragraph 2

The study and practice of eugenics is often associated with the atrocities propagated by the Third Reich under the reign of Adolf Hitler.

_____ **Q.** Hitler committed countless war crimes in efforts to study eugenics.

_____ **R.** In contemporary practice, these alterations in farming practices have allowed scientists to create genes of rice that are resistant to floods, preventing the starvation of millions in the global south.

_____ **S.** Eugenics has been used in farming practices for millennia, though.

_____ **T.** With possession of the intellectual property rights, these MNCs can restrict the use of dominant seeds, even as these seeds take over neighboring farms due to travel by air and water.

_____ **U.** Even in this case, people worry about the ramifications of homogenized seeds owned by multi-national corporations, or MNCs.

Paragraph 3

The standard movie, like the standard essay or fiction novel, is traditionally broken down into three major sections with bookends on each side.

_____ **Q.** Next, we are introduced to the characters and the setting.

_____ **R.** At the beginning of the movie, the viewer will normally see a few credits roll while environmental elements are presented.

_____ **S.** At last, the characters work to resolve this conflict.

_____ **T.** Once we appreciate the characters, we are then normally presented with the major conflict of the story.

_____ **U.** Once the conflict is resolved, the credits roll.

CONTINUE ON TO THE NEXT PAGE ➡

Paragraph 4

Lawns present one of the largest global issues for international welfare.

_____ **Q.** Manicured lawns have a long history in regal environments, but with the democratization of home ownership in suburbs, lawns have also come under the possession of average citizens.

_____ **R.** Lawns provide home owners with a place that their children may play and offers an aesthetic contrast to the industrialized urban landscape.

_____ **S.** While these lawns are coveted, they are often created in housing developments that already have a dearth of water.

_____ **T.** For example, as people have migrated from the rust belt to the southern half of the United States, they have established their homes and lawns in previous deserts.

_____ **U.** Arizona and California have already seen a plethora of emergency droughts, due to overtaxing their natural reservoirs.

Paragraph 5

It may be strange to outside observers that Iowa and New Hampshire, the first states to hold caucuses and elections in primary elections, have so much power in US presidential politics.

_____ **Q.** Political elections center on perception and framing; therefore, winning the first elections makes a candidate seem more electable and thus increases the chance of people voting for him or her.

_____ **R.** Electors from these states are not rewarded more seats at the nomination convention than other states, but that does little to enervate their political potency.

_____ **S.** The two states are amongst the smaller in the union, yet president nominees will have spent far more time in those two states than any other during their election run.

_____ **T.** Not only does this scheduling allow the people in these states to have greater influence on the early rhetoric of the presidential election, but they also provide huge boons to local economies.

_____ **U.** A contemporary presidential election injects billions of dollars into economies and a disproportionate amount of this goes towards the media conglomerates present in Iowa and New Hampshire.

CONTINUE ON TO THE NEXT PAGE ➡

Logical Reasoning
Practice Test 4 (Paragraphs 11-20)

DIRECTIONS: This section requires you to closely analyze the problems and choose the correct answer choice. Exclusively use premises provided within the text. Pay close attention to the rules, setups, and wording.

11. Francesca is either going to the movies or to miniature golf. If she goes to miniature golf, then she will go with Joseph. If she goes to the movies, then she will go with Beth.

    What must be true?

    A. If she does not go to the movies with Beth, then she must be going somewhere with Joseph.

    B. If she does not go miniature golfing, then she will go the following week.

    C. Francesca is not going to the rodeo.

    D. If she goes to the movies, then she is not going somewhere with Jordan.

    E. If she goes to miniature golf, then she is not going somewhere with Beth.

12. Todd goes to the bank every morning. On Sundays he is only able to access the ATM in front of the bank.

    If Todd goes to an ATM in the morning, then what must be true?

    F. It must be Sunday.

    G. It could be Sunday.

    H. It could not be any day but Sunday.

    J. The main bank must be closed.

    K. Todd needs cash.

224

CONTINUE ON TO THE NEXT PAGE →

13. If Theresa gets an A on her upcoming test, then she will go to a water park. If she fails, then she will be punished. If Theresa gets a B, then what do we know?

    A. She will not go to a water park
    B. She will not get punished
    C. She will try harder the next time
    D. Theresa didn't want to go to a water park
    E. None of the above

14. There are three groups of students attending a science fair. Each group has three students. Anne is in the same group as Dan. Dan is not in the same group as Chris or Grahm. Florence is in group three along with Ben. Grahm is in group 2. Henry and Jorge are in the same group.

    What group is Chris in?

    F. 1
    G. 2
    H. 1 or 2
    J. 1 or 3
    K. 3

Questions 15 and 16 refer to the following information.

Uncover the code below. Each letter corresponds to a word in the line directly below it. A letter **may not** be directly above its corresponding word.

A	B	C	D	E	means...
Door	Farm	Car	Home	Ant	
D	C	B	F		means...
Bike	Ant	Door	Car		
D	A	C	E		means...
Farm	Ant	Home	Door		

15. What word corresponds with B?

    A. Farm
    B. Car
    C. Door
    D. Ant
    E. Home

16. What word corresponds with A?

    F. Farm or Bike
    G. Car or Door
    H. Door
    J. Home
    K. Home or Farm

17. Jerimiah likes listening to rock music. Everyone at Jerimiah's school that likes listening to rock music wants to go to the upcoming concert at the local music hall. Some of Jerimiah's friends do not want to go to the upcoming rock show.

What must be true?

A. Jerimiah is going to go to the rock show.

B. If Jerimiah does not go to the show, then he doesn't actually like listening to rock music.

C. Some of Jerimiah's friends do not like listening to rock music.

D. Some of Jerimiah's friends will be going to the rock concert.

E. Some of Jerimiah's friends would go to the concert if Jerimiah went.

18. Thomas will go fishing if it is not raining and/or snowing. If Thomas does not go fishing, then he will stay home.

What must be true?

F. If it is raining, then Thomas will not got fishing.

G. If he goes fishing, then it must not be raining.

H. If he is not at home then it must be raining or snowing.

J. If he does not stay home, then he will go fishing.

K. If rains but does not snow then he will not stay home.

19. Corina is standing in line for coffee along with four other people. She is standing fourth in line. Behind her is Jennifer. In front of her is Timothy. Timothy is standing next to Kaitlyn.

What must be true?

A. Ben must be first in line.

B. Exactly two different people could be third in line.

C. Ben could be second in line.

D. Either Timothy or Kaitlyn is second in line.

E. Corina must be next to Ben.

20. Ten students stand in line with ten teachers. Each student is paired with one teacher. The students are Anne, Beth, Caitlyn, Derik, and Ethan. The teachers are Francine, George, Henry, Icarus, and Jordan. Anne is paired with George. Caitlyn is either paired with Francine or Henry. Ethan is not with Jordan. Derik is paired with Henry. Who is Beth paired with?

F. Jordan

G. Icarus

H. Henry

J. Francine

K. George

CONTINUE ON TO THE NEXT PAGE ➡

Reading
Practice Test 5 (Questions 21-50)

DIRECTIONS: Analyze the passages below, and answer the commensurate questions. Only use information provided within the passage for your answers. There is only one answer for each question.

Long ago, when you were a little boy or a little girl—perhaps not so very long ago, either — were you never interrupted in your play by being called in to have your face washed, your hair combed, and your soiled apron exchanged for a clean one, preparatory to an introduction to Mrs. Smith, or Dr. Jones, or Aunt Judkins, your mother's early friend? And after being ushered into that august presence, and made to face a battery of questions which were either above or below your capacity, and which you consequently despised as trash or resented as insult, did you not, as were gleefully vanishing, hear a soft sigh breathed out upon the air, — "Dear child, he is seeing his happiest days?" In the concrete, it was Mrs. Smith or Dr. Jones speaking of you. But going back to general principles, it was Commonplacedom expressing its opinion of childhood.

There never was a greater piece of absurdity in the world. I thought so when I was a child, and now I know it; and I desire here to brand it as at once a platitude and a falsehood. How the idea gained currency, that childhood is the happiest period of life, I cannot conceive. How, once started, it kept afloat, is equally incomprehensible. I should have supposed that the experience of every sane person would have given the lie to it. I should have supposed that every soul, as it burst into flower, would have hurled off the imputation.

I can only account for it by recurring to Lady Mary Wortley Montague's statistics, and concluding that the fools are three out of four in every person's acquaintance.

I for one lift up my voice emphatically against the assertion, and do affirm that I think childhood is the most undesirable portion of human life, and I am thankful to be well out of it. I look upon it as no better than a mitigated form of slavery. There is not a child in the land that can call his soul, or his body, or his jacket his own. A little soft lump of clay he comes into the world, and is moulded into a vessel of honor or a vessel of dishonor long before he can put in a word about the matter. He has no voice as to his education or his training, what he shall eat, what he shall drink, or wherewithal he shall be clothed. He has to wait upon the wisdom, the whims, and often the wickedness of other people. Imagine, my six-foot friend, how you would feel, to be obliged to wear your woollen mittens when you desire to bloom out in straw-colored kids, or to be buttoned into your black waistcoat when your taste leads you to select your white, or to be forced under your Kossuth hat when you had set your heart on your black beaver: yet this is what children are perpetually called on to undergo. Their wills are just as strong as ours, and their tastes are stronger, yet they have to bend the one and sacrifice the other; and they do it under pressure of necessity.

CONTINUE ON TO THE NEXT PAGE ➡

21. What is this passage mostly about?

A. Why it is great to be a child.

B. Why being told what to do is bad.

C. To prove that people are fools.

D. To illustrate that, contrary to popular belief, childhood is the worst time of life.

E. To discuss one's childhood mishaps.

22. What does the author imply about the belief that childhood is the happiest time of one's life?

F. It is a commonly held belief.

G. It is a lie we tell ourselves.

H. It is never true.

J. It is always true.

K. It is a belief never held by children.

23. What do we know about the author's childhood?

A. She was never allowed to decide what she would wear.

B. She was never allowed to leave the house when she wanted.

C. She did not prefer it to her adult life.

D. She was happier at the time of her childhood.

E. She had no friends during her childhood.

24. What is one reason listed as to why childhood is considered by the author to be the worst time in one's life?

F. At the time there were no child labor laws.

G. You need to focus too much on school.

H. You do not get to play as much as when you are an adult.

J. You do not get to boss people around as much as when you are an adult.

K. Many important decisions are not in your control.

25. Why does the author ask the six-foot friend to imagine needing to wear mittens?

A. To illustrate how distasteful mittens are.

B. To illustrate that we take for granted our right to decide mundane actions.

C. The illusion requires a cold habitat.

D. The author believes her friend would look good in mittens.

E. To illustrate why children dislike mittens.

26. What, if true, would most strongly weaken the author's main claim?

F. Children are given some decision making.

G. Adults are not entirely free to decide everything.

H. Making decisions can be tiresome.

J. People are happiest when others decide what is good for them.

K. Modern toys are more fun to play with than old toys.

When we read in history that Antigonus was very much displeased with his son for presenting him the head of King Pyrrhus his enemy, but newly slain fighting against him,
5 and that seeing it, he wept; and that Rene, Duke of Lorraine, also lamented the death of Charles, Duke of Burgundy, whom he had himself defeated, and appeared in mourning at his funeral; and that in the battle of
10 D'Auray (which Count Montfort obtained over Charles de Blois, his competitor for the duchy of Brittany), the conqueror meeting the dead body of his enemy, was very much afflicted at his death, we must not presently
15 cry out (as did Petrarch): "And thus it happens that the mind of each veils its passion under a different appearance. Melancholy beneath a smiling visage, happy beneath a somber air."

When Pompey's head was presented to
20 Caesar, the histories tell us that he turned away his face, as from a sad and unpleasing object. There had been so long an intelligence and society betwixt them in the management of the public affairs, so great a community of
25 fortunes, so many mutual offices, and so near an alliance, that this countenance of his ought not to suffer under any misinterpretation, or to be suspected for either false or counterfeit.

30 In judging of these accidents, we are to consider how much our souls are oftentimes agitated with diverse passions. And as they say that in our bodies there is a congregation of diverse humors, so too is there in the soul.
35 Thence it is, that we see not only children, who innocently obey and follow nature, often laugh and cry at the same thing, but not one of us can boast, what journey he may have in hand that he has the most set his heart upon,
40 but when he comes to part with his family and friends, he will find something that troubles him within; and though he refrain his tears yet he puts foot in the stirrup with

a sad and cloudy countenance.

27. What is this passage mostly about?

A. Reasons we distrust our enemies.

B. Reasons that we love our enemies.

C. Reasons why it is never wise to kill your enemy.

D. Reasons why we may feel joy and sadness over the same occurrence.

E. Reasons why adults are similar to children.

28. According to the passage, who was victorious in the war between Antigonous and King Pyrrhus?

F. King Pyrrhus

G. Antigonous

H. D'auray

J. Caesar

K. None of the above.

CONTINUE ON TO THE NEXT PAGE ➡

29. How best could the beliefs of Petrarch be described?

   A. One should always take into consideration how someone feels.

   B. It is unwise to kill one's enemy.

   C. It is wise to lie about one's emotions.

   D. A person's outward emotions rarely indicate their internal feelings.

   E. People should never be trusted.

30. What is not cited as a reason Caesar was upset about the death of his former foe?

   F. Near alliance

   G. Mutual offices

   H. Similar managerial styles

   J. Familial ties

   K. Similar beliefs

31. The author's discussion most nearly relates to which of the following scenarios?

   A. Someone is sad because they have been slighted by a friend.

   B. Someone is happy because they have won a sporting championship.

   C. Someone is glad, even though they were fired from their job.

   D. Someone is angry, even though they normally do not get angry.

   E. Someone is happy, even though others have been sad in the same situation.

32. Tears are meant to represent what emotion throughout the passage?

   F. Happiness

   G. Sadness

   H. Confusion

   J. Determination

   K. Excitement

CONTINUE ON TO THE NEXT PAGE ➡

My life has always been a continuous struggle with ill-health and ambition, and I have mastered neither. I try to reassure myself that this accursed ill-health will not affect my career. I keep flogging my will in the hope of winning through in the end. Yet at the back of my mind there is the great improbability that I shall ever live long enough to realize myself. For a long time my hope has simply been to last long enough to convince others of what I might have done – had I lived. That will be something. But even to do that I will not allow that I have overmuch time. I have never at any time lived with any sense of security. I have never felt permanently settled in this life—nothing more than a shadowy *locum tenens*, a wraith, a festoon of mist likely to disappear any moment.

At times, when I am vividly conscious of the insecurity of my tenure here, my desires enter on a mad race to obtain fulfillment before it is too late...and as fulfillment recedes ambition obsesses me the more. I am daily occupied in calculating with my ill-health: trying to circumvent it, to carry on in spite of all. I conquer each day. Every week is a victory. I am always surprised that my health or will has not collapsed, that, by Jove! I am still working and still living.

One day it looks like appendicitis, another stoppage, another threatened blindness, or I develop a cough and am menaced with consumption. So I go on in a hurricane of bad dreams. I struggle like Laocoon with the serpents—the serpents of nervous depression that press around the heart tighter than I care to admit. I must use every kind of blandishment to convince myself that my life and my work are worthwhile. Frequently I must smother and kill (and it calls for prompt action) the shrill voice that cries from the tiniest corner of my heart, "Are you quite sure you are such an important fellow as you imagine?" Or I fret over the condition of my brain, finding that I forget what I read, I lose in acuteness of my perceptions. My brain is a tumefaction. But I won't give in. I go on trying to recollect what I have forgotten, I harry my brain all day to recall a word or name, I attack other folk importunately. I write things down so as to look them up in reference books – I am always looking up the things I remember I have forgotten

33. What is this passage mostly about?

A. A writer's attempt to struggle through illness and self-loathing.

B. An author's relationship to memory.

C. The importance of friends.

D. The impact of illness on one's career.

E. Ways to avoid depression.

34. Why does the author never feel "settled?"

F. He believes illness will kill him at any moment.

G. He does not believe his work is very good.

H. He is worried that others will not believe his work is very good.

J. He is worried that he will never finish his work.

K. He is worried that others are doing better work than him.

CONTINUE ON TO THE NEXT PAGE ➡

35. What is one impact of the author's bad health?

A. It makes him a better author.

B. It is sometimes the inspiration for his work.

C. It makes him more intelligent.

D. His work is always a study of his own health.

E. It gives him bad dreams.

36. Why does the author always write down his thoughts?

F. He is an author.

G. As a way to fight off insanity.

H. So that he may remember lost knowledge.

J. To give himself purpose in life.

K. To convince himself that he is a good author.

37. What does the author imply about himself?

A. He is of good health.

B. He does not always have confidence in himself.

C. He is insane.

D. He has never actually been ill.

E. He is perfectly healthy.

38. *Locum tenens* most closely means:

F. Locust

G. Wraith

H. Loco teen

J. Local teen

K. Local tenant

We hear it maintained by people of more gravity than understanding, that genius and taste are strictly reducible to rules, and that there is a rule for everything. So far is it from being true that the finest breath of fancy is a definable thing, that the plainest common sense is only what Mr. Locke would have called a mixed mode — subject to a particular sort of acquired and an definable tact. It is asked, "If you do not know the rule by which a thing is done, how can you be sure of doing it a second time?" And the answer is, "If you do not know the muscles by the help of which you walk, how is to you do not fall down at every step you take?"

In art, in taste, in life, in speech, you decide from feeling, and not from reason; that is, from the impression of a number of things on the mind, which impression is true and well founded, though you may not be able to analyze or account for it in the several particulars. In a gesture you use, in a look you see, in a tone you hear, you judge of the expression, propriety, and meaning from habit, not from reason or rules; that is to say, from innumerable instances of like gestures, looks, and tones, in innumerable other circumstances, variously modified, which are too many and too refined to be all distinctly recollected, but which do not therefore operate the less powerfully upon the mind and eye of taste.

Shall we say that these impressions (the immediate stamp of nature) do not operate in a given manner till they are classified and reduced to rules, or is not the rule itself grounded, upon the truth and certainty of that natural operation? How then can the distinction of the understanding as to the manner on which they operated be necessary to their producing their due and uniform effect upon the mind? If certain effects did not regularly arise out of certain causes in mind as well as matter, there could be no rule given for them: nature does not follow the rule, but suggests it.

Reason is the interpreter and critic of nature and genius, not their law-giver and judge. He must be a poor creature indeed whose practical convictions do not in almost all cases outrun his deliberate understanding, or does not feel and know much more than he can give reason for. Hence the distinction between eloquence and wisdom, between ingenuity and common sense. A man may be dexterous and able in explaining the grounds of his opinions, and yet may be a mere sophist, because be only sees one half of a subject. Another may feel the whole weight of a question, nothing relating to it may be lost upon him, and yet he may be able to give no account of the manner in which it affects him, or to drag his reasons from their silent lurking places.

39. What is this passage mostly about?

A. Why people need to discuss their feelings using reason.

B. The importance of reason in explaining one's emotions.

C. Why feelings should have priority over reason.

D. Why it is important to be in touch with one's feelings.

E. Why we should not take science so seriously.

CONTINUE ON TO THE NEXT PAGE ➡

40. What does the author imply about Mr. Locke?

    F. He does not give priority to feelings over rules.

    G. He is in agreement with the author.

    H. He is very intelligent.

    J. He is very unintelligent.

    K. There is no reason to study Mr. Locke.

41. What does the author believe to be the relationship between feelings and reason?

    A. The author believes that reason comes before feelings.

    B. The author believes that reason and feelings are distinct.

    C. The author believes that reason is used to provide explanation for one's feelings.

    D. The author does not believe in reason.

    E. The author believes reason should never be used to justify feeling.

42. What would be an example of how the author believes the relationship between feelings and reason to operate?

    F. A person believes he should feel happy for a friend and then feels happy.

    G. A person is taught that he should hate someone else and develops hatred for that person.

    H. A person feels ill at the thought of hurting an animal and then becomes a vegetarian.

    J. A person hates math but learns it anyway.

    K. A person wants to buy a car, but cannot afford it.

43. What does the author imply about an individual who does not use reason adeptly?

    A. He/She is more intelligent than one who does use reason adeptly.

    B. He/She is less intelligent than one who does use reason adeptly.

    C. He/She has greater common sense than one who uses reason adeptly.

    D. He/She is not necessarily wrong in his/her beliefs.

    E. He/She should not hold beliefs.

44. What does the author imply about the man who "may be able to give no account of the manner in which it affects him?"

    F. He can be wiser than the person who is able to argue their point effectively.

    G. The person is wiser than someone who can argue their point correctly.

    H. The person would understand his position more closely if he could discuss it using rules.

    J. The man could feel stronger about his belief.

    K. The man will never need to argue for his beliefs.

CONTINUE ON TO THE NEXT PAGE ➡

A house should be built with the summer in view. In winter one can live anywhere, but a poor dwelling in summer is unbearable. Deep water does not give a cool sensation. Far cooler is a shallow running stream. A room with sliding doors is lighter than one with doors on hinges. When the ceiling is high the room is cold in winter and difficult to light. As for construction, people agree in admiring a place with plenty of spare room, as being pleasing to the eye and at the same time useful for all sorts of purposes.

There is a charm about a neat and proper dwelling house, although this world, it is true, is but a temporary abode. Even the moonshine, when it strikes into the house where a good man lives in peaceful ease, seems to gain in friendly brilliancy.

The man is to be envied who lives in a house, not of the modern, garish kind, but set among venerable trees, with a garden where plants grow wild and yet seem to have been disposed with care, verandas and fences tastefully arranged, and all its furnishings simple but antique.

A house which multitudes of workmen have devoted all their ingenuity to decorate, where rare and strange things from home and abroad are set out in array, and where even the trees and shrubs are trained unnaturally — such is an unpleasant sight, depressing to look at, to say nothing of spending one's days in there. Nor, gazing on it, can one but reflect how easily it might vanish in a moment of time.

The appearance of a house is in some sort an index to the character of its occupant.

Once in the month of September I passed over the plain of Kurusu and sought out a certain village among the hills beyond, when, threading my way far down a narrow moss-grown path, I came upon a lonely hut. There was never a sound to greet me, save the dripping of water from a pipe buried in fallen leaves, but I knew that someone lived there, for sprays of chrysanthemum and maple leaves bestrewed the shelf before the shrine, and "Ah!" thought I, "In such a place a man can spend his days." But as I stood and gazed in wonder, I perceived in the garden beyond a great orange tree, its branches weighted down with fruit. It was strongly closed in on all sides by a fence. This broke the spell, and I thought to myself, "If only that tree had not been there!"

45. What is this passage mainly about?

- **A.** The author's distaste for modern architecture.
- **B.** The author's belief that orange trees are a detriment to one's dwelling.
- **C.** What makes for a good house.
- **D.** The author's belief that open-space is necessary for a good house.
- **E.** Those tendencies in architectural design that can detract from a house's aesthetic beauty.

46. Home design should be structured based on one's experience in which season?

- **F.** Winter
- **G.** Summer
- **H.** Fall
- **J.** Spring
- **K.** Houses should be great year-round.

CONTINUE ON TO THE NEXT PAGE ➡

47. What is a listed reason for why people like open spaces in homes?

   A. It is a sign of wealth.

   B. The space can be used for a multitude of purposes.

   C. It can allow you to put up more decorations.

   D. People should not have open spaces in their home.

   E. It will go nicely with the high ceilings.

48. The author would most likely prefer to live in what type of habitat?

   F. Urban environment with many cultural activities.

   G. Suburban environment with a nice lawn.

   H. Rural environment with wild trees.

   J. Rural environment with a nice lawn.

   K. An apartment complex in a rural environment.

49. What reason does the author provide as to why one should not fully manicure one's residency?

   A. It will remind them of the temporal nature of their existence.

   B. It will be too costly.

   C. It will not allow for new things to be put on display.

   D. It is too time consuming.

   E. It requires too much space.

50. What would have made the house noted at the end of the passage more preferable to the author?

   F. More trees

   G. More space

   H. Better location

   J. The removal of the orange tree and fence.

   K. Shorter ceilings.

CONTINUE ON TO THE NEXT PAGE →

75 MINUTES • 50 QUESTIONS

Select the best answer from the choices given by carefully solving each problem. Bubble the letter of your answer on the answer sheet. Please refrain from making any stray marks on the answer sheet. If you need to erase an answer, please erase thoroughly.

Important Notes:

1. There are no formulas or definitions in the math section that will be provided.
2. Diagrams may or may not be drawn to scale. Do not make assumptions based on the diagram unless it is specifically stated in the diagram or question.
3. Diagrams are not in more than one plane, unless stated otherwise.
4. Graphs are drawn to scale, therefore, you can assume relationships according to the graph. If lines appear parallel, then you can assume the lines to be parallel. This is also true for right angles and so forth.
5. Simplify fractions completely.

*THIS EXAM IS MORE DIFFICULT

Practice Test 5* (Questions 51-100)

51. Find the next term in the series:
0, 1, 1, 2, 4, 7, 13, 24...

   A. 28

   B. 37

   C. 44

   D. 48

   E. 81

52. Which is true about A and B?

$$A = \sqrt{65} - 9$$
$$B = \sqrt{50} - 8$$

   F. $A = B$

   G. $A > B$

   H. $A > 1$

   J. $B > A$

   K. $A + B > 0$

CONTINUE ON TO THE NEXT PAGE ➡

53. Which is a solution of the following equation?

$$\frac{(x^2 + x - 6)}{(x - 2)} = 0$$

- **A.** -2
- **B.** -3
- **C.** 0
- **D.** 2
- **E.** 3

54. John is stacking boxes directly upon each other. He stacks at 1 box per minute initially and every minute after that, his stacking rate increases by 1 box per minute. If each box is 5 inches tall, in how many minutes will the stack be 30 inches tall.

- **F.** 2 min
- **G.** 3 min
- **H.** 5 min
- **J.** 6 min
- **K.** 30 min

55. A Dilob has a mass of 20.2 milligrams. What is the Dilob's mass in grams?

- **A.** 0.0202 g
- **B.** 0.202 g
- **C.** 2.02 g
- **D.** 20.2 g
- **E.** 202 g

56. Jesse goes to the store. He buys a magazine for $8. Then he sells it for $10 and buys it back again for $11. He finally sells it for $12. What was his profit?

- **F.** -$1
- **G.** $0
- **H.** $2
- **J.** $3
- **K.** $5

57. If $f(\gamma) = 2f(\delta)$ and $\gamma = 2\delta$, what is a possible function for f?

- **A.** x
- **B.** x^2
- **C.** $2x^2$
- **D.** $\sqrt{x}$
- **E.** 0

58. A substance's length doubles every hour. At 2PM it was 3 meters. What was the length at 12PM that same day?

- **F.** 0.375 meters
- **G.** 0.5 meters
- **H.** 0.75 meters
- **J.** 1 meter
- **K.** 1.5 meters

CONTINUE ON TO THE NEXT PAGE ➡

59. Which is true of these three functions?

$$f = x^{x^4}$$
$$g = (x^x)^4$$
$$h = x^{4^x}$$

A. $f = g = h$

B. $f = g$

C. $h = g$

D. $f = g + h$

E. $f \neq g$

60. Linda scored a 66, 82, 81, and 92 on her English exams. What score must Linda obtain on the next math test, to have an average of exactly 84?

F. 84

G. 87

H. 95

J. 99

K. 100

61. If today is Saturday, what day of the week will it be in 365 days from now?

A. Monday

B. Tuesday

C. Thursday

D. Friday

E. Sunday

62. What is the remainder of $7,700,000,000,202$ divided by **9**?

F. 0

G. 1

H. 2

J. 3

K. 8

241

CONTINUE ON TO THE NEXT PAGE ➡

63.

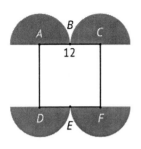

In the figure above $\overline{AB} = \overline{BC} = \overline{DE} = \overline{EF}$ and the side of the square is 12. Points B and E are the midpoints of the square. Find the area of the shaded region.

A. 12π

B. 24π

C. 36π

D. 72π

E. 144π

64. $8^{x+3} = 64^{3x}$, what is the value of x?

F. $\frac{1}{2}$

G. $\frac{3}{5}$

H. $\frac{5}{3}$

J. 2

K. 3

65. If $A \bullet\!\bullet B = AB\left(\frac{A}{B}\right) - 2^{3}$,

then what is the value of $3\bullet\!\bullet(6\bullet\!\bullet2)$?

A. 1

B. $13\frac{3}{7}$

C. $14\frac{3}{7}$

D. $13\frac{7}{4}$

E. $21\frac{3}{7}$

66. If the average of 11 numbers is 15, then what is the sum of these 11 numbers?

F. 15

G. 26

H. 121

J. 165

K. 225

242

CONTINUE ON TO THE NEXT PAGE ➡

67. What is the average of
$(9b - 7) + (7 - 3b) - (-3 - 3b) + (6 + 3b)$

- **A.** $3b + \dfrac{9}{4}$

- **B.** $\dfrac{9}{4}b + 3$

- **C.** $3b + 2$

- **D.** $2b + 3$

- **E.** $3b + \dfrac{4}{9}$

68. $\dfrac{y^{-1} \cdot y^{3} \cdot y^{4} \cdot y^{5} \cdot y^{6}}{y^{6} \cdot y^{5} \cdot y^{4}}$

- **F.** y^{-4}
- **G.** y^{-2}
- **H.** 1
- **J.** y^{2}
- **K.** y^{4}

69. If the pattern continues, what will be the 50th symbol?

★ ♥ → ← * ↑ ★ ♥ → ← ...

- **A.** ←
- **B.** *
- **C.** ★
- **D.** ♥
- **E.** ↑

70. A trapezoid has base lengths in the ratio of 2:6. If the area of a trapezoid is 260 and the altitude is 5, then what is the length of the longer base?

- **F.** 13
- **G.** 20
- **H.** 26
- **J.** 65
- **K.** 78

71. $\dfrac{4}{9}$ is the square root of what number?

- **A.** $\dfrac{1}{2}$

- **B.** $\dfrac{2}{3}$

- **C.** $\dfrac{8}{18}$

- **D.** $\dfrac{16}{81}$

- **E.** $\dfrac{3}{2}$

CONTINUE ON TO THE NEXT PAGE ➡

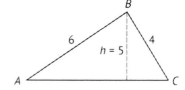

72. In the following system of equations,
$3x + 7y = 24$
$9x + 4y = 21$

What is (x,y)?

F. $(1, 1)$

G. $(1, 3)$

H. $(3, 1)$

J. $(2, 4)$

K. $(4, 2)$

---

73. If a b / c d means $\sqrt{abcd}$, then

what is the value of 1 12 / 3 4

A. 3

B. $\sqrt{12}$

C. $\sqrt{24}$

D. 12

E. 144

---

74. Which of the following is bigger, the first or the second? Assume X does not equal Y

First: $\dfrac{X}{X - Y}$ Second: $\dfrac{Y}{Y - X}$

F. They are equal

G. First

H. Second

J. Not enough information

K. One of these is undefined

75.

Figure not drawn to scale

In the figure above, the triangle ABC has an area of 20 square inches, where the height is 5 inches. If a square has the same perimeter as the triangle above, then what is the area of the square?

A. 8 sq.in

B. 18 sq.in

C. 20 sq.in

D. 20.25 sq.in

E. 25.50 sq.in

---

76. The following table shows the class test average score in Ms. Jones' Biology class over the years she has been teaching for. What is the median class test score for the years shown?

Average Test Score in Ms. Jones' Biology Class

Year	2007	2008	2009	2010	2011	2012	2013	2014	2015
Avg. Test Score	74	83	74	71	92	84	69	89	91

F. 74

G. 83

H. 84

J. 89

K. 92

CONTINUE ON TO THE NEXT PAGE ➡

77. The wheels of a car have a diameter of 10 meters. If the speed of the car is 50 meters per hour, how many revolutions does one wheel make in **one hour**?

A. $\dfrac{1}{2\pi}$

B. 5

C. $\dfrac{50}{\pi}$

D. 10

E. $\dfrac{5}{\pi}$

78. A circle is inscribed in a square. What is the probability that a penny, if thrown, will fall in the shaded region below?

F. 2π

G. 1

H. $\pi - 2$

J. $1 - \dfrac{\pi}{4}$

K. $\left(\dfrac{\pi}{2}\right)$

79. What is: $\dfrac{(10\%) \cdot (10\%)}{100\%}$?

A. 1%

B. 10%

C. .001

D. 1

E. 50%

80. The greatest integer function of x, gives the largest integer that is less than x and is represented by: $\lfloor x \rfloor$, what is $\lfloor 10\% \rfloor + 1$?

F. 0

G. 1

H. 1.1

J. 11

K. 11%

81. Sara is stuck in a circular field. She knows that the area of the circular field is 100 square meters. She walks at a speed of 10 meters per minute. How long will it take her to walk from one end of the circular field to the other end assuming she must cross through the center.

A. $\dfrac{100}{\pi}$

B. $\sqrt{\dfrac{100}{\pi}}$

C. $2\sqrt{\dfrac{100}{\pi}}$

D. $10\sqrt{\dfrac{100}{\pi}}$

E. $0.2\sqrt{\dfrac{100}{\pi}}$

82. The Fibonacci Sequence involves taking two previous numbers and adding them together to get the next. If the first two Fibonacci numbers are 0 and 1, what is the mean of the first 5 Fibonnaci numbers?

F. $\dfrac{5}{6}$

G. $\dfrac{7}{6}$

H. $\dfrac{7}{5}$

J. 1

K. 2

83. If

1 slack = x vaks
9 vaks = 12 hips,

How many slacks are in 24 hips?

A. 2

B. $\dfrac{9}{x}$

C. $\dfrac{18}{x}$

D. $\dfrac{x}{9}$

E. $\dfrac{x}{18}$

84. What is the value of $\dfrac{11^2}{10^2}$?

F. 12.1

G. 121

H. .121

J. 1.21

K. 1.12

246

CONTINUE ON TO THE NEXT PAGE ➡

85. $(\breve{ab}) = a + b - b^2$ then what is the value of this expression when $a = 5$ and $b = 2$?

A. 2

B. 3

C. 4

D. 5

E. 7

---

86. How many nonpositive integers are **between** -3 and 5?

F. 1

G. 3

H. 4

J. 6

K. 8

---

87. A number is squared and added to its reciprocal. If that number is represented by x, what is the expression?

A. $x^2 + 1$

B. $x^2 + \dfrac{1}{x}$

C. $x^2 + \dfrac{1}{x^2}$

D. $\dfrac{x^4 + 1}{x^2}$

E. x

88. If I increase the size of a ball by 50% two times in a row, what is the percent increase assuming that the initial size of the ball was 20.

F. 10%

G. 25%

H. 50%

J. 75%

K. 125%

89.

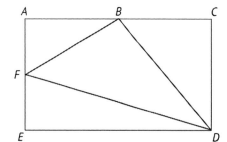

In the figure above, the rectangle *ACDE* has an area of 440 square meters. The points *B* and *F* are the midpoints of the sides *AC* and *AE* respectively. What is the area of the triangle, *BCD*?

A. 56

B. 110

C. 200

D. 220

E. Not enough information is given

CONTINUE ON TO THE NEXT PAGE ➡

90. The least common multiple of two numbers, x and y can be represented by:

$LCM(x, y)$. The following is true for the concept of the least common multiple:

If we can find integers, a and b for both x and y respectively such that $ax = by = LCM(x, y)$, then ax or by is the least common multiple of x and y.

What is the least common multiple of $\sqrt{2} \cdot \pi$?

- **F.** $\pi\sqrt{2}$
- **G.** $2\pi\sqrt{2}$
- **H.** 2π
- **J.** $2\pi^2$
- **K.** Does not exist

91. For how many values of x is the function not equal to 1?

$$f(x) = \frac{x - 3}{x - 3}$$

- **A.** 0
- **B.** 1
- **C.** 2
- **D.** 3
- **E.** ∞

92. If today is Monday, what day will it be in 49^2 from now?

- **F.** Tuesday
- **G.** Wednesday
- **H.** Thursday
- **J.** Monday
- **K.** Sunday

93. If $f(x) = x^3$, then how many times greater is $f(4)$ then $f(2)$?

- **A.** 2
- **B.** 3
- **C.** 4
- **D.** 8
- **E.** 10

94. Convert $\frac{3}{40}$ to a decimal.

- **F.** 0.0075
- **G.** 0.075
- **H.** 0.06
- **J.** .75
- **K.** 7.5

CONTINUE ON TO THE NEXT PAGE ➡

95. How many prime numbers are between 4 and 16 inclusive?

  A. 2

  B. 3

  C. 4

  D. 5

  E. 6

96. How many perfect squares are between 9 and 25 exclusive?

  F. 0

  G. 1

  H. 2

  J. 3

  K. 4

97. An octagon, a triangle and a circle all have the same perimeter (circumference for the circle). Which is true of the areas of these shapes? (O = area of octagon, T = area of triangle, and C = area of circle).

  A. $O < T < C$

  B. $O < C < T$

  C. $O = T = C$

  D. $C > T = O$

  E. $C > O > T$

98. If $\left(\frac{x}{y}\right) = x^2$, then what is $\left(\frac{x}{y}\right) - \left(\frac{x}{y}\right)^2$?

  F. x^2

  G. $x^2 y$

  H. x^4

  J. $x^2(1 - x^2)$

  K. $x^2(1 + x^2)$

99. In a scaled drawing, 1 millimeter represents 150 meters. How many square millimeters on the drawing represent 1 square meter?

  A. $\dfrac{1}{150}$

  B. $\dfrac{1}{22,500}$

  C. $\dfrac{150}{22,500}$

  D. 120

  E. 22,500

249

CONTINUE ON TO THE NEXT PAGE ➡

100. A rectangle is drawn on a coordinate plane. If the coordinates of one corner of the rectangle is (0,-5) and the coordinates of the opposite corner is (7, 3), then what is the area of the rectangle?

    F.   -56

    G.   -21

    H.   21

    J.   56

    K.   105

THIS IS THE END OF THE TEST. IF THERE IS TIME REMAINING, YOU MAY CHECK YOUR ANSWERS TO PART 1 OR PART 2.

SHSAT PRACTICE TEST 5
ANSWER KEY

PART 1 (VERBAL)

Scrambled Paragraphs

1. T, R, S, U, Q
2. Q, S, R, U, T
3. R, Q, T, S ,U
4. Q, R, S, T, U
5. S, R, Q, T ,U

Logical Reasoning

11. A
12. G
13. E
14. K
15. B
16. K
17. C
18. J
19. D
20. F

Reading

21. D	44. F
22. F	45. C
23. C	46. G
24. K	47. B
25. B	48. H
26. J	49. A
27. D	50. J
28. G	
29. D	
30. J	
31. C	
32. G	
33. A	
34. F	
35. B	
36. H	
37. B	
38. G	
39. C	
40. F	
41. C	
42. H	
43. D	

PART 2 (MATHEMATICS)

Math

51. C	63. D	75. D	87. B	99. B
52. J	64. G	76. G	88. K	100. J
53. B	65. A	77. E	89. D	
54. G	66. J	78. J	90. K	
55. A	67. A	79. A	91. B	
56. J	68. J	80. G	92. J	
57. A	69. D	81. E	93. D	
58. F	70. K	82. H	94. G	
59. E	71. D	83. C	95. C	
60. J	72. G	84. J	96. G	
61. E	73. D	85. B	97. E	
62. F	74. J	86. G	98. J	

To calculate your score visit our web site
and download excel calculator:
www. einstein-academy.com/calc

SCRAMBLED PARAGRAPHS

1. **T, R, S, U, Q**

    T: "However" indicates that the following sentences will be different in content from the introductory sentence. This is the case.

    R: R introduces the concept that S, U, and Q must follow. It is possible to make logical sequencing rules such as:

    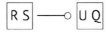

    These can prove beneficial in scramble paragraphs like this. Here, R may be difficult to place, but RS clearly comes before UQ, and thus R needs to go second.

    S: S is an example of the topic introduced in sentence R.

    U: "This primordial mode of perception" references the topics discussed in S and R.

    Q: The concept of "internal grammars" was introduced in sentence U.

2. **Q, S, R, U, T**

    Q: Q connects Hitler to the introductory sentence. C indicates a break in topics, and so Q must come before.

    S: The use of the word "though" indicates that the following sentences will be different from the prior sentences. R, U, and T all relate to a new topic from the introductory sentence and sentence Q.

    R: "These alterations in farming practices" references the uses of eugenics in farming, as seen in sentence S.

    U: "Even here though" indicates something problematic with the previous statement. U goes on to discuss issues with homogenized seeds, something that may arise due to practices discussed in sentence R.

    T: "These MNCs" uses the abbreviation introduced in sentence U.

3. **R, Q, T, S, U**

R: This paragraph goes in order of the sections. "Beginning of the movie" indicates that this is the beginning of the discussion.

Q: "Next" follows from the beginning.

T: "Once we appreciate the characters" refers to the topic discussed in sentence Q.

S: S concludes the actions of the characters discussed in T.

U: The credits roll after the conflict is resolved.

4. **Q, R, S, T, U**

Q: R, S, T, and U all have clear referrals to sentences outside of the introductory sentence. Q introduces the specific issue discussed further in subsequent sentences.

R: R discusses the home owners introduced in sentence Q.

S: "These lawns" refer to the lawns introduced in sentence R.

T: T provides an example of a place where there is a "dearth of water," as discussed in sentence S.

U: U expands on the example begun in sentence T, providing more particular details.

5. **S, R, Q, T, U**

S: S comments on why outsiders may view the situation as odd, as discussed in the introductory sentence.

R: Presidential nominees refers to the presidential nominees introduced in sentence S.

Q: Q provides the reason why they have the political potency mentioned in sentence R.

T: U must follow T, as they both relate to a new topic from R and Q.

U: U provides details concerning the economic boon mentioned at the end of sentence T.

LOGICAL REASONING

11. A The rules should be written as:

$$[M \rightarrow \cancel{G}; G \rightarrow \cancel{M}]$$
$$[G \rightarrow J; \cancel{J} \rightarrow \cancel{G}]$$
$$[M \rightarrow B; \cancel{B} \rightarrow \cancel{M}]$$

Note that two rules are bi-conditional. If Francesca does not go to the movies with Beth, then she did not go to the movies. If she did not go to the movies, then she must have gone miniature golfing. If she went miniature golfing, then she went with Jordan. Thus, A is correct.

12. G The logical statements should read:

$$S \rightarrow FATM$$
$$\cancel{FATM} \rightarrow \cancel{S}$$

Going to the ATM in the morning does not lead to any necessary truths. However, it does necessarily leave open the possibility that it could be Sunday. It could also be any other day, thus why F and H are wrong. J and K are irrelevant information.

13. E Getting a B does not satisfy any logical statements, thus it does not let us know anything.

14. K This is a pairing game. First place F, B, and G in their respective groups. A and D cannot be in group 2 with G, and would not fit in group 3, thus must be in group A. H and J can only fit in group 2. C cannot be with D, thus he must be in group 3.

15. B Note the third rule, as it is very important to this question. The third rule can change depending on the text. When the rule states that the two elements of the pair cannot be on top of each other, you will often depend heavily on the rule. C/D and Door/Ant are both in all three rows. However, C is over Ant and must thus be paired with Door. D must be paired with Ant. A, B, and E are all in two rows. Write them out with all four of the possibilities: Farm, Car, and Home. Now look for letters that are over these words, looking at one letter at a time. B is over farm and is not in a same line pair as home, so must be

with car. A and E can each be with either farm or home. The final chart should look like:

C = Door/~~Ant~~
D = ~~Ant~~/~~Door~~
A = Farm/~~Car~~/Home
B = ~~Farm~~/Car/~~Home~~
E = Farm/~~Car~~/Home
F = Bike

16. K

17. C Establish the following logical chain:

$$[J \rightarrow RM \rightarrow C; \cancel{C} \rightarrow \cancel{RM} \rightarrow \cancel{J}]$$

Some of Jerimiah's friends do not want to go to the concert, which places them at the beginning of the logical chain that involves not liking to listen rock music. Thus, C is the correct answer.

18. J Right down all rules:

$$[\cancel{S} \& \cancel{R} \rightarrow F; \cancel{F} \rightarrow S \text{ or } R]$$
$$[\cancel{F} \rightarrow H; \cancel{H} \rightarrow F]$$

If he does not stay at home, he will necessarily go fishing, thus J is correct.

19. D Once you place C and J in their respective locations, there are two possible boards. Complete both boards such that it looks like:

$$\frac{J}{5} \quad \frac{C}{4} \quad \frac{T/K}{3} \quad \frac{T/K}{2} \quad \frac{B}{1}$$

$$\frac{J}{5} \quad \frac{C}{4} \quad \frac{B}{3} \quad \frac{T/K}{2} \quad \frac{T/K}{1}$$

In both games, T/K is in the 2 position, thus the answer is D.

20. F Fill in the two rules that can be directly plugged into the board. Since D is with H, C must be with F. As E is not with J, he must be with I. This leaves B and J as the final pair. The answer is thus F.

READING COMPREHENSION

21. D All three paragraphs involve statements reinforcing this answer choice.

22. F Noting the position as coming from "Commonplacedom" indicates that it is a commonly held belief.

23. C As she notes that childhood is the worst time of one's life, we can infer that she prefers adult life.

24. K This is the focus of the third paragraph. Childhood is, according to the author, a time of one's life where one has little agency over their own life. It is this lack of agency which repulses her.

25. B Choosing to wear mittens is a mundane action. Being denied the ability to decide an action as simple as simple this helps to support the author's claim.

26. J The author's main claim is that people should not prefer childhood because they have no agency over their lives during that time. However, if people instead prefer to have all decisions made for them, then this would no longer be a good explanation as to why it is not a good time of one's life.

27. D This is the focus of all three paragraphs. No other answer appears in this many paragraphs.

28. G This answer derives from lines 1-5. Antigonus's son presents the head of King Pyrrhus, indicating that Pyrrhus lost the battle.

29. D Petrarch's quote occurs in lines 15-18. In both examples, the outward appearance of the person discussed belies their inner emotions.

30. J All other answer choices can be explicitly found within the passage.

31. C In this example, something that makes a person sad is also giving them a certain level of happiness. A and B are expected emotional responses and are not conflicting. D does not indicate whether the angry person is also happy. E does not indicate whether the particular situation is such that they are both happy and sad.

32. G The passage uses tears as a contrary emotional response to laughter or happiness. Sadness is the opposite of happiness and is often associated with the tears noted in the passage.

33. A This passage is in diary form, detailing the author's severe illness and depression due to illness. This theme occurs in all paragraphs. No other answer is as prevalent.

34. F The sentences surrounding the phrase "unsettled"(line 16) discuss his fear of imminent death.

35. B This passage is an essay created by the author, and thus is sometimes the inspiration for his work. D uses extreme language.

36. H The sentence this answer is derived from directly follows from a discussion of the author's concern that his brain is not functioning properly.

37. B This answer derives from lines 43-45.

38. G This answer derives from line 17.

39. C This answer occurs in all paragraphs. The author's primary argument is that one has feelings and reason is then used to explain those feelings. Thus, the feelings are prior to the rational argumentation.

40. F Mr. Lock is used as an example of those who believe rational reasons and rules should be used to judge the world as opposed to feelings.

41. C This answer derives from line 47.

42. H In this example, an individual has an emotional response which then leads to rationalized action.

43. D The author notes that one can be correct in their beliefs, even if they are not proficient at explaining their beliefs.

44. F This answer derives from line 53-65. The distinction between eloquence and wisdom is particularly salient.

45. C This answer occurs in the most paragraphs. Other answer choices only occur in one or two paragraphs.

46. G This answer derives from line 1.

47. B This answer derives from line 12.

48. H This description most closely follows the criteria for a proper habitat, as presented by the author.

49. A This answer derives from lines 33-35. Gazing upon a dwelling that is well manicured reminds you that it could "vanish in a moment of time." This recognition of the mortality of life is frowned down upon by the author.

50. J This answer derives from lines 53-55. The tree and fence "broke the spell."

Practice Test 5 (Answers and Explanations)

51. C After inspection, it can be seen that if you sum the first three terms, you get the next term. If you continue this pattern of adding the previous three terms to get the next, you can find the next term in the series to be, $7 + 13 + 24 = 44$. The answer is C.

52. J For this problem, we can assume that A is greater than B. If we do this, we can follow the steps,
$\sqrt{65} - 9 > \sqrt{50} - 8$
$\sqrt{65} > \sqrt{50} + 1$ and then squaring both sides and simplifying,
$7 > \sqrt{50}$, which is impossible since the square root of 49 is 7. Since this is a contradiction, we know that our original assumption was incorrect and that, B is greater than A instead. The answer is J.

53. B This equation can be factored as,
$$\frac{(x-2)(x+3)}{(x-2)} = (x+3) = 0,$$
so $x = -3$. The answer is B.

54. G During the first minute, he stacks one box. During the second minute, he stacks 2 more boxes on that 1 box he had originally. During the third minute, he stacks 3 more boxes on everything making the total 6 boxes, and since each box is 5 inches tall, that is 30 inches in total. It took 3 minutes to reach 30 inches. The answer is G.

55. A We simply must divide by 1000 to convert from miligrams to grams. 0.0202g is the answer or answer choice A.

56. J If we assume negative values for costs and positive values for profit, we can write,
$-\$8 + \$10 - \$11 + \$12 = +\$3$, so his profit is \$3 or answer choice J.

57. A Substituting $Y = 2\delta$ into the function gives us,
$f(2\delta) = 2f(\delta)$ which only happens for a non-constant linear function. The only non-constant linear function shown is, x, or answer choice A.

58. F 11AM is 3 hours before 2PM. If the length doubles every hour, then three hours before, it was $\frac{1}{2^3}$ the length at 2 pm or $(\frac{3}{8}) = 0.375$ meters. In other words, we have to cut the length in half three times. The answer is F.

59. E None of these functions are equal to each other. The answer is E.

60. J Using the definition of averages and using x as the score for the next test, we have:

$$\frac{66 + 82 + 81 + 92 + x}{5} = \frac{321 + x}{5} = 84,$$

which simplifies to $x = 420 - 321 = 99$, or answer choice J.

61. E Every 7 days from Saturday, it will be Saturday again. 7 can go into 365, 52 times with a remainder of 1 day. So it will be 1 day after Saturday, which is Sunday.
The answer is E.

62. F A number is divisible by 9 if all of the digits of that number sum up to a number divisible by 9, which in this case, does. The answer is 0 or answer choice F.

63. D The length of AB is 6, since B is the midpoint of AC. The radius of each semicircle is then, 6 and there are 4 identical semicircles, which is equivalent to 2 circles. The area of 1 circle is 36π, so the area of both circles is 72π, or answer choice D.

64. G This equation can be simplified to,
$$8^{x+3} = (8^2)^{3x} = 8^{6x}$$
, so $x + 3 = 6x$, or $x = (\frac{3}{5})$.
The answer G.

65. A The right hand side of the equation simplifies to $A^2 - 8$. So, we only need to worry about the first number and not what is in the parentheses.
$3^2 - 8 = 1$. The answer is A.

66. J We simply have to multiply 11 by 15 to find the sum. the answer is 165 or answer choice J.

67. A Adding all of the terms and dividing by 4 gives,
$$\frac{12b + 9}{4} = 3b + \frac{9}{4}$$
The answer is A.

68. J This simplifies to, $\frac{y^{17}}{y^{15}} = y^2$
The answer is J.

69. D Each symbol repeats every 6 symbols later. For example, the first symbol appears at position 1, 7, 13 and so on. So, the second symbol will appear at 2, 8, 14, ..., 50. The answer is D.

70. K The area of a trapezoid with bases a and b and altitude, h, is: $A = \frac{(a + b)h}{2}$ and we know what h is and we know what A is. Plugging those in and solving for $a + b$ gives us, $a + b = 104$. We also know the ratio of the base lengths if $(\frac{2}{6})$ which means, $\frac{a}{b} = \frac{2}{6}$ or $3a = b$. Plugging this into $a + b = 104$ and solving for b gives us a value for b of, $b = 78$ or answer choice K.

71. D The square root of $(\frac{16}{81})$ is $(\frac{4}{9})$. The answer is D.

72. G Multiplying the first equation by -3 and adding it to the second equation gives, $-17y = -51$ or $y = 3$. If $y = 3$, then we can plug that value into the first equation and solve for x to give us $x = 1$. The solution is $(1, 3)$. The answer is G.

73. D Multiplying all of the numbers in the trapezoid and taking the square root of that gives us, $\sqrt{144} = 12$ The answer is D.

74. J This answer depends on the signs of X and Y so the answer is J.

75. D If we call the unknown side, AC, x, we have that the perimeter of the triangle is, $P = 10 + x$ and the area is $(\frac{5}{2})x = 20$. We can solve for x to get $x = 8$, which means the perimeter of the triangle is, 18, which is also the perimeter of the square. All of the sides of a square are equal and the area is the side length squared. So, the area of the square is $(\frac{18}{2})^2$ square inches = 20.25 square inches. The answer is D.

76. G To solve this problem, we must align the scores in order from least to greatest (or greatest to least) and find the middle number. The middle number is 83, so the answer is G.

77. E In one hour, the car travels 50 meters and the circumference of the wheel is $2\pi r = 10\pi$, with a radius of 5 meters. Given this, we can find the number of revolutions that occur in one hour. This will be 50 meters divided by 10π which is $\frac{5}{\pi}$ The answer is E.

78. J To find this probability, we must divide the area of the shaded region by the area of the square. Let's say that the radius of the circle is r. Then, the side length of the square is $2r$. The area of the square is then, $4r^2$. The area of the circle is πr^2 and the area of the shaded region is the difference between these two areas, $r^2(4 - \pi^2)$, and once we divide this by $4r^2$, we get:

$$\frac{r^2(4 - \pi^2)}{4r^2} = 1 - \frac{\pi}{4}$$

which is answer choice J.

79. A We know that 100% = 1, so we can simplify this to just 10% times 10%, which is 0.01 or 1%. The answer is A.

80. G 10% = 0.1. The greatest integer less than 0.1 is 0. 0 + 1 = 1. The answer is G.

81. E We know that the area is 100 square meters, so we can find the diameter (2 times the radius, r) by equating, $\pi r^2 = 100$, which gives a diameter of,

$$2r = \sqrt{\frac{100}{\pi}}$$ and dividing this by her speed gives us the time it takes for her to traverse the diameter which is,

$$0.2\sqrt{\frac{100}{\pi}}.$$ The answer is E.

82. H Using this formula of adding the previous 2 terms to get the next, we have for the first 5 terms, 0, 1, 1, 2, 3 which sums to 7. The mean is $(\frac{7}{5})$ or answer choice H.

83. C If there are 9 vaks in 12 hips, then there are 18 vaks in 24 hips. There are $(\frac{18}{x})$ slacks in 24 hips or 18 vaks. The answer is C.

84. J This simplifies to,

$$(\frac{11}{10})^2 = (1.1)^2 = 1.21,$$

or answer choice J.

85. B Plugging in the values for a and b into the equation gives us, $5 + 2 - 2^2 = 3$. The answer is B.

86. G The integers that are nonpositive within that range are, -3, -2, -1. There are 3 integers. It does not specify whether the question asks for inclusivity or exclusivity, but there is no answer for exclusivity. So the answer is G.

87. B A number squared is x^2. It's reciprocal is ($\frac{1}{x}$). The sum is, $x^2 + \frac{1}{x}$. The answer is B.

88. K If the original size is 20, then it increases by 50%, the size will be 30. Then the size will be 45 if we increase it by 50% again. The percent increase from 20 to 45 is 125%. The answer is K.

89. D Labeling the sides AB and BC as x, respectively and the sides, AF and FE as y, respectively, we can represent the area of the rectangle as, $4xy = 440$. This means that $xy = 110$. The area of triangle BCD is $2xy$ or 220. The answer is D.

90. K Since $\sqrt{2}$ and π are both irrational, there are no integers, a and b that can satisfy the definition of $LCM(x, y)$. The answer is K.

91. B This function is undefined and not equal to 1 when the denominator is 0, which occurs when $x = 3$. The answer is 1, or answer choice B.

92. J Since 49^2 is divisible by 7, the answer is still Monday. The answer choice is J.

93. D $f(4)$ can be written as 4^3 or 2^6. $f(2)$ can be written as 2^3. The question becomes, how much greater is 2^6 than 2^3. The answer is 2^3 greater, or 8 times greater. The answer is D.

94. G ($\frac{3}{40}$) = 0.075. The answer is G.

95. C There are four prime numbers between 4 and 16 inclusive. They are: 5, 7, 11, 13. The answer is C.

96. G The only perfect square between 9 and 25 exclusive is 16. The answer is G.

97. E The more sides the figure has, the bigger the area, holding the perimeter constant. So, an octagon would have a bigger area than a triangle, and a circle would have the largest area. The answer is E.

98. J Plugging in what the formula tells us gives us,

$x^2 - x^4 = x^2(1 - x^2)$ or answer J.

99. B If 1 mm represents 150 m, then 1 sq. mm represents 22,500 sq. m. So then, 1 sq. m. is simply ($\frac{1}{22,500}$) sq. mm. The answer is B.

100. J If we draw the two points that represent the corners of the rectangle, we see that the rectangle would look like this:

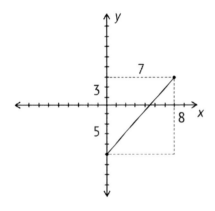

The area is 8 • 7 = 56. The answer is J.

CPSIA information can be obtained at www.ICGtesting.com
Printed in the USA
BVOW04s0906040216

435416BV00005B/107/P